Active Learning and Student Engagement

This book examines significant issues in geography teaching and learning from the perspectives of an international network of academic geographers and postgraduate students. Drawing on classroom experiences and research in a wide variety of educational settings, the authors describe conceptually interesting and practical applications for enhancing student learning through inquiry, problem-based learning, field study, online collaboration, and other highly engaging forms of pedagogy. Other chapters focus on approaches for improving the experiences of distance learners, strategies for enhancing the employability of geography students, and preparing students to engage ethical issues in the discipline.

An international audience of educators will find much of value through the use of comparative examples, literature reviews encompassing research in multiple national contexts, and an underlying awareness of the diversity of practices in higher education internationally.

This book is a collection of articles previously published in two special issues of the *Journal of Geography in Higher Education*.

Mick Healey is Professor of Geography, University of Gloucestershire, UK, and Senior Adviser for Geography for the National Subject Centre for Geography, Earth and Environmental Sciences. He is a National Teaching Fellow and Senior Fellow of the Higher Education Academy and has twice been awarded the *Journal of Geography in Higher Education* Biennial Award for Promoting Excellence in Teaching and Learning.

Eric Pawson is Professor of Geography, University of Canterbury, New Zealand. He is a national teaching award winner, a former Head of Department, and member of the Social Science Panel of the Royal Society of New Zealand's Marsden Research Fund.

Michael Solem is Educational Affairs Director at the Association of American Geographers, where he directs several federally funded initiatives supporting geography education in the United States and internationally. His research (with Ken Foote) on geography faculty development was recognized by the *Journal of Geography in Higher Education's* Biennial Award for Promoting Excellence in Teaching and Learning.

Active Learning and Student Engagement

International Perspectives and Practices in Geography in Higher Education

Edited by Mick Healey, Eric Pawson and Michael Solem

LONDON AND NEW YORK

First published 2010
by Routledge

2 Park Square, Milton Park, Abingdon, Oxon, OX14 4RN
Simultaneously published in the USA and Canada
by Routledge
711 Third Avenue, New York, NY 10017

Routledge is an imprint of the Taylor & Francis Group, an informa business

First issued in paperback 2012

© 2010 Taylor & Francis

Typeset in Times by Value Chain, India

All rights reserved. No part of this book may be reprinted or reproduced or utilised in any form or by any electronic, mechanical, or other means, now known or hereafter invented, including photocopying and recording, or in any information storage or retrieval system, without permission in writing from the publishers.

British Library Cataloguing in Publication Data
A catalogue record for this book is available from the British Library

ISBN13: 978-0-415-56492-2 (hbk)
ISBN13: 978-0-415-63398-7 (pbk)

Contents

Acknowledgments   vii

Introduction   1
Mick Healey, Eric Pawson and *Michael Solem*

Section A
Re-imagining ourselves as learners

1. Co-learning: re-linking research and teaching in geography   11
   Richard Le Heron, Richard Baker & Lindsey McEwen

2. 'None of us sets out to hurt people': the ethical geographer and geography curricula in higher education   22
   William E. Boyd, Ruth L. Healey, Susan W. Hardwick, Martin Haigh with *Phil Klein, Bruce Doran, Julie Trafford & John Bradbeer*

Section B
Engaging students in inquiry

3. Experimenting with active learning in geography: dispelling the myths that perpetuate resistance   39
   Regina Scheyvens, Amy L. Griffin, Christine L. Jocoy, Yan Liu & Michael Bradford

4. Problem-based learning in geography: towards a critical assessment of its purposes, benefits and risks   58
   Eric Pawson, Eric Fournier, Martin Haigh, Osvaldo Muniz, Julie Trafford & Susan Vajoczki

5. Where might sand dunes be on Mars? Engaging students through inquiry-based learning in geography   72
   Rachel Spronken-Smith, Jo Bullard, Waverly Ray, Carolyn Roberts & Artimus Keiffer

6. International perspectives on the effectiveness of geography fieldwork for learning   88
   Ian Fuller, Sally Edmonson, Derek France, David Higgitt & Ilkka Ratinen

Section C
New spaces of learning

7. Developing and enhancing international collaborative learning   103
   David Higgitt, Karl Donert, Mick Healey, Phil Klein, Michael Solem & Susan Vajoczki

8. E-learning for geography's teaching and learning spaces   116
   Kenneth Lynch, Bob Bednarz, James Boxall, Lex Chalmers, Derek France & Julie Kesby

9. Strength in diversity: enhancing learning in vocationally-orientated, master's level courses   131
   Lindsey McEwen, Janice Monk, Iain Hay, Pauline Kneale & Helen King

10. Teaching geography for social transformation   150
    Jane Wellens, Andrea Berardi, Brian Chalkley, Bill Chambers, Ruth Healey, Janice Monk & Jodi Vender

Section D
Beyond the classroom

11. Community engagement for student learning in geography   167
    Sarah Witham Bednarz, Brian Chalkley, Stephen Fletcher, Iain Hay, Erena Le Heron, Audrey Mohan & Julie Trafford

12. Variations in international understandings of employability for geography   181
    Paul Rooney, Pauline Kneale, Barbara Gambini, Artimus Keiffer, Barbara Van Drasek & Sharon Gedye

13. Internationalizing professional development in geography through distance education   194
    Michael Solem, Lex Chalmers, David DiBiase, Karl Donert & Susan Hardwick

Conclusion

14. Reflecting on student engagement   208
    Eric Pawson, Mick Healey & Michael Solem

Index   215

Acknowledgments

The chapters in this book were previously published in two symposia in the *Journal of Geography in Higher Education (JGHE)*, in volume 30 (1), 2006 and volume 32 (1), 2008. We are grateful to Martin Haigh, Editor of *JGHE*, for suggesting that we should draw them together as a book about active learning methods in geography and how these can enhance levels of student engagement; and to Louise Glenn and Steve Thompson of Routledge for their support in turning this idea into a reality.

The two symposia were the outcome of workshops held by the International Network for Learning and Teaching Geography in Higher Education (INLT)[1], as is explained in the first chapter. As the current co-chairs of the INLT, we have grouped the papers thematically, written new opening and concluding chapters, and short section introductions. But the book would not exist were it not for our INLT colleagues from nine different countries who authored the original papers.

The papers have been assembled as originally published, without any updating, apart from authors' institutional affiliations. We are grateful to Alison Holmes, Keith Comer and Lane Perry III of the University Centre for Teaching and Learning at the University of Canterbury, for debate, ideas and references during our preparation of the introduction and conclusion. We are also grateful to the UK Geography Earth and Environmental Science Subject Centre who have supported INLT over the last decade.

Mick Healey
Department of Natural and Social Sciences
University of Gloucestershire,
Cheltenham, UK

Eric Pawson
Department of Geography
University of Canterbury,
Christchurch, NZ

Michael Solem
Association of American Geographers
Washington, DC, USA

October 1, 2009.

Note

[1] The INLT is free to join for anyone interested in geography in higher education. Further details are available at: www.geog.canterbury.ac.nz/inlt/

Introduction

MICK HEALEY, MICHAEL SOLEM AND ERIC PAWSON

There is growing evidence to show that engaging students is a pre-requisite to enhancing student learning, retention and achievement (Healey *et al.*, forthcoming, 2010; Healey & Roberts, 2004; Ramsden, 2003). There appears to be a desire by virtually all educators, almost as a *cri de coeur,* for more student engagement (Bryson & Hand, 2007). Bryson *et al.* (2008, 1) define engagement as a concept which "encompasses the perceptions, expectations and experience of being a student and the construction of being a student". Barnett & Coate (2005, 165), furthermore, suggest that "the test of an effective curriculum is 'engagement': Are the students individually engaged? Are they collectively engaged?" The chapters in this book show that active learning is a key way in which to engage students. The challenge, according to Barnett & Coate, is that: "A complex and uncertain world requires curricula in which students as human beings are placed at their centre ... A curriculum of this kind has to be understood as the imaginative design of spaces where creative things can happen as students become engaged" (2005, back cover). This volume presents many creative ways of engaging students through active learning, both in the classroom and beyond.

The chapters developed from two workshops organized by the International Network for Learning and Teaching Geography in Higher Education (INLT) and held in Glasgow, UK and Brisbane, Australia (Healey, 2006a; Pawson, 2008). Since it was established in 1999, the INLT has evolved an effective process of bringing academics from several different countries together to reflect collaboratively on aspects of teaching and learning (Hay *et al* 2000; Hay, 2008; Healey, 2006b). Well before the meetings in Glasgow and Brisbane, participants were allocated to groups of five or six depending on their preferred topics, and accounting as far as possible for a balance of nationality, gender and experience. Each group, under the leadership of their chair, was asked to develop a 2,500 word discussion paper on their topic, which was put on-line for a month long debate prior to the workshop. The 48-hour workshop consisted of a mixture of plenary and group sessions interspersed with social activities. By the end of the workshop each group had prepared an outline draft of a final paper, which they then had another two to three months to reshape before final editing and submission to the *Journal of Geography in Higher Education (JGHE)*. The following 13 chapters are the papers published in *JGHE* following refereeing and reworking.

The introduction and last chapter of the collection have both been specially written for this book.

The nature of active learning and student engagement

Active learning is the key to student learning. As Chickering & Gamson (1987, 3) point out:

> "Good practice uses active learning techniques. Learning is not a spectator sport. Students do not learn much just sitting in classes listening to teachers, memorizing prepackaged assignments, and spitting out answers. They must talk about what they are learning, write reflectively about it, relate it to past experiences, and apply it to their daily lives. They must make what they learn part of themselves."

Gibbs (1998, 9) puts this another way: "It is not enough just to do, and neither is it enough just to think. Nor is it enough simply to do and think. Learning from experience must involve linking the doing and the thinking."

One of the most effective ways of linking the doing and the thinking is engaging students in inquiry-based learning. According to the UK's Centre for Active Learning (CeAL), active learning "focuses on inquiry in the field, studio, laboratory and classroom, using real sites, community-related and employer linked activities" (Healey et al., 2005a). More than simply 'learning by doing', this approach enables students to construct theoretical understanding through reflection on practical activities.

The CeAL approach to active learning is inquiry-based. It works best, they suggest, when students undertake thought-demanding activities, because this ensures a reflective and research-minded approach to their learning (Elton, 2005; Healey, 2005a; Kaufmann & Stocks, 2004). This means of active learning thus helps to maintain close synergistic relationships between our teaching, research and knowledge transfer strategies and practices (Healey et al., 2005a). Badley (2002, 451) argues for "seeing both research and teaching as different forms of learning". Healey (2005b, 183), moreover, suggests that "undergraduate students are likely to gain most benefit from research in terms of depth of learning and understanding when they are involved actively, particularly through various forms of inquiry-based learning." In later work, Healey and Jenkins (2009, 6) argue that "all undergraduate students in all higher education institutions should experience learning through and about research and inquiry."

Kuh (2009), based on work in the US on high impact activities, argues that active learning and student engagement are closely interrelated:

> "A growing body of evidence suggests that – when done well – some programs and activities appear to engage participants at levels that elevates their performance across multiple engagement dimensions and desired outcomes such as grades, deep learning, and persistence. These high-impact activities include first-year seminars, writing-intensive courses, common intellectual experiences, learning communities, service learning, undergraduate research, study abroad and other experiences with diversity, internships, and capstone courses and projects".

Furthermore, he suggests that institutions should "structure the curriculum and other learning opportunities so that *one high-impact activity is available to every student every year"* (Kuh 2008, 19-20, emphasis in original). A good example of embedding inquiry-based learning in the curriculum comes from Miami University, Ohio (Hodge *et al.*, 2008). They suggest that the time has come to move on from the paradigm shift from teaching to learning, advocated by Barr & Tagg (1995), to one based on inquiry.

The rationale and theory behind active learning and student engagement

The key idea behind active learning and student engagement is experiential learning. According to Kolb (1984, 38) 'Learning is the process whereby knowledge is created through the transformation of experience'. Kolb's theory presents a way of structuring and sequencing the curriculum at module and programme levels so that students, taking account of their diverse set of learning styles and needs, go through a range of activities which reflect the *cyclical* nature of learning (Fielding, 1994; Healey & Jenkins, 2000). This involves four stages which, paraphrasing Kolb, may be referred to as experiencing, reflecting, generalising and testing (Cowan, 1998). A key feature of Kolb's argument is that in the spirit of social constructivism, ie starting where the learner is, we need to recognise that students favour different learning styles (just as teachers favour different teaching styles). The logic of this observation is that to recognise the diversity of student backgrounds and needs in our classrooms we should design a variety of learning and assessment experiences which address each of the stages of the learning cycle (Healey *et al.*, 2005b).

CeAL has extended Kolb's approach to include the 'teaching for understanding' perspective because it requires that we attend to the *kinds* of experience we design for our students (Fig. 1). The strength of the 'teaching for understanding movement' (Blythe & Associates, 1998; Perkins, 1999) in the US is in its emphasis on crafting thought-demanding experiences for student learning. Its proponents insist that simply 'having' knowledge is insufficient because learners need to go through 'performances of understanding' fully to comprehend their subject. Although developed with school children in mind, this coupling of knowing and doing can be readily translated to the university context and has been used by the UK 'Enhancing Teaching-Learning Environments for Undergraduate Courses' project, because it supports an understanding of how theoretical mastery is achieved through active learning (Entwistle, 2003).

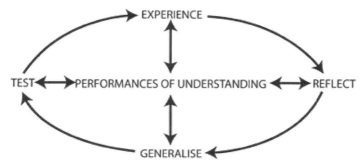

Figure 1.1 *The CeAL approach to active learning.*
Source: Healey, *et al.*, 2005a; drawing on ideas from Kolb, 1984; Cowan, 1998; and Perkins, 1999.

The practice of active learning and student engagement in geography

Geography provides a useful context for exploring approaches to active learning and student engagement in higher education, for several reasons. First, geographers are by nature sensitive to 'diversity' and its many cultural and demographic manifestations, not the least of which concerns the increasingly diverse character of college and university students. If we are to take to heart Kolb's (1984) view of learning as a process of creating knowledge through the transformation of experience, then attention to the diversity of experiences that students bring with them into higher education implies a need to understand where they 'come from' and 'are now'. After all, our past and present experiences are a reflection of our geographies – the cities, towns and rural areas where we spent our formative years, our travel experiences, the cultural dimensions of our childhood, the labour markets where we sought employment, the friendships we made, and how all of these things are shaped by the globalizing forces of economic change, social technologies, and political integration. Geographers are well positioned to help students make sense of the complex circumstances in which they are beginning their higher education and what their varied geographies afford for their future careers.

Hence the need for 're-imagining ourselves as learners', which is the theme linking the first two papers in this collection. It is an empowering thought when one realizes the contribution one can make to the learning of others, by virtue of the experiences we carry with us. When these experiences are pooled in a learning environment - whether a traditional classroom, in a workplace internship, or in the field - opportunities arise for 'co-learning' within a community defined by a collective of experiences. This topic is the focus of the paper by Le Heron *et al*. A geography course, the authors note, might engage students and move them toward 'transformed experiences' via such signature geographical practices as field study, spatial analysis, and interdisciplinary collaboration. In all of these modes of geography education we can see important principles in motion: learning as a process of interacting with the social environment (Vygotsky, 1962), instruction that engages different cognitive styles (Kolb, 1984), and engaging students in the ways geographers think and work (ie, as captured by the CeAL notion of understanding via performance in Figure 1.1).

Because re-imagining learners and learning in geography is a process spanning a discipline with scores of specializations, educators carry the additional responsibilities of framing that process to provide students with practical experiences rooted in the sorts of ethical issues that frequently arise. The chapter by Boyd *et al.* warns that much of educational practice divorces ethics from the learning process, making it difficult for many students to understand the ethical considerations underlying the work they do and the decisions they make as geographers and users of geographic technologies. Active learning, however, provides immediate opportunities for introducing students to the ways geographers approach ethical issues by making this an explicit component of the learning process. The potential result is the 'ethical geographer' attuned to the moral facets of spatial data and technologies and the ways geographers can contribute towards more socially responsible societies.

Many geographers use inquiry as a means to engage students actively in the learning of geography. This theme is explored in more detail by the next four papers in this volume. As the paper by Scheyvens *et al.* notes, once educators take the step of adopting active learning techniques, it becomes a natural setting for teaching geographical content and skills, giving students a hands-on taste of how geographers examine the world using spatial concepts and mapping technologies. And the discipline itself provides an almost limitless amount of case material for which to engage students as problem solvers. Whether investigating source pollution in a local watershed or tracking the international spread of a virus, geography offers the spatial analytical perspective needed to address issues and problems facing the world's people, places, and environments. Thus, geography education ought to equip students with the competences they will need as future workers and citizens. To accomplish this aim, the papers Pawson *et al.* and Spronken-Smith *et al.* assess the ways in which problem-based and inquiry learning are being employed in the discipline, and provide insight into using these methods to create authentic contexts for geographic learning. Further connecting the process of learning and doing geography is the traditional yet ever evolving practice of field study, the subject of the paper by Fuller *et al.* Perhaps no other approach to active learning in geography offers students a more powerful opportunity to experience all aspects of the discipline, from cultural studies to environmental analysis, from field mapping using GPS to classical observational techniques.

And with a subject this rich and varied, it is unsurprising that geographers are at the forefront evincing new environments in which to engage students as active learners. The next set of four papers explores new spaces of learning. In recent years geographers have launched broad-based initiatives to build collaborations among students and educators, many of which are based on innovative applications of information and communication technologies. This trend seems to rest on the premise that pedagogy itself must change in a way that reflects the nature of the discipline being taught. In the case of geography, which is concerned with international issues, it seems most appropriate that geographers would seek to 'internationalize' the processes of teaching and learning as a means for promoting global literacy. Many of these initiatives are critically examined in the chapter by Higgitt *et al.*

Further evidence of the new geographies of active learning is presented in the chapter on e-learning by Lynch *et al.* The virtual world of blogs, podcasts, chat rooms, and social networking has charted new spaces in which learning occurs and has provided educators with more tools for creatively engaging their students beyond traditional classroom walls. Observing the importance of building and maintaining a sense of community of learners, the authors remind us that effective practices for online instruction, much like active learning in a traditional setting, should be connected to principles of social constructivism such as those described earlier in this introduction.

The chapter by McEwen *et al.* extends the conversation beyond undergraduate level to include postgraduate students in masters and doctoral programs. This is an important issue because research on faculty development in geography (Solem & Foote 2006) indicates that pedagogical techniques learned early in professional development persist into the first years of faculty appointment. The implication here is that the sooner future faculty are engaged in methods of active learning, the more likely they will adopt and experiment with those practices as they begin their teaching careers. Similar arguments apply for geographers who leave their degree programs for careers outside of education. This, in turn, can ultimately benefit students who, as noted in the chapter by Wellens *et al.*, may enter their future careers more prepared to apply their geographical education for the good of their neighbourhoods, nations, and the international community.

This theme of connecting students beyond the classroom into issues facing society underpins the last set of three chapters. Many geographers are advocates of the types of service learning approaches described in the chapter by Bednarz *et al.*, in which students participate in community-based projects as part of their higher education program. This is another example of how the geography of active learning can be conceived. Many students who experience these approaches – or any of the approaches described in this book – are much more aware of the value of geographic knowledge, skills, and perspectives in preparing them for careers in business, industry, government, and non-profit organizations, the theme addressed in the chapter by Rooney *et al.* As the demand for graduate-level training in geography continues to rise in the labour market (Solem, Cheung & Schlemper, 2008), so too will the access to geography programmes in higher education. The paper by Solem *et al.* examines issues in serving the needs of professional learners in the international workforce through expanded online course and certification offerings.

The conclusion to the book reflects on the practice of student engagement, past, present and future. It is a concept that has been around for a long time. We have argued that active learning is one of the best ways to encourage the majority of students to be engaged. So, we might ask, why is active learning not more widely practiced? It may be that many of the approaches to active learning and the evidence of their effectiveness are not sufficiently well known amongst faculty and their managers. It is our intention that this book will help to rectify this. It is also important that, based on the experiences of our own classes, we communicate to others how methods such as inquiry-based, problem-based, and service learning work for those students who are otherwise poorly engaged. That is the challenge that this book lays down.

References

Badley, G. (2002) "A really useful link between teaching and research," *Teaching in Higher Education*, 7(4), pp. 443-455.

Barnett, R. & Coate, K. (2005) *Engaging the Curriculum in Higher Education*, Maidenhead: McGraw Hill/Open University Press.

Barr, R.B. & Tagg, J. (1995) "From teaching to learning – a new paradigm for undergraduate education," *Change*, November/December, pp. 13-25.

Blythe, T. & Associates (1998) *The Teaching for Understanding Guide*, San Francisco: Jossey Bass.

Bryson, C. & Hand, L. (2007) "Do staff conceptions of good teaching and learning approaches align with enhancing student engagement?", in *Enhancing Higher Education, Theory and Scholarship, Proceedings of the 30th HERDSA Annual Conference [CD-ROM]*, Adelaide, 8-11 July.

Bryson, C., Hand, L. & Hardy, C. (2008) "The student perspective on enhancing their experience of, and engagement with, their studies, paper presented to SEDA Conference," *Engaging with Student Expectations*, London, 8-9 May.

Chickering, A. W. & Gamson, Z. F. (1987) "Seven principles for good practice," *AAHE Bulletin*, 39, pp. 3-7.

Cowan, J. (1998) *On Becoming an Innovative University Teacher: Reflection in Action*, Milton Keynes: Open University Press.

Elton, L. (2005) "Scholarship and the research teaching nexus," R. Barnett (ed.) *Reshaping the University: New Relationships Between Research, Scholarship and Teaching*, pp. 108-118, Maidenhead: McGraw-Hill/Open University Press.

Entwistle, N. (2003) "Concepts and conceptual frameworks underpinning the ETL project, Enhancing Teaching-Learning Environments for Undergraduate Courses," *Occasional Report* 3. Available at: www.etl.tla.ed.ac.uk/publications.html. Accessed 14 September 2009.

Fielding, M. (1994) "Valuing difference in teachers and learners: building on Kolb's learning styles to develop a language of teaching and learning," *The Curriculum Journal*, 5(3), pp. 393-417.

Gibbs, G. (1988) *Learning by Doing: A Guide to Teaching and Learning Methods.* London: Further Education Unit. Available at: www2.glos.ac.uk/gdn/publ.htm#other Accessed 14 September 2009.

Hay, I. (2008) "Postcolonial practices for a global virtual group: the case of the International Network for Learning and Teaching Geography in Higher Education (INLT)," *Journal of Geography in Higher Education*, 32(1), pp. 15-32.

Hay I., Foote, K & Healey, M. (2000) "From Cheltenham to Honolulu - the purposes and projects of the International

Network for Learning and Teaching (INLT) Geography in Higher Education," *Journal of Geography in Higher Education*, 24(2), pp. 221-227.

Healey, M. (2005a) "Linking research and teaching. Exploring disciplinary spaces and the role of inquiry-based learning," R. Barnett (Ed.) *Reshaping the University: New Relationships Between Research, Scholarship and Teaching*, pp. 30-42, Maidenhead: McGraw-Hill/Open University Press.

Healey, M. (2005b) "Linking research and teaching to benefit student learning," *Journal of Geography in Higher Education*, 29(2), pp.183-201.

Healey, M. (2006a) "International perspectives on selected issues in the learning and teaching of geography in higher education," *Journal of Geography in Higher Education*, 30(1), pp. 63-64.

Healey, M. (2006b) "From Hawaii to Glasgow: INLT five years on," *Journal of Geography in Higher Education*, 30(1), pp. 65-75.

Healey, M. & Jenkins, A. (2000) "Learning cycles and learning styles: the application of Kolb's experiential learning model in higher education," *Journal of Geography*, 99, pp. 185-95.

Healey, M. & Jenkins, A. (2009) *Developing Undergraduate Research and Inquiry*, York: Higher Education Academy. Available at: www.heacademy.ac.uk/assets/York/documents/resources/publications/DevelopingUndergraduate_Final.pdf. Accessed 14 September 2009.

Healey, M., Jenkins, M. & Roberts, C. (2005a) "Researching and evaluating active and inquiry-based learning in Geography in higher education," Paper presented to *Researching and Evaluating Research-based Learning in CETLs Symposium*, C-SAP, University of Birmingham, Birmingham, 15 December. Available at: http://resources.glos.ac.uk/ceal/resources/cealpresentations/0506.cfm. Accessed 14 September 2009.

Healey, M., Kneale, P., Bradbeer, J. (2005b)" Learning styles among geography undergraduates: An international comparison," (with other members of the INLT Learning Styles and Concepts Group) *Area* 37 (1), pp. 30-42.

Healey, M., Mason O'Connor, K. & Broadfoot, P. (forthcoming, 2010) "Reflecting on engaging students in the process and product of strategy development for learning, teaching and assessment: an institutional example," *International Journal for Academic Development*.

Healey, M. & Roberts, J. (eds) (2004) *Engaging Students in Active Learning: Case Studies in Geography, Environment and Related Disciplines*, Cheltenham: University of Gloucestershire, Geography Discipline Network and School of Environment. Available at: http://resources.glos.ac.uk/ceal/resources/casestudiesactivelearning/index.cfm. Accessed 14 September 2009.

Hodge, D., Haynes, C., LePore, P., Pasquesi, K. & Hirsh, M. (2008) "From inquiry to discovery: developing the student as scholar in a networked world." *Keynote Address at the Learning Through Enquiry Alliance. Inquiry in a Networked World Conference,* June 25-27, University of Sheffield. Available at: http://networked-inquiry.pbworks.com/About+the+LTEA2008+keynote. Accessed 14 September 2009.

Kauffman, L.R. & Stocks, J.E. (2004) *Reinvigorating the Undergraduate Experience: Successful Models Supported by SF's AIRE/RAIRE Program.* Washington DC: Centre for Undergraduate Research. Available at: www.cur.org/publications/AIRE_RAIRE/toc.asp. Accessed 14 September 2009.

Kolb, D. A. (1984) *Experiential Learning: Experience as a Source of Learning and Development*, New York: Prentice Hall.

Kuh, G. D. (2008) *High-impact Educational Practices: What They Are, Who Has Access To Them, And Why They Matter*, Washington, DC: Association of American Colleges and Universities.

Kuh, G. D. (2009) "High impact activities: what they are, why they work, who benefits," C. Rust (ed.) *Improving Student Learning through the Curriculum,* pp. 20-39, Oxford: Oxford Centre for Staff and Learning Development, Oxford Brookes University.

Pawson, E. (2008) "The INLT symposium: Brisbane 2006," *Journal of Geography in Higher Education,* 32(1), pp. 33-36.

Perkins, D. (1999) "The many faces of constructivism," *Educational Leadership,* 57(3), pp. 6-11.

Ramsden, P. (2003) *Learning to Teach in Higher Education* (2nd ed.), London: RoutledgeFalmer.

Solem, M., Cheung, I. & Schlemper, B. (2008) "Skills in professional geography: an assessment of workforce needs and expectations," *The Professional Geographer,* 60(3), pp. 1-18.

Solem, M. & Foote, K. (2009) "Enhancing departments and graduate education in Geography: a disciplinary project in professional development," *International Journal of Researcher Development,* 1(1), pp. 11-28.

Vygotsky, L. (1962) *Thought and Language*, Cambridge, Mass.: MIT Press.

Section A: Re-Imagining Ourselves as Learners

The first two chapters in this book propose new environments for learning in higher education. In chapter 1, Le Heron *et al.* discuss ways in which research and teaching, which became increasingly separated in the last decades of the twentieth century, could be re-linked. The authors propose that the concept of "co-learning", by which multifarious stakeholders in higher education work together in learning communities, provides a pedagogically sound and empowering way ahead. Seeking to dissolve the teaching-research dichotomy, the authors propose strategies based on reaching out to other disciplines, showcasing the applied nature of geography, field-based education, and developing internationally responsive curricula. One of the tenets of such a re-imagining of learning will undoubtedly require geography educators to renew their attention to matters of professional ethics. Boyd *et al.* (chapter 2) find that the provision of ethical learning is relatively weak at both undergraduate and graduate levels, resulting in the "disengaged graduate". This person stands in contrast to the expectations of sets of graduate attributes that highlight the need for the highest standards of ethical behavior. The authors then explore the barriers to, as well as more productive pathways towards, the production of the "Ethical Geographer", someone in whom ethical practice is embedded as the result of ongoing considered reflection.

Co-learning: Re-linking Research and Teaching in Geography

RICHARD LE HERON*, RICHARD BAKER** & LINDSEY MCEWEN[†]

*School of Environment, University of Auckland, New Zealand, **The Fenner School of Environment and Society, Australian National University, Australia, [†]Pedagogic Research and Scholarship Research Institute (PRSI), University of Gloucestershire, UK

ABSTRACT *What might geography in 'the universities' look like if geographers seriously confronted the growing dichotomy between research and teaching? This challenge goes to the heart of 'the university' as a site of learning. The authors argue that the globalizing character of higher education gives urgency to re-charting the university as an environment that prioritizes co-learning as the basis for organizing educational activities in geography and potentially beyond discipline boundaries. By co-learning is meant systematic approaches to maximizing the synergies between research and teaching activities to capitalize on prior learning and experiences of all involved. The authors' argument is that feedback gained through co-learning will reshape the nature and quality of both research and teaching environments as we know them. Four methodological framings of co-learning, derived from established practice in geography, are presented, to highlight possible directions of development that are especially strategic in the current context of globalizing higher education. It is suggested that with strategies that explicitly maximize co-learning, the development of geography could occur in distinctive ways that would not happen if research and teaching were progressed in isolation.*

Introduction

This paper considers what geography in 'the universities' might look like should geographers seriously confront the current dichotomy between research and teaching.[1] This is not simply that geographical research and teaching are carried out physically in the same department but an explicit and targeted approach to their co-development. Globalizing trends in higher education give urgency to re-charting 'the university' as an environment for learning where engagement is conducted in ways that prioritize *co-learning* as the basis for organizing educational activities. By co-learning we mean *coordinated and targeted approaches to maximizing the synergetic relationships between research and teaching such that their symbiotic development capitalizes on prior learning and experiences of all involved and feeds back positively on the nature and quality of both research and teaching environments.* We argue that with co-learning the development of geography could be dramatically different.

Our claim is that there are clear risks to the ability of those practising collectively as geographers in higher education to deliver learning opportunities. These derive from continuing moves to privilege or prioritize either research or teaching over the other and from making artificial distinctions between these spheres through a plethora of institutional rules and national governmental strategies. The emerging international scene now features university league tables, branding and quality assurance dimensions. These often separate out teaching and research and perpetuate a myth that they are unrelated activities. What is the evidential basis of the claim? Governmental modes of assessment and differential funding are acting to extend this divide. In the UK, for example, national mechanisms separately judge teaching (the Quality Assurance Agency) and judge and reward research (the Research Assessment Exercise (RAE)). In New Zealand a Performance Based Research Funding (PBRF) regime has been instituted (an equivalent in Australia is scheduled) and a universities teaching audit is pending (a teaching quality ranking exercise has been recently completed in Australia). In the case of the UK, a division of academic labour is emerging around RAE high-scoring universities and departments in comparison with those with not-so-high or low scores (and exacerbated by related rationalization of geography units). The extent of this division has increased exponentially since the first RAE in 1992 and the most recent assessment in 2001, with the total pot of research funding going to an increasingly smaller number of institutions. In the three countries some departments, seen increasingly as units of assessment instead of disciplinary homes, are reassigning teaching responsibilities. In New Zealand and Australia, low graduate enrolments in many subjects at some universities mean academic staff are effectively decoupled from this traditional arena of learning. For instance, two New Zealand geography groupings accounted for over 60 percent of PhD enrolments in the subject in 2004. This situation, while springing from underfunding and difficulties of recruiting students, has the unfortunate effect of restricting what some staff may be able to count as research-related activities. New Zealand's PBRF calculation procedures include 15 per cent for 'contribution to research environment' and the payment formula to universities is progressively taking account of academic unit scores, built up from individual PBRF scores.

Recent debate (Holmes, 2002; Johnston, 2002; Thrift, 2002; Gregson, 2003; Fincher, 2004; Herbert & Matthews, 2004) over geography's future misses at least one key issue: the nature of learning processes that might shape the discipline's contribution in the foreseeable future. An urgent priority is a reconceptualization aimed at exploring how geography could focus educational encounters and practices on co-learning. Such an agenda highlights a range of different dimensions to those presently being debated in the geography literature and, indeed, in the education literature (even Biggs's (2003) manifesto for quality learning at university does not mention co-learning in the index). First, that reconceptualization creates space to rethink what 'engaging to learn' might mean, within the discipline, in departmental strategy, programme design, courses and fieldwork. Second, it reopens the debate about who might populate 'communities of learners' and the relationships and interactions they might have. Existing categories and labels used to describe the present system may curtail discussion. Third, it focuses on the strategic work of 'framing' as an explicit part of creating learning processes. As a subject that has emphasized both personal 'a-ware-ness' and 'a-where-ness' about others (Massey & Thrift, 2002), geographers as a broad community may have the individual and collective capacities to encourage alternative learning frameworks in education through the demonstration effects of their practices. Asking questions about the distinctive nature of learning and learners, as Castree (2005) argues, yields useful insights into geography's future in higher education. We make a case that developing a culture of co-learning may be an invaluable intervention at this moment in the discipline. In arguing for a reconceptualization of research and teaching we are not simply calling for integration of these areas, since any attempt to do so would retain the conventional views on research and teaching. Nor are we attempting to justify a pedagogic career route in the universities (although this deserves serious attention). Rather we wish to elevate for collegial, managerial and student attention a potential strategy concerning geographic practice that offers a potentially different direction. Thus, we come to co-learning not because it is a pedagogic fad or an opportunity to secure subsidized inputs to research, but because it is a radical departure from much existing practice and because it might enhance both research and teaching as we understand them. But in order to begin our argument we immediately come up against the conventional wisdom in the current higher education academy: that there are two distinct areas of endeavour, research and teaching.

As geographers we identify the emerging international context as one that demands new approaches to learning and to facilitating innovative types of learning environments, and different institutional structures to aid the uptake of different educational practices (Robertson, 2004; Ward, 2004). Growing numbers of international students and the increasing international movement of especially postgraduate students and the rise of alliances amongst universities present new opportunities (and challenges) to explore geographies of life, land and livelihood. We suggest that the research and teaching binary, the distinction that defined the academy in much of the twentieth century, is an inadequate heuristic to guide the design of the educational menu of geography in a globalizing educational order. Instead, with widened access, we propose a model of co-learning amongst participants who, without traditional restraints of hierarchy, actively contribute insight from their varied backgrounds, academic, vocational and life experiences, skills and capacities.

We suspect how co-learning is perceived as an idea is very dependent on context, especially national degree structures and whether discussion centres on undergraduate or graduate study. The UK system, for instance, with quotas of students specializing in the discipline, differs sharply from the Australian and New Zealand systems, where students major or minor in subjects for their degree, with a maximum of half of the degree being geography. Thus, new student arrivals in the different countries are likely to be different. This difference counts. Students in Australia and New Zealand are often older or returnees to study taking a range of subjects. What is less apparent is the extent to which the UK system is represented by the Russell group mix of students or the mix found in other universities (which may be closer to the Australia and New Zealand experience rather than that of the Russell group). But more fundamentally, at the graduate level, the difference plays out in the post-university experience of many (if not most) PhD enrolees. Exploring co-learning is therefore a very real possibility.

Why do we advocate this direction? Our reasoning stems from structural, organizational and personal assessments. Foremost, universities—at least as we have experienced them—are broadening their entry at undergraduate and postgraduate levels and exhibit increasingly diverse ethnic, age and career-stage mixes. The UK's Higher Education Council for England (HEFCE), for example, is working strategically to embed widening access and improving participation in HEIs so to equip people to operate productively within the global knowledge economy. This compositional effect widens the life and work experiences that geographers can draw on to create co-learning opportunities in their teaching and research. At the level of the university or institution, we argue the research–teaching split restricts how learning (and research) might be approached. To our surprise, we found we had come to similar conclusions about exploring co-learning from quite different backgrounds, regardless of nationality, field in geography and career paths. To us, co-learning is an approach that could cascade far beyond the subject of geography. Much educational practice used by geographers already approximates or stands as examples of what we envisage to be co-learning. Many publications from the International Network of Learning and Teaching include examples (Healey *et al.*, 2000) and the course design followed by Cook (2000) is illustrative. This includes the high status of the *Journal of Geography in Higher Education* as recognized by impact factors in education as well as geography and growing appreciation in education circles that place and space affect learning.

The organization of this paper reflects these views. The opening discussion outlines a conceptual redirection rather than a prescriptive model of co-learning. As far as we can tell the particular wording of co-learning is relatively new. We then draw attention to the effects of the way educational activities are named. In particular, we argue that the research and teaching dichotomy is played out at all levels, from national governmental policy, through institutional interpretation to the personal decision-making on links and priorities (and associated tensions). Most of this paper, however, is devoted to illustrating how geography is both an exciting and fruitful field for innovative exploration of co-learning *and* an example of how space and place are integral to the concept of co-learning. We present four methodological framings of co-learning, derived from established practice in geography, to highlight possible directions of development that are especially strategic in the current context of globalizing higher education. Here, geography is foundational, in the sense that it is both a subject of relevance to understanding human and planetary issues *and* a context in which learning relationships are placed and linked. These framings are offered as illustrative examples of how geographers might reassess the potential and contribution of their contemporary practices.

In outlining the framings we draw on our own growing understandings of co-learning opportunities in and through geography in higher education. In many respects, collaboration for this paper under the metaphor of co-learning meant we had to confront the principles by which we had practised as educators. At one stage we had thought that individual biographies with examples of our introductions to co-learning would be an effective way to illustrate the value of the strategy. As we refined our argument, however, we realized our key intervention should be to sketch the wider landscape of co-learning possibilities open to geographers. We hope the following more general explorations help readers re-conceptualize their educational practices, towards co-learning.

Dimensions of Co-learning

Defining co-learning is neither easy nor straightforward. This arises in part because to name what we already attempt to do differently immediately collides with the assumptions, preferences and power relationships of existing orders of doing things. A likely response on first thinking about co-learning is to point to the presumed links between research and teaching to show that co-learning is already established practice and that any claims about co-learning are merely reinventing the wheel of educational practice. Indeed, this aspect cannot be sidestepped.

Several conceptualizations directly tackle the issue. Boyer (1990) recasts the academy in terms of a number of scholarships, a classification aimed at highlighting the intersection of research and teaching. Others have shown how research and teaching might feed into each other (Jenkins *et al.*, 2003). Healey (2005a, 2005b), for example, evaluates the complexity and contested nature of the research–teaching nexus from different national and institutional contexts. He states: "The development of such research-based curricula provides challenges to staff across the sector, not the least because they may lead to finding new ways for staff and students to work together" (Healey, 2005a, p. 183). Co-learning can be promoted as one such way.

So far we have avoided using the word 'students'. This use of 'flat' language has been deliberate. Our contention is that companion dichotomies (some with implicit hierarchies)—staff/student, lecturer/student, student/community, student/practitioner—precondition how we approach the research and teaching dichotomy. By giving centre stage to the university as a site for learning, and to learning as the distinguishing activity of all those involved in the academy (a perspective articulated by Boyer with his politically inspired classification), we believe the agenda of understanding and working on a changing world takes on a different complexion. Thus, the premium, at all levels, is in devising frameworks (frames-to-do-work) that assemble human and other resources, appropriate to particular lines of enquiry. While groups assembled for learning are made up of individuals or groups with experiences that equate to or exceed those of the organizers and authority figures and teachers are learners, learning opportunities are diminished if the insight sourced from outside the academy is ignored. Such suggestions are, of course, often the bread and butter of seminars, workshops, buzz groups, role-play activities and problem-based learning. We also acknowledge differences in difficulties and opportunities that the approach might face in human and physical geography. This stems from how knowledge is constructed within the discipline and its sub-disciplines. In physical geography there is a strong element of gaining declarative and procedural knowledge, before allowing functional knowledge. At lower levels of the curriculum the emphasis is on building blocks in terms of knowledge and skills but co-learning could be introduced by the third year and potentially earlier, with mature student groups with more extended prior learning experiences. For example, the exploration, investigation and explanation of unknown landscapes through real or virtual fieldwork can be excellent vehicles for facilitating co-learning within physical geography. What we are highlighting in this paper is the difference on the one hand between local or ad hoc examples and experimentation with the educational possibilities gained through the serendipity of those brought together in the learning environment, and on the other a *system-wide and systematic reorganization to explore co-learning as an educational strategy*.

Encountering Worlds through Mobility

Geographic fieldwork is an arena where practices relating to co-learning are quite visible, yet the wider advantages that might come from focusing explicitly on this dimension are still largely latent. What shape might co-learning informed field experiences take? Geographers value highly work in the field, whether on pedagogical grounds or because of the socialization (perceived as being into geography) connected with fieldwork. We acknowledge these positions but also view fieldwork differently. Rather, our main premise is that fieldwork can be seen as a way to maximize co-learning. However, even the extensive literature made available through the INLT on fieldwork fails to pick up on the scope to extend the range, content and nature of learning processes integral to activities in the field. From a co-learning perspective, both socialization strategies and knowledge-production strategies can be accented in fieldwork. Stated somewhat differently, learning *can* encompass the cognitive and the performative. But our rationale differs from the usual justifications. Instead of regarding the group or team activities of fieldwork (which are widespread in human and physical geography fieldwork) as primarily nurturing pro-geography feelings, we would stress the opportunities of group, individual-in-group and 'wider community' work for building an ethos of co-learning. The standard repertoire of activities in geography fieldwork experiences consists of a wide range of co-learning opportunities. These span guest contributor(s), panel discussions involving local politicians or organizational representatives or community gatekeepers, group reporting of findings to peers and the communities that they are researching (co-learning with), debates over conflicting explanations for observed patterns of space and place, and interviews with different stakeholders. These are rich opportunities for co-learning within a heterogeneous learning community.

Naming the co-learning dimensions of these important educational strategies would begin to expose the social construction of all knowledge and shift understanding of expertise by revealing the underlying social relationships in which expertise is accumulated. Everyone involved in fieldwork finds themselves in some way in the position of co-learner. Students, academics, community members and external contributors/scene-setters can all learn much from each other especially if fieldwork is constructed and organized in a way that is sensitive to co-learning opportunities. Students and staff alike can learn by listening or conversing with local experts who are voicing or demonstrating how knowledge about place, interactions, phenomena or outcomes is produced. Students can learn from each other and other co-learners if opportunities are provided for them to share the insights that their different worldviews provide, capitalizing on different sociocultural perspectives and prior learning experiences of the group. Again, shared reflection on and explanation of the unknown can capitalize on different knowns that are available in or to the group. Fieldwork can also provide important learning opportunities for communities being visited if reporting back opportunities are given for both visitor and hosts to reflect on what they have learnt.

The World Wide Web and other emerging electronic formats such as multi-cast and grid access conferencing links provide new opportunities for co-learning between students, academics and community members.[2] Creating informal social spaces is a key for much of this co-learning. That generations of geography graduates recall mostly fondly the social life of fieldwork should not be discarded as an incidental point. Maximizing the opportunity for this development of a sense of community has traditionally had other benefits, not the least in increasing the attractiveness of geography in the educational marketplace and in helping to retain and give a social and intellectual home to students who might without this sense of community drift elsewhere. This is an advantage of tradition and practice that is available to geographers. That the educational advantages continue to be construed mainly in such terms, however, is a blockage to further developing geography as a source of innovation in education practice.

A great opportunity from fieldwork lies in the trend to develop geographical courses and programmes in international frameworks. With increasing student mobility and cross-credit arrangements within university alliances, a new era appears to be dawning. Courses built around comparative cultural and landscape analysis in several countries, virtual fieldtrips contextualizing features of cities or landscapes in different states and countries, explorations of difference within cities or landscapes are all available. Geographers are conducting reflective enquiry on fieldwork (Welch & Panelli, 2003; Panelli & Welch, 2005). The cross-cultural dimensions of these framings of geographical fieldwork extend the nature of co-learning opportunities (see also Fuller *et al.*, this issue).

A key to the pedagogic value of fieldwork is thus the way it brings together people from different worlds. This integrative strategy is an explicit recognition that groups formed to ensure or reflect diversity, interests, affiliation, prior learning and vocational experience, cultural background and gender are potentially critical elements in constituting effective environments and relationships for co-learning. Once more, this is hardly a novel suggestion. Workshops, seminars and brainstorming sessions are the daily diet of the university. We contend, however, that organizing to make explicit the lines of encounter, whether through role playing, representation (e.g. citizens' juries) or structured opportunities to share reflections on what individuals have learnt, establishes a basis for co-learning along multiple axes. This could include 'expected' dialogue amongst those articulating different perspectives and positions on issues (e.g. around a specific resource management issue or alternative indexes and indicators of national development) and the 'unexpected' engagement from hearing why and how the arguments of others are expressed as they are (Hickey & Lawson, 2005).

Travelling Knowledge and Experts

A second framing draws heavily on actor-network thinking. The study of the spatial and temporal contexts associated with the circulation of ideas, models, artefacts and experts is a different route by which co-learning might be explored. This involves extending the scope of learning by delving into the agency implicated in the production, translation and use of knowledge. The analogy of the seed planted and growing differently in different soils—and with the hands of the experienced or inexperienced gardener (!)—is helpful. An illustrative question is: How do geography textbooks travel? Such questioning begins to reveal key actors—authors, publishers, readers, reviewers. Critical accounts give pointers. Textbooks require translation, a performance task essential to the communication of knowledge and understanding. Such understanding is achieved in context, the elements of which bear closely on how translation occurs. Smith's (2003) anecdote about Haggett's *Geography: A Regional Synthesis* is a rare statement of the processing needed to make the learning of others possible. Australasian replacements of the universalist textbook for introductory human geography, first in New Zealand (*Introducing Human Geography: Encountering Place*,

Oxford University Press, Melbourne) and then in Australia (*Introducing Human Geography: Globalization, Difference and Inequality*, Longman, Melbourne), illustrates the potency of making place-in-wider-space matter. Putting different locals/locales into circulation (in the form of a textbook, or travelling expert) poses fresh challenges for geographic enquiry, irrespective of field. In many respects, exploring space–time journeys enables one of geography's methodological strengths (Harvey, 2000) to be applied in new settings.

Another illustrative question is 'do we speak a common geographical language?' within geography internationally. Different cultures can use different languages for description, explanation and articulation of ideas, whether in understanding landscape processes or in evaluating human interventions. A good example is the terminology used to describe river environments; for example, what is construed by 'wild' rivers or 'wilderness' or 'wastelands' may be value-laden, culturally determined and favour some interests above others. Co-learning has the potential to expose co-learners to those differences in preparation for future engagement with different perspectives—a transferable skill.

Applying the Discipline

Another framing reflects on the potential of bringing examples of applied geography to the co-learning environment. Applied geography is about putting geography to use and lends itself to many forms of inquiry and active learning, such as problem-based learning. Our experience highlights that, within such frameworks, when research and teaching are connected they motivate students to work towards addressing the wide range of social and environmental problems. The potential for co-learning in problem-solving activities around human–environment relations and sustainable development is high. Potential subject foci and stimuli are varied (e.g. determining flood hazard management, waste management or sustainable tourism development strategies in developed or developing world contexts). Potential foci for debate within the co-learning environment include how theoretical principles are applied within geographical problem-solving or on what criteria environmental management options are evaluated. The former may involve both the application of a shared theoretical literature but with different interpretations, and engagement with different theoretical literatures (based on previous experience outside geography) and their application to a shared environmental management problem. A key question is therefore the application of which knowledge and skills for whom—a decision-making process that will be informed by prior experiences and sociocultural factors. In documenting human–environment relations geographers are always revealing issues of equity and inequality (e.g. who gets or does not get what, where and why). The potential for co-learning is maximized where groups of learners examine the research evidence from different human and physical geographical specialisms, and other disciplinary experiences and sociocultural perspectives are co-located in the same learning environment (Baker, 1997). Here there is potential for the learning environment to capitalize on resources (literature, data, specialist software) drawn together for funded live research projects and for the debates to benefit all those participating (including the researcher). For the student, there is the valuable opportunity to co-learn in the research process; for the researcher, the opportunity to view the evidence in different ways and to reflect on the specifics of learning by participants.

Engaging with other Disciplines

Geography has an extensive history of projects that transcend disciplinary boundaries and hence co-learning skills have long been at the heart of geography giving us valuable communication skills for multi- and inter-disciplinary working. Examples are numerous: consider, in the development of geography, the importance of Sauer's communication with geographers and social anthropologists, or the political/policy geographers' engagement with both policy and politics. Physical geographers, when engaging in inter-disciplinary discussion on environmental management problems, need to tailor their language and spatial and temporal perspectives to communicate effectively with different disciplinary specialists, e.g. engineers, geologists and ecologists (see Newson, 1992 for discussion concerning physical geography and its integration with neighbouring disciplines). Similarly, in debating the adaptation and mitigation impacts of climate change, geographers now need to engage routinely in debates with climatologists, environmental scientists, social scientists and landscape architects, to identify a few. At the Cheltenham Climate Change Forum in 2001, for example, geographers acted as facilitators for inter-disciplinary and multi-organizational stakeholder debate regarding climate change impacts in the South West Region, UK.

However, despite this long history of inter-disciplinary initiatives, analyses of the conduct of cross-disciplinary projects, as distinct from ungrounded rhetoric concerning gains from such interactions, are few. The status of disciplinary as against inter-disciplinary research and learning also is debated (see the increasing inter-disciplinarity of national research assessment (RAE) in the UK and the mushrooming of inter-disciplinary courses at many universities in the response to perceived student and market demand). Such Master's courses (e.g. in environmental management) that draw across students with prior learning experiences in different cognate disciplines and varied life skills can be particular fruitful locations for co-learning. Field-based discussion with different disciplinary specialists (including geographers) can facilitate new insights into familiar or 'known' landscapes or can explore competing explanations for 'unknown' landscapes.

Gregson (2003) foresees a post-disciplinary future, a horizon of opportunity towards which geographers might move. In the main, much inter-disciplinary activity embraced by geographers has been quite narrow in scope, consisting of small research or teaching teams. A three-country workshop series on the theme of 'Beyond globalization: subjectivation and governmentality' exemplifies the potential of co-learning as an organizing metaphor.[3] The workshops sought to extend participants' understanding of how governing is increasingly accomplished through techniques centred on knowledge, information and calculation. The workshop format was seen as a framework for engagement; the intent was open, to be informed as much as to inform. Each workshop was co-organized by three facilitators and consisted of approximately 25 participants. Workshop processes and the theme were kept constant. Who attended differed, in spite of advertising from geography departments, but about half at each workshop had a background in human geography. Significantly the concerns of each group could be traced to the mix of those involved. In Canberra (two days) where geographers dominated, the interest was subjectivity ahead of spatiality. In Auckland (two days) indigenous issues and the cultural studies background of many pressed discussion towards space and place. Those from outside geography who attended in Seattle (one day), in contrast, came from English literature and cultural studies and wished to interrogate spatiality *and* subjectivity.

The example illustrates two things. First, by deliberately constituting cross-disciplinary groups who would otherwise have not met and using mainstream educational techniques to run the workshop, a stage was set for different learning work. Second, by approaching the workshop as a co-learning exercise from conception to operation, perspectives on a shared but differently interpreted and utilized literature were articulated and discussed reflexively.

Conclusions

This paper is a multiple argument about the potential for co-learning as a key area in the debate around the present widely accepted and relatively uncontested teaching–research dichotomy. It has argued that geographers should be turning a critical eye to the practices of the academy, revisiting areas of traditional strength such as fieldwork and reframing these in the twenty-first century to maximize co-learning opportunities among multifarious stakeholders in higher education. This of course is a shift away from the traditional student/teacher view. It has argued, further, that developing a different conception of how the academy might work is needed in order to formalize the benefits of co-learning. The learning environment now comprises a community of co-learners, with different sociocultural backgrounds and different prior disciplinary, educational and life experiences. It has argued that use of the insight of geography to help refresh on-the-ground educational practices in the spirit of co-learning will not only benefit the subject but will also cascade to other disciplines. However, we stopped short of providing in the paper a worked example of a curriculum, believing this is for others to develop (through co-learning!). This goes to the very heart of our claim. As one referee put it: "Can universities still be considered sites for learning?" We contend that one key strategy to answer this question in the affirmative is through developing an environment that prioritizes *co-learning* as the basis for organizing educational activities in geography.

Our final comment draws on the University of Strathclyde INLT workshop process. The present paper, with its explicit working of space, place and environment, emerged from an engagement at the workshop of geographers with quite diverse backgrounds and fields of interest. What became apparent in the discussions was the sudden re-positioning of much geographic philosophy and practice that occurred in the group once co-learning as an idea had been made visible. We see co-learning as being central to geography futures.

Acknowledgements

The generous and helpful comments of the two anonymous referees are gratefully acknowledged. Mick Healey was also very supportive of the shift from research and teaching links to co-learning that occurred in our group discussion at the University of Strathclyde INLT meeting.

Notes

[1] This paper grew out of discussions at the INLT Workshop, University of Strathclyde, Glasgow, August 2004. Other members of the Linking Teaching and Research Group who contributed to discussions were John Bradbeer (University of Portsmouth, UK), Alan Jenkins (University of Warwick and Oxford Brookes University, UK) and Gabor Mezosi (University of Szeged, Hungary).

[2] An example relating to the use of the web for co-learning is shown at http://www.sres.anu.edu.au/people/richard_baker/teaching/epp/index.html

[3] The series was organized by Richard Le Heron and Wendy Larner (then Sociology, University of Auckland), with the third co-organizer, respectively at the Canberra, Auckland and Seattle workshops, Kathie Gibson (Geography, ANU), Rosemary du Plessis (Sociology, Canterbury) and Kim England (Geography, University of Washington).

References

Baker, R. (1997) Landcare: policy, practice and partnerships, *Australian Geographical Studies*, 35(1), pp. 61–73.
Biggs, J. (2003) *Teaching for Quality Learning at University: What the Student does*, 2nd edn (Buckingham: SRHE and Open University Press).
Boyer, E. (1990) *Scholarship Revisited* (Princeton: Princeton University Press).
Boyer Commission on Educating Undergraduates in the Research University (1998) *Reinventing Undergraduate Education* (Stony Brook: State University of New York at Stony Brook).
Castree, N. (2005) Whose geography? Education as politics, in: N. Castree, A. Rogers & D. Sherman (Eds) *Questioning Geography*, pp. 294–307 (Oxford: Blackwell).
Cook, I. (2000) 'Nothing can ever be the case of "us" and "them" again': exploring the politics of difference through journal writing, *Journal of Geography and Higher Education*, 24(1), pp. 13–27.
Fincher, R. (2004) Geography and futures, *Australian Geographical Studies*, 42(3), pp. 299–306.
Fuller, I., Edmondson, S., France, D., Higgitt, D. & Ratinen, I. (2006) International perspectives on the effectiveness of geography fieldwork for learning, *Journal of Geography in Higher Education*, 30(1), pp. 89–101.
Gregson, N. (2003) Discipline games, disciplinary games and the need for a post-disciplinary practice: response to Nigel Thrift's 'The future of geography', *Geoforum*, 34(1), pp. 5–7.
Harvey, D. (2000) *Cartographic identities: Geographical knowledges under globalization*, paper presented at the 29th IGC meeting, Seoul, South Korea, August 2000.
Healey, M. (2005a) Linking research and teaching to benefit student learning, *Journal of Geography in Higher Education*, 29(2), pp. 183–199.
Healey, M. (2005b) Linking research and teaching: exploring disciplinary spaces and the role of inquiry-based learning, in: R. Barnett (Ed.) *Reshaping the University: New Relationships between Research, Scholarship and Teaching* (Milton Keynes: Open University Press, forthcoming).
Healey, M., Foote, K. & Hay, I. (Eds) (2000) *JGHE* Symposium: international perspectives on learning and teaching geography in higher education, *Journal of Geography in Higher Education*, 24(2), pp. 217–298.
Herbert, D. & Matthews, J. A. (2004) *Unifying Geography: Common Heritage, Shared Future* (London: Routledge).
Hickey, M. & Lawson, V. (2005) Beyond Science? Human Geography, interpretation and critique, in: N. Castree, A. Rogers & A. D. Sherman (Eds) *Questioning Geography*, pp. 96–114 (Oxford: Blackwell).
Holmes, J. (2002) Geography's emerging cross-disciplinary links: process, causes, outcomes and challenges, *Australian Geographical Studies*, 40, pp. 2–20.
Jenkins, A., Breen, R., Lindsay, R. & Brew, A. (2003) *Reshaping Teaching in Higher Education: Linking Teaching with Research* (London: Kogan Page).
Johnston, R. (2002) Reflections on Nigel Thrift's optimism: political strategies to implement his vision, *Geoforum*, 33(4), pp. 421–425.
Massey, D. & Thrift, N. (2002) The passion of place, in: R. Johnston & M. Williams (Eds) *A Century of British Geography*, pp. 275–299 (Oxford: Oxford University Press).
Newson, M. (1992) Twenty years of systematic physical geography—issues for a new environmental age, *Progress in Physical Geography*, 16(2), pp. 209–221.
Panelli, R. & Welch, R. (2005) Teaching research through field studies: a cumulative opportunity for teaching methodology to human geography undergraduates, *Journal of Geography in Higher Education*, 29(2), pp. 255–277.
Robertson, S. (2004) The WTO/GATS: changing geographies of power and the education services industries. Paper presented at the Association of American Geographers Meeting, Philadelphia, 19 March.
Smith, W. (2003) Haggett, P. 1972 Geography: A Modern Synthesis. Harper & Row, London in 'Textbooks that moved generations', *Progress in Human Geography*, 28(5), pp. 671–674.
Thrift, N. (2002) The future of geography, *Geoforum*, 33, pp. 291–298.
Ward, D. (2004) Panel contribution, 'Perspectives on Globalization/Trade/Neoliberalism/Higher Education', Association of American Geographers Meeting, Philadelphia, 16 March.
Welch, R. & Panelli, R. (2003) Teaching research methodology to geography undergraduates: rationale and practice in a human geography programme, *Journal of Geography in Higher Education*, 27(3), pp. 255–272.

'None of Us Sets Out To Hurt People': The Ethical Geographer and Geography Curricula in Higher Education[1]

WILLIAM (BILL) E. BOYD*, RUTH L. HEALEY**, SUSAN W. HARDWICK†, MARTIN HAIGH‡ with PHIL KLEIN^, BRUCE DORAN§, JULIE TRAFFORD¶ & JOHN BRADBEER#

*School of Environmental Science and Management, Southern Cross University, Australia, **Department of Geography and Development Studies, University of Chester, UK, †Department of Geography, University of Oregon, USA, ‡Department of Anthropology and Geography, Oxford Brookes University, UK, ^Geography Program, University of Northern Colorado, USA, §The Fenner School of Environment and Society, Australian National University, Australia, ¶Student Learning Centre, University of Auckland, New Zealand, #Bucks Cross, Devon, UK

ABSTRACT *This paper examines ethics in learning and teaching geography in higher education. It proposes a pathway towards curriculum and pedagogy that better incorporates ethics in university geography education. By focusing on the central but problematic relationships between (i) teaching and learning on the one hand and research on the other, and (ii) ethics and geography curricula, the authors' reflections illustrate how ethics may be better recognized within those curricula. They discuss issues affecting teaching and learning about ethics in geography, and through identification of a range of examples identify ways to enhance the integration of ethical issues into university geography curricula.*

Introduction

There is a trend in higher education to define graduate attributes, the professional, scholarly and personal characteristics expected of graduates of university courses arising from their university studies. At Southern Cross University, for example, this is expressed as graduates being more than the sum of the knowledge acquired through their studies and extends to the skills, values and attitudes essential for gaining employment and advancing lifelong learning. These graduate attributes include ethical and professional standards, expressed as "Understanding and a commitment to the highest ethical and environmental standards, sustainability, sensitivity to moral issues and conflicts, and relevant professional and environmental legislation and regulations".

While this intention is laudable, we might ask whether universities actually produce graduate geographers skilled for practical and ethical engagement with their scholarly, professional and personal worlds. If not, how can they? Currently the system allowing this is weak, and integration of ethical thought and practice into geography curricula in higher education is relatively ineffective, especially at undergraduate level.[2] How can this situation be improved? In considering this challenge, the authors restrict the notion of ethics as ethical ways of thinking. This aligns well with geographical practice, providing ethics as practical reflection on professional and/or personal behaviour, rather than as higher level conceptual ethics or theorizing: we are concerned about ethics for living versus ethics for ethics' sake.

Academic integrity, rigor, fairness, and equity are integral to the geographer's working life. The ethics of the act of teaching are significant; an extensive literature on ethical and moral dimensions of school teaching makes this point. Among the characteristics of professionalism are self-regulation and the promotion of professional codes based on ethical principles (e.g. HEA, 2006; TDA, 2006), which, while these may be viewed as part of the new managerialism (Deem, 1998; Mahony & Hextall, 2000; Nixon et al., 2001; Nixon 2003), may equally be seen as codifying traditional professional values or creating a new professionalism. Furthermore, teachers may differ significantly from other professionals in that they must be above moral censure: as their professional knowledge is about what constitutes a good life, they have ethical duties to students, the discipline, institutions, and the wider natural and social world to demonstrate the living of a 'good' life (Macfarlane, 2004). Geography educators, for example, should not just teach, for instance, sustainability, but live it. What we teach matters: we are communicating information that can affect young people's attitudes (Forsyth & Maier, 2006). Our paper examines ethics in learning and teaching geography in universities, through reflection on our individual experiences as university academics,[3] providing examples of how ethics may be integrated into university geography curricula, thus offering suggestions to both academics and students as producers and consumers of geographical knowledge.

Because university teaching and research are so closely intertwined (a key defining character of university education), it is necessary to discuss research and ethics (e.g. Glassick et al., 1997; Healey, 2005; Le Heron et al., 2006). Teaching and learning about ethics is inevitably linked to research in two ways. First, issues of ethics are logically embedded in work done by the student as researcher, regardless of whether the research is input to coursework or research per se; student projects all engage students as producers of geographical knowledge and as co-researchers with their supervising academics. They share all the ethical considerations an academic must consider; this is especially so, and often explicit, in the apprenticeship model of research candidature and supervision, while it is more commonly only implicit, and unlikely to be acknowledged, in coursework studies. Second, ethics plays a central role for the student as a consumer and producer of geographical knowledge, where students need to understand the ethical considerations related to the research they are studying. In some parts of geography—notably the social and cultural geographies such as gender, queer, health and indigenous studies—this is explicit. Elsewhere—the physical geographies, for example—it may be less so, although recent trends towards professional training in geography (e.g. in environmental studies or management) place greater emphasis on professional codes and modes of conduct, themselves ethics-based.

The Roles of Ethics and Ethical Considerations in Geography in Higher Education

In framing this issue, the authors' collective experience identifies a conceptual model of the role of ethics in university geography curricula. At present, ethics is at best patchy within the curriculum (Figure 1). Undergraduate and research postgraduate pathways are different, and connections between them weak or invisible. Ethics largely only impinges on research students via ethics clearance processes, which act as impediments and define methodology. Issues of ethics are, in many cases, invisible. The aim is to create ethical behaviour amongst research students and graduates, although this is usually better achieved through specific content rather than by underlying principle. The undergraduate pathway, alternatively, largely relies on implicit statements of ethical matters, with some (limited) introduction of ethics content into the curriculum; content is, at best, patchy, and rarely approaches any sequential development of ethical skills throughout a course. For many students ethical issues are never encountered. The result is the disengaged graduate.

How do we, as university geographers, progress to a pedagogical and curriculum situation that better aligns to achieving graduate outcomes such as those articulated in the introduction? In a desirable situation (Figure 2), undergraduate and postgraduate experiences would be closer and overlapping, with undergraduate pathways, for example, providing a stronger ethical basis for postgraduate studies, and the latter being more closely integrated into undergraduate curricula. Undergraduate studies would be designed to provide explicit, diverse and sequential development of ethical understanding and practices. This would require vertical development of ethical content (knowledge content, skills practices, and the evolution of scholarly behaviour) and horizontal alignment of content and practice throughout a degree program, enhancing students' skills

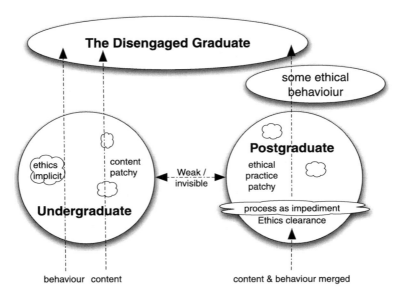

Figure 1. A conceptual model of the role of ethics and ethical matters in teaching and learning of geography in higher education, with the focus on the student as a consumer of geographic knowledge. The model is derived from the authors' collective experiences

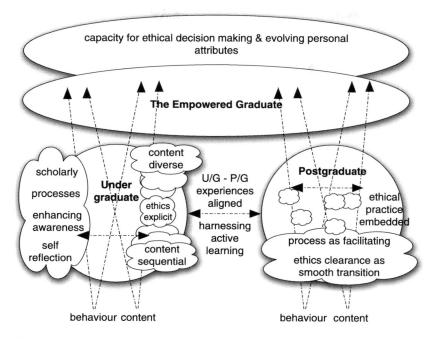

Figure 2. A conceptual model of the role of ethics and ethical matters in an enhanced teaching and learning of geography in higher education, where the focus is on the student working towards the empowered graduate. This model reflects the collective experiences and aspirations of the authors

of self-awareness and reflection. The result would be an empowered graduate with well-developed capacity for ethical decision-making and evolving personal attributes.

Ethics—a Complex of Concepts and Behaviours

Ethics, whether allied to a geography curriculum or applied more broadly, is a commonly-used label concerning a complex of concepts and behaviours (Israel & Hay, 2006): "the systematic study of morality concerned with what it is to make a moral judgement" (Smith, 2000, p. 231). Kimmel (1988) distinguishes ethics as the distinction between right and wrong, from morals as usual or normal behaviour, effectively the distinction between metaethics and normative ethics. Metaethics concerns the "analysis or logic of moral concepts" (Hay, 1998, p. 57), and underlies moral views, seeking and exploring meaning and function of, and justification for, normative judgements: the meaning behind what is right and what is wrong. In contrast, the theory of normative ethics proposes solutions to moral problems; normative ethics offer the moral norms that guide what should or should not be done in situations (Hay, 1998, p. 57). This is the basis that generally underlies university ethics procedures.

Although Hay (1998, p. 57) argues that normative ethics are more important for "the day-to-day practice of geography", here we suggest it is important to consider both normative ethics and metaethics in addressing ethics within learning and teaching. Students need to understand both their own moral views and the foundations of ethical considerations, and the behavioural or normative aspects of ethical action, to develop appropriate levels of scholarly and professional behaviour and, in a geographic context, empathy for the people they work with and the environments they work in.

A further distinction is important. If we consider normative ethics as having institutional and personal components, then it is possible to view ethics as representing the structured and reasoned response to issues supported by academic bodies and codified in universities into mandated rules and procedures. On the other hand, morals encompass the judgements about issues or dilemmas that have to be made by an individual. Both ethics and morals combine to determine actions within research *sensu lato*, and have to be examined and cultivated when learning and teaching ethical practice within geography. Ethical positions may vary: whose side is the geographer on when acting as a geographer? Whose values are influencing him/her? What ideologies does he/she hold? What are his/her personal preferences for one type of method as opposed to another? (to paraphrase Denzin, 1970, pp. 341–342). Research and teacher positionality will affect the answer to these questions, as it indeed influences all of an academic's scholarly position (Cloke, 1994). Consideration of ethical bases and decision-making within geographical curricula provides a foundation for structured examination of positionality, thus allowing the student to engage the relationships between him/herself and his/her studies or research as social activities (cf. Cloke, 1994).

The literature on current ethical practice makes a convincing argument that prescriptive ethical procedures are "in fundamental opposition to moral thinking" (Hay & Foley, 1998, p. 171). Research procedures used in universities are argued to induce a situation where, once ethical approval is achieved, the student or researcher is freed from the necessity to think ethically (Kearns *et al.*, 1998). This position counters the logical ethical position of perceiving ethics as implicated in every part of the research process, teaching, and life. If this is the case, ethics clearance procedures can ultimately undermine ethical practice, and may defeat the reason for being. Common examples of the effects of ethics clearance on ethical practice include interesting spatial and temporal variations in what is deemed ethical within, for example, a single institutional committee, with similar studies being treated very differently on different submissions. For some researchers, it remains a puzzle that they are only required to obtain formal ethics approval when dealing directly with human participants or animals, whereas there can equally be ethical issues concerning the use of publicly available written and spoken information, computer software, taking samples from the field, etc. Equally puzzling can be the common practice of obtaining blanket approvals for undergraduate student projects or for teaching material used in teaching, or that ethics approval may not be required for research by non-academic organizations.

Peach (1995) argues how consequentialist and deontological approaches to normative ethics have dominated the Western world. Consequentialist approaches seek the greatest balance of good over evil; deontological approaches emphasize "collective rationality and the importance of moral laws as 'categorical imperatives'" (Hay 1998, p.59). The latter view provides the basis of prescriptive procedures that universities and research bodies demand or encourage of researchers (e.g. ARC 2005; ESRC, 2005). Such frameworks for ethics tend to be better developed for research than for teaching. A recent Ethics Symposium (WACT, 2004), for example, asked: How do ethics impact on our everyday work as teachers? Why should teachers engage in discussion about ethics? Who should decide who guides our decision-making? Why does the teaching profession even want or need a Code of Ethics? In this context, it is unsurprising that the first real opportunity students have to learn about ethics is through submitting proposals to ethics committees for research work. This often has a negative learning outcome as students become entangled in bureaucratic procedures, blinding them to the positive advantages of best practice and the fundamental importance of appropriate behaviour. Ethics becomes a barrier or impediment to student progress rather than an enhancement, and makes the supervising academic's task harder. If for no other reason than this, it is incumbent on curricula to engage issues of ethics long before the student requires a bureaucratic encounter with ethics approval.

Ethical meaning emerges from discourse, context and culture. There is an uneven ethical global landscape, often expressed as different expectations among different universities (Howitt 2005). The study by Healey *et al.* (2005) of students in the US, Australia and UK provides a good example. Ethical clearance is considered unnecessary for a test project in the UK, whereas the same project required ethics clearance in Australia. In the US different institutions may have widely varying ethics policies for students and faculty. One of the authors (Klein) has experienced parallel outcomes in the AAG's Center for Global Geography Education project in which collaboration between universities in Barcelona and Pennsylvania resulted in project design varied to be suited to each country's circumstances, variation that raised the ethical issue of inequitable treatment of students engaged in the project, given that some appeared to have learning opportunities denied others. It is clear that research is "undertaken in a social context, and ... cannot be divorced from its social and cultural settings" (Howitt, 2005, p. 319).

Prescriptive procedures and ethics committee advice, therefore, can lead to unethical actions within certain contexts (Grayson, 2004); confidentiality and anonymity, for example, cannot always be guaranteed from a legal perspective (Vujakovic & Bullard 2001). The introduction of the recent anti-terrorism bill in the UK (Curtis & Taylor, 2005) could make guaranteeing anonymity in certain contexts more difficult; similar conditions may apply in Australia with the recent re-writing of sedition laws (e.g. AVCC, 2006). Since early 2006, some US funding agencies have added stipulations that their funds not be used in any way to support terrorist groups. This highlights the differentiation introduced above between ethics and morals: "the moral person is not one who blindly follows ethical codes, no matter how enlightened" (Diener & Crandalld 1978, p. 4). Ethical judgement becomes extremely personal, since "we all have very different personal or local views of what is right and wrong ... we have every right to follow what we feel is morally acceptable, unless it is harming another" (Robinson, 2005, p.6).

An Example: Ethics, Vulnerable Groups, and Conducting Ethical Research with Refugees

To put these ideas into a context, we provide a case study reflection on the comparative experiences of students and faculty as they engage with ethical practice in their research, drawing on Healey's and Hardwick's student-centred refugee research projects. Within research ethical procedures, refugees are frequently perceived to need greater protection than other groups. However, while it is important to consider how the research may address issues possibly not arising with other groups, working with refugees should not be considered distinctly different from working with any other group; all groups should be protected from harm. The overarching ethical view within refugee research is that research should be done *with*, rather than *for* or *on* refugees (Hynes, 2003). Working with potentially vulnerable people demands that researchers need "honest self-appraisal over motives, definitions, interpretations and accountability plateaus" (Teariki, 1992, p. 86). This provides the basis of our ethical reflections from two of the authors, a student and an academic respectively.

Healey's main dilemma in working with refugees is whether it is appropriate to intrude on the lives of particularly powerless people, just to complete a student project; this highlights a student's immediate agenda, his/her own scholarly development, against the subjects' needs. In disturbing people's lives, "information provided by the refugee must not only *not* be used to oppress, but if trust is to be restored, it must also be rendered meaningful" (Daniel & Knudsen, 1995, p. 5). Healey's work raised several ethical issues: how to examine refugees' experiences without re-igniting the traumas that caused them to become refugees; the practical problem of identifying and accessing interviewees; and ensuring participants did not feel undue pressure to participate. Although all research provides the opportunity for participants to decline, it is often harder than it appears, or than academics think, to do so, especially for people whose understandings of English and academic culture may be limited. Healey also encountered ethical issues in writing up (e.g. Healey, 2006), where ethical clearance had proposed that interviewees were automatically given confidentiality (Kimmel, 1988); it was not anticipated that not all participants may want anonymity (Grinyer, 2002). The student's ethical clearance in this case was static, coming at one point in time, and consequently in conflict with the nature of ethical practice and the changing ethical issues arising within the research.

Hardwick's experience, from the perspective of a faculty member engaged in learning and teaching ethics, highlights the particular challenge of finding ways to work within an ethical framework on refugee research. She has directed graduate students on refugee issues in the US Pacific Northwest, documenting migration pathways, spatial patterns, and adjustment experiences of refugee groups now residing in the region. Hardwick's ethical issues largely reflect the dramatically changing international political situation, with tightening of refugee admissions policies and the imposition of Homeland Security restrictions. The project's research maps of refugee residential patterns have now become potentially dangerous political documents, and the project databases now contain information potentially useful to law-makers intent on tracking down so-called 'illegals'. Ethically, Hardwick finds herself caught between supporting the greater good of her students' research and larger questions of the safety and security of refugee communities. Although the project regularly submits to her university's Human Subjects Protocol for ethics clearance, the emerging politically charged issues are not accounted for in university policies. Hardwick has established, with refugee groups, a strict code of research ethics, but still questions whether this is enough to protect the lives of people who must safeguard their legal status and economic security in the world they now live in, and whether the public maps generated by the project give away too much information. Only one thing is clear, she claims: the lives and landscapes of vulnerable groups grow ever more vulnerable. By continuing to discuss, debate, and act upon concerns to protect interviewees, her group continues to hope that published and unpublished research outcomes will support rather than harm refugees.

A Desirable Future: A Model for Enhancing the Ethical Capacity of Geography Students

The key to including ethics in university geography is that, for ethics education to be relevant to the contemporary university geography student and to be effective in developing a new generation of ethical geographers, geography educators need to move from prescribed ethical practice towards embedded ethical considerations (see Figure 2). Ethics are, after all, "socially embedded, fluid, and contextual and that ethical practice cannot be routinized" (Hay 1998, p. 72). Ethical teaching within geography, therefore, needs to concentrate on teaching students to think ethically within the context of their own studies or research, so that they can be flexible in their approach to ethical practice where necessary. This then becomes part of a package allowing students greater self-determination and authority over their own scholarship and work, through their closer understanding of foundations and principles, and of their practical abilities in critical and informed analysis. Of course, this situation is neither easy nor unambiguous: "are we more interested in making ethical decisions on the basis of the consequences of our actions or on the basis of some notions of 'justice'?" (Hay, 1998, p. 60). Perhaps the next generation of geographers will be better equipped to tackle and answer this question.

In general, work on ethics in higher education has focused on research rather than on learning and teaching. Hay (1998) calls for geographers to become a greater part of the debate on ethics in teaching and learning; Vujakovic & Bullard (2001) provide useful ideas to assist in focusing on an ethics and teaching theme. Given both Hay's and Vujakovic and Bullard's comments we reflect on our own experiences here—especially Haigh's Ethical Geographer course development (below), Healey's and Hardwick's work with refugees and immigrants (above), and Boyd's broad-brush approach to integrating ethical considerations across scholarship (below). Equally, it would be possible to consider issues in geography laboratory settings, ethics in collaborative assignments, and ethics and problem-based learning. Within the literature, Hay and Foley's (1998) take on ethics and citizenship provides valuable contributions towards the goal of teaching ethical geography.

Alongside the inappropriateness of prescribed ethical practice, it is necessary to engage students with a responsibility to the 'Other' and to their moral self-conscience, rather than to the guardians of a code of ethics (Hay 1998). Such an approach sits comfortably with the growth of the new humanities (e.g. Fiske, 1989; Stock, 1993; Fuery & Mansfield, 1997) and its influence on contemporary cultural geography and cultural influences on social geography (e.g. Short, 1991; Porteous, 1996; Gelder & Jacobs, 1998). However, in the authors' countries, most teaching of ethics is still part of a research methods course. Such teaching is largely designed to meet prescribed institutional ethical procedures, in which an ethics lesson is often simply another tick box to the rest of the course, making ethics appear secondary to other curriculum content. More importantly, it runs the risk of focusing on bureaucratic aspects of ethics clearance, and thus creates an environment, as indicated above, in which students view ethics as a hindrance rather support for their research. By considering ethics this way, there is a serious risk that geography students are not recognized as moral active agents within their education and learning. Jackson (1993) argues that students should be re-conceptualized as embodied subjects rather than detached observers: teaching and learning ethics in geography becomes about educating 'responsible citizens' (Hay & Foley, 1998), and thus ethics should be the basis of everything taught within geography, the foundation of the discipline. It is thus argued that ethics in university geography should be embedded in every part of the curriculum. In a contemporary geographical scholarly context, it is critical for ethics to emphasize empathy, and to be actively taught in collaboration with other faculty and students; this social aspect of teaching and learning emphasizes the core value of ethics as a social mechanism and process.

Two predominant loci of ethics can be found in undergraduate geographical curricula. First, where ethics are introduced into coursework they are largely subsumed into a broader agenda of 'cultural studies'. Cultural geography, as reconfigured over the last decades, fundamentally engenders issues of ethical and moral dilemmas, concerns for personal and group identity and expression of identity, the place of minority groups, and articulation of identities through behaviour within geographical and social space. Such an intellectual agenda is primarily concerned with issues of ethics, especially concerning relationships between people; students are thus confronted with ethical matters. Second, and especially with the growth of environmental management and studies within geography, ethics are introduced in the form of students' understanding and command of professional codes and behaviours; this, however, is more likely to take the form of training rather than reflective engagement. Boyd & Taffs (2002, p. 259) for example, extol students to "conduct work in as environmentally a friendly way as possible, and adhere to relevant codes of practice ... and laws". They support this call with exercises for undergraduate students to collect examples of codes of ethics for different environmental disciplines, and to consider how, for example, such codes enhance fieldwork, and how they compare between academic and professional branches of the discipline.

Embedding Ethics and Ethical Behaviour in Higher Education Geography Curricula

Having argued that the inclusion of ethics and education of ethical thinking and practice within geographical curricula needs to be widened from the current narrow views of ethical practice within research, it remains to illustrate how this may be done. To close, we offer two illustrative case studies. The first draws on the experiences of one of the authors, Boyd, in introducing teaching and learning of ethics into his own geography courses and research. Some of this concerns non-ethics-specific curriculum adaptation. Environmental management teaching and learning, for example, often focuses upon technocratic and bureaucratic processes, and can become apparently value-neutral; it is the perfect medium for discussing and introducing matters of ethical concern. Boyd does this by raising issues of environmental concern, community and political action, and environmental custodianship (Boyd & Laird, 2006), indigenous conceptions of environment, science as a social construction, and the roles and effects of social values on social behaviour, building on social construction theory (Jackson & Penrose, 1993), and cognitive ownership (Boyd et al., 2005), methods that are not overtly 'ethical' but inevitably raise ethical questions, questions of personal relationships and responsibilities, appropriate behaviour, collaboration and cooperation in professional activities, the self versus the group, etc.

While intercultural and cross-cultural communication is not a mainstream component in many geography curricula, it is a fundamentally geographic phenomenon. Studies in indigenous geography provide ample opportunity to cover topics as varied as heritage and natural resource management to housing, and to develop students' inherent cultural awareness, empathy, and sensitivity (e.g. Boyd, 1996, 1999). In parallel to this, as a director of a local Aboriginal cultural mapping project, Boyd has had the opportunity to be explicit in clarifying relationships that we, as academics, have with Aboriginal communities. This has worked through a Memorandum of Understanding which redefined the roles of academics, the university, and the community as partners, in part articulating the notion that teaching and learning extends beyond the university to the community, democratizes scholarship and de-authorizes the academic as 'expert' and sole author

(Greenwood & Levin, 1998). Finally, Boyd makes considerable use of Cloke (1994) as a valuable trigger for students and staff starting to engage in personal reflection on their scholarship, encouraging all project students to compose short autobiographies as part of the methods section of their research reports; this has been extended to a short self-interview exercise with three postgraduate students, in which the team reflected on the conceptual bases for their scholarship; the result was an, as yet, unpublished paper entitled "Finding a home: talking cultural geography".

The Ethical Geographer: Developing a Coursework Ethics in Geography Module

The second case study is a teaching module, *The Ethical Geographer*, recently introduced at Oxford Brookes University in the UK. This module examines an alternative way of teaching ethics in geography, and moves towards a greater emphasis on ethics within the university. The module articulates a particular interest in engaging more than just the ethics of the research, as is most commonly done by geographers. The focus is on geographers' activities as citizens, and the staff delivering this module try to address what one of the authors, Haigh, describes as "the wide-eyed and radical idea that the things geographers do could be more useful". Haigh was offered the opportunity to realize these ideas when his university department added a new course to the Honours component of its geography programme, a unit that he shares with a colleague. The module builds on four foundations: ethics (formally described), empathy (aspects of emotional intelligence and Emotional Quotient (EQ), environment (especially educational aspects of personal responsibility for sustainable development), and employment (which thus far basically refers to business ethics). It aims to encourage learners to consider their own personal goals and development, and the ambition is to persuade geography graduates to apply an ethical filter to everything they do, their studies, research and, more importantly, their everyday lives. The course first ran in 2006, and initial impressions are that the students seem content. The staff, however, are currently looking for other methods that can make this programme more effective.

In the module introduction, Haigh makes it clear that the module is designed to engage students in an exploration of what is described as "some largely unexplored territory", the students' self, equipping them with reflective tools and techniques to help them make the best of their own futures. The study guide introduction reminds students that the mark of a reflective practitioner is self-awareness, while the mark of a good citizen is conscience, one, it is hoped, that is clear because the citizen has self-evaluated his/her life and is satisfied that his/her actions are right, appropriate and morally correct. The introduction does admit a more controversial concept, that "the mark of a successful person is someone who knows who they want to be in the future, who is able to rise above the rough and tumble of everyday life, and who can, ultimately, say I was the best that I could be for me, for others, and for my world". The module is presented as an honours-level course, and so contains higher level undergraduate challenges and expectations of academic skills, capabilities and maturity. It is anticipated that students will become autonomous and self-motivated learners, with a solid grounding in a wide range of personal transferable skills: problem-solving, critical and lateral thinking, information retrieval, personal time management, team working and presentation. In other words, it addresses issues of ethics from a position of grounded reality and experience rather than theory, which is a strong behavioural or pragmatic process approach. Acknowledging that students will be entering "a realm where there are no easy answers and no universally accepted answers", it uses challenges to work out their own positions on key issues. Assessment is based on the skills with which they tackle the questions rather than specific answers themselves. Rather than prescribing ethical practices for students to research, this module aims to provide them with the skills to think ethically in all aspects of their lives.

The ethics component of the module introduces ethics as the systematic study of right and wrong, and so provides the framework for the whole module. The theme of empathy concerns the appreciation of beliefs and emotional understanding, and in doing so introduces students to psychogeography, the examination of landscapes in terms of their symbolic and emotional impact. However, at this stage, the module introduces a new, multicultural spin on the topic, an overview of ways different societies create their world picture; this emphasizes the contextual or positionality issues considered above. The environment component comprises what is probably the module's most explicit and conventional geographic content, paying homage to the *United Nations Decade of Education for Sustainable Development*, and concerning personal responsibilities and lifestyle and helping all people to live as if the future matters. This section also grants the opportunity for students to engage in practical environmental action through tree planting. Finally, the module turns to look at students' future, encouraging them to assess their current state and life goals through the writing of a personal statement; students need to reflect upon their current preparedness and needs and to construct a portfolio, such as they might need for a future employer, that illustrates their present capabilities and future potential.

Conclusion

This paper has come a long way. Commencing with a view that ethics is poorly integrated into university geography education, we have drawn on our own collective experiences, albeit in the Anglocentric university system, to identify impediments to integration of ethical education, and identify a desirable context for ethics education in geography curricula. We have drawn also on our experience to provide examples of engagement of ethical education in geography curricula, focusing on a practical or grounded approach rather than a theoretical one. It remains to be assessed whether we have, however, really answered the question posed above: How do we, as university geographers, progress to a pedagogical and curriculum situation that better aligns to achieving graduate outcomes such as those articulated in the introduction? While Figure 2 offers a schematic suggestion of a desirable position to be in, Haigh's module, for example, has yet to run long enough or to be evaluated critically to indicate if this is truly a model for a way forward. Likewise, our other experiences, drawn upon here to illustrate impediments, issues or small-scale teaching and learning approaches to the issue, have also yet to be fully tested. Nevertheless, they do represent a growing awareness of the need to better incorporate ethics education into university geography curricula.

Acknowledgements

The authors were all either present at the International Network for Learning and Teaching Geography in Higher Education (INLT) meeting in Brisbane (June 2006) or have communicated with the meeting group through the internet discussion. They acknowledge the many inputs provided by members of the INLT workshop and comments from others in the internet discussion. They especially wish to acknowledge the contributions and support of Eric Pawson and Iain Hay.

Notes

[1] This title draws from an illuminating statement in Israel & Hay's recent book (2006, p. 1): "It is disturbing and not a little ironic that regulators and social scientists find themselves in this situation of division, mistrust and antagonism. After all we each start from the same point: that is, that ethics matter. Indeed, we share a view that ethics is about what is right, good and virtuous. None of us sets out to hurt people."

[2] The author group considered this matter during the INLT workshop in Brisbane and its lead-up discussion, and while we focused in part on issues affecting the relative lack of teaching and learning of ethics in university geography criteria, and thus appear to be dwelling on the impediments to such curricula, it should be noted that we also discussed positive examples of how such obstacles and impediments to successfully integrating ethics into teaching geography could be overcome. This paper attempts to capture this balance.

[3] We acknowledge that the authorship has a distinct Anglo-American-Australian emphasis. This will influence our discussion of issues, both culturally and pedagogically.

References

ARC (Australian Research Council) (2005) *Research Ethics*. Available at http://www.arc.gov.au/grant_programs/research_ethics.htm (accessed May 2006).

AVCC (Australian Vice-Chancellors' Committee) (2006) *Media Releases 2006, 27 April 2006, Sedition Laws not appropriate for universities*. Available at http://www.avcc.edu.au/content.asp?page = /news/media_releases/2006/avcc_media_15_06.htm (accessed May 2006).

Bondi, L. (2005) The place of emotions in research: from partitioning emotion and reason to the emotional dynamics of research relationships, in: J. Davidson, L. Bondi & M. Smith (Eds) *Emotional Geographies*, pp. 231–246 (London: Ashgate).

Boyd, W. E. (1996) The significance of significance in cultural heritage studies: a role for cultural analogues in applied geography teaching. *Journal of Geography in Higher Education*, 20(3), pp. 295–304.

Boyd, W. E. (1999) Teaching cultural diversity to environmental science university students: Humanities-science culture clash and the relative effectiveness of three exercises confronting socio-cultural images and values, in: J. A. Kesby, J. M. Stanley, R. F. McLean & L. J. Olive (Eds) *Geodiversity: Readings in Australian Geography at the Close of the 20th Century*, pp. 213–223 (Canberra: School of Geography & Oceanography, Australian Defence Force Academy).

Boyd, W. E., Cotter, M. M., Gardiner, J. & Taylor, G. (2005) Rigidity and a changing order...disorder, degeneracy and daemonic repetition: fluidity of cultural values and cultural heritage management, in: T. Darvill, C. Mathers & B. Little (Eds) *Heritage of Value, Archaeology of Renown: Reshaping Archaeological Assessment and Significance*, pp. 89–113 (Gainesville: University Press of Florida).

Boyd, B. & Laird, W. (2006) *Analysing Global Environmental Issues: A Skills Manual*, 2nd edn (Sydney: Pearson).

Boyd, B. & Taffs, K. (2002) *Mapping the Environment: A Professional Development Manual* (Frenchs Forest: Pearson).

Cloke, P. (1994) (En)culturing political economy: a life in the day of a 'rural geographer', in: P. Cloke, M. Doel, D. Matless, M. Philips & N. Thrift (Eds) *Writing the Rural: Five Cultural Geographers*, pp. 149–190 (London: Chapman).

Curtis, P. & Taylor, M. (2005) Law-breakers in the library. *Guardian*, 8 November.

Daniel, E. V. & Knudsen, J. C. (Eds) (1995) *Mistrusting Refugees* (Berkeley, CA: University of California Press).

Deem, R. (1998) 'New managerialism' and higher education: the management of performances and cultures in the United Kingdom, *International Studies in the Sociology of Education*, 8(1), pp. 47–70.

Denzin, N. (1970) On ethics and the politics of doing sociology, in: *The Research Act*, pp. 314–343 (Chicago: Aldine).

Diener, E. & Crandall, R. (1978) *Ethics and Values in Social and Behavioural Research* (Chicago: University of Chicago Press).

ESRC (2005) *Research Ethics Framework* (Swindon: Economic and Social Research Council).

Fiske, J. (1989) *Understanding Popular Culture* (London & New York: Routledge).

Forsyth, A. S. & Maier, J. N. (2006) Affective outcomes of a world geography course, *Journal of Geography*, 105(2), pp. 59–74.

Fuery, P. & Mansfield, N. (1997) *Cultural Studies and the New Humanities: Concepts and Controversies* (Melbourne: Oxford University Press).

Gelder, K. & Jacobs, J. M. (1998) *Uncanny Australia: Sacredness and Identity in a Postcolonial Nation* (Carlton South: Melbourne University Press).

Glassick, C. E., Huber, M. T. & Maerof, G. I. (1997) *Scholarship Assessed: Evaluation of the Professoriate* (San Francisco: Jossey Bass).

Grayson, P. (2004) How ethics committees are killing survey research on Canadian students, *University Affairs*, Available at http://www.universityaffairs.ca (accessed January 2007).

Greenwood, D. J. & Levin, M. (1998) *Introduction to Action Research: Social Research for Social Change* (Thousand Oaks, CA: Sage Publications).

Grinyer, A. (2002) The anonymity of research participants: assumptions, ethics and practicalities. *Social Research Update* 36. Available at http://www.soc.surrey.ac.uk/sru/SRU36.html (accessed January 2007).

Hay, I. (1998) Making moral imaginations: research ethics, pedagogy, and professional human geography, *Ethics Place and Environment*, 1(1), pp. 55–76.

Hay, I. & Foley, P. (1998) Ethics, geography and responsible citizenship, *Journal of Geography in Higher Education*, 22(2), pp. 169–183.

HEA. (Higher Education Academy) (2006) *The UK Professional Standards Framework for Teaching and Supporting Student Learning in Higher Education* (Higher Education Academy, York). Available at http//:www.heacademy.ac.uk/regandaccr/StandardsFramework.pdf (accessed February 2006).

Healey, M. (2005) Linking research and teaching to benefit student learning, *Journal of Geography in Higher Education*, 29(2), pp. 183–201.

Healey, M., Kneale, P. & Bradbeer, J. (2005) Learning styles among geography undergraduates: an international comparison, *Area*, 37(1), pp. 30–47.

Healey, R. L. (2006) Asylum seekers and refugees: a structuration theory analysis of their experiences in the UK, *Population, Space and Place*, 12(4), pp. 257–271.

Howitt, R. (2005) Human ethics, supervision and equity: ethical oversight of student research, *Journal of Geography in Higher Education*, 29(3), pp. 317–320.

Hynes, T. (2003) The issue of 'trust' or 'mistrust' in research with refugees: choices, caveats and considerations for researchers, *New Issues in Refugee Research* (London: UNHCR).

Israel, M. & Hay, I. (2006) *Research Ethics for Social Scientists* (London: Sage Publications).

Jackson, P. A. (1993) Changing ourselves: a geography of position, in: R. J. Johnston (Ed.) *The Challenge for Geography*, pp. 198–214 (Oxford: Blackwell).

Jackson, P. A. & Penrose, J. (Eds) (1993) *Constructions of Race, Place and Nation* (London: UCL Press).

Kearns, R., Le Heron, R. & Romaniuk, A. (1998) Interactive ethics: developing understanding of the social relations of research, *Journal of Geography in Higher Education*, 22(3), pp. 297–310.

Kimmel, A. J. (1988) *Ethics and Values in Applied Social Research* (London: Sage Publications).

Le Heron, R., Baker, R. & McEwen, L. (2006) Co-learning: re-linking research and teaching in geography, *Journal of Geography in Higher Education*, 30(1), pp. 77–87.

Macfarlane, B. (2004) *Teaching with Integrity: The Ethics of Higher Education Practice* (London: Routledge).

Mahony, P. & Hextall, I. (2000) *Reconstructing Teaching: Standards, Performance and Accountability* (London: Routledge).

Nixon, J. (2003) Professional renewal as a condition of institutional change: a manifesto of hope, *International Studies for the Sociology of Education*, 13(1), pp. 3–15.

Nixon, J., Marks, A., Rowland, S. & Walker, M. (2001) Towards a new academic professionalism: a manifesto of hope, *British Journal of Sociology of Education*, 22(2), pp. 227–244.

Peach, L. (1995) An introduction to ethical theory, in: R. L. Penslar (Ed.) *Research Ethics: Cases and Materials*, pp. 13–26 (Bloomington: Indiana University Press).

Porteous, J. D. (1996) *Environmental Aesthetics: Ideas, Politics and Planning* (London & New York: Routledge).

Robinson, S. (2005) Ethics and employability, in: *Learning and Employability*, pp. 1–25 (York: Higher Education Academy). Available at http://www.heacademy.ac.uk/resources.asp?process=full_record&section=generic&id=584 (accessed October 2007).

Short, J. R. (1991) *Imagined Country: Society, Culture and Environment* (London and New York: Routledge).

Smith, D. M. (2000) Geography and ethics, in: R. J. Johnston, D. Gregory, G. Pratt & M. Watts (Eds) *The Dictionary of Human Geography*, 4th edn, pp. 231–234 (Oxford: Blackwell).

Stock, B. (1993) Reading, community and a sense of place, in: D. Duncan & D. Ley (Eds) *Place/Culture/Representation*, pp. 314–328 (London and New York: Routledge).

TDA (Training and Development Agency) (2006) *Professional Standards for Classroom Teachers* (London: Training and Development Agency). Available at http:www.tda.gov.uk/upload/pdf/d/draft_revised_ standards_for_classroom_teachers_6_apr_06.pdf (accessed June 2006).

Teariki, C. (1992) Ethical issues in research from a Maori perspective, *New Zealand Geographer*, 48(2), pp. 85–86.

Vujakovic, P. & Bullard, J. (2001) The ethics minefield: issues of responsibility in learning and research, *Journal of Geography in Higher Education*, 25(2), pp. 275–283.

WACT (Western Australian College of Teaching) (2004) *Ethics for the Teaching Profession.* Available at http://www.collegeofteaching.wa.edu.au/ethics.html (accessed May 2006).

Section B: Engaging Students in Inquiry

The four chapters in this section outline effective practices in student-led inquiry, a key area of active learning. Scheyvens *et al.* (chapter 3) try to dispel the myths that fuel resistance against active learning, and counter them by providing worked examples and by using the voices of students who have benefited from the deeper learning that can result. Pawson *et al.* (chapter 4) undertake a critical assessment of the purposes, benefits, and risks of problem-based learning, and explore its applications internationally in geography. Another set of examples is provided in chapter 5 by Spronken-Smith *et al.*, the focus of which is on inquiry-based learning. Like problem-based learning, the authors view student inquiry as a subset of active learning, with a focus on question-driven, student-centered methods. One of the signature components of geographic inquiry is fieldwork, a subject specifically addressed in chapter 6 by Fuller *et al.* They draw on research spanning three continents and conclude that the strongest theme concerning the effectiveness of fieldwork from a student perspective is "the hands-on experience of the real world that fieldwork provides across cultures and continents". In sum, these four chapters set forth signposts to guide students and faculty toward effective learning in the geography classroom.

Experimenting with Active Learning in Geography: Dispelling the Myths that Perpetuate Resistance

REGINA SCHEYVENS*, AMY L. GRIFFIN**, CHRISTINE L. JOCOY[†], YAN LIU[‡] & MICHAEL BRADFORD[§]

*School of People, Environment and Planning, Massey University, New Zealand, **School of Physical, Environmental and Mathematical Sciences, University of New South Wales-ADFA, Australia, †Department of Geography, California State University, Long Beach, USA, ‡Humanities and Social Studies Education Academic Group, National Institute of Education, Singapore, §School of Environment and Development, University of Manchester, UK

ABSTRACT *While some geographers have embraced active learning as a means to engage students in a course, many others stick to conventional teaching methods. They are often deterred by suggestions that it can be difficult to implement active learning where students have no prior knowledge of a subject, that active learning requires too much work of lecturers and students, and that there are significant institutional constraints to implementing active learning. In this article the authors draw on their experiences of utilizing active learning in five different countries before dispelling myths which continue to constrain the uptake of active learning methods. Finally, they provide simple guidelines for successful integration of active learning in geography courses.*

Introduction

The term *active learning* covers a wide variety of learning strategies aimed at encouraging active student participation in learning ('learning-by-doing'). Active learning requires more than simple activity, however; rather it should also encourage thinking and reflection on learning activities (Bonwell & Eison, 1991). For some time now geographers and others in related disciplines have recognized the value of promoting active learning in the university setting. By utilizing learning strategies that can include small-group work, role play and simulations, data collection and analysis, active learning is purported to "increase student interest and motivation and to build students' critical thinking, problem solving and social skills" (Hanson & Moser, 2003, p. 18). Healey & Jenkins (2000) show how using a range of different teaching methods, as is common when promoting active learning, is appropriate in terms of responding to students' different learning styles. Certainly this approach adds variety to a course, thus helping to arouse students' curiosity and retain interest and attention.

Given the strengths of active learning noted above, some geographers have enthusiastically adopted an active learning approach with its philosophy running through every aspect of their teaching. However, it is apparent that more of us have simply chosen to experiment with some of the methods of active learning. One question we will examine in this paper, therefore, is whether one can achieve good learning outcomes in a course by 'experimenting' with active learning methods from time to time, or whether it is necessary to embrace this learning philosophy wholeheartedly in the design and overall concept for a course or degree programme.

The main aim of this paper is, however, to explore some concerns that have been raised with regard to the application of active learning. Many geographers still feel that there are significant problems to adopting an active learning approach, arguing, for example, that it can be difficult to implement active learning where students have no prior knowledge of a subject, that active learning requires too much work of lecturers and students, and that there are significant institutional constraints to implementing active learning. The authors have direct experience of working in a wide range of tertiary institutions in England, Singapore, Australia, United States, and New Zealand, so will provide examples of their own experiences in utilizing active learning before spelling out, and dispelling, a number of myths that have been perpetuated about active learning methods. Finally, we provide a number of simple guidelines for successful integration of active learning in geography courses.

Approaches to Active Learning

What constitutes active participation is typically expressed by what it is not—students passively listening to a lecture delivered by a lecturer. While student note-taking provides some measure of activity during a lecture, such action is typically limited to copying what the lecturer has provided, an activity that may easily be void of learning. Moreover, in a traditional classroom setting, it is quite possible for students to get by *without* taking an active part in the learning process. A teacher-focused information transfer approach to education primarily involves information recall or fact recognition, thinking of the lowest order on most taxonomies of thinking skills (see Houghton, 2003 for a review of these taxonomies). Marton & Säljö (1976) first described two radically different student approaches to learning: the surface and deep approaches to learning. In the surface approach, students learn to reproduce knowledge (e.g. by regurgitating facts in an exam), whereas in the deep approach, they make sense of or develop meaning from knowledge.

There are numerous reports of individual students who take a deep approach in one context, and a surface approach in others (e.g. Gibbs, 1992), suggesting that students can and do change their approach to learning, and that we do have at least some ability to influence the approach that they take. A common goal of the strategies and methods of active learning is the facilitation of higher-order thinking skills, not just knowledge and recall of facts, but comprehension, application, analysis, synthesis and evaluation of knowledge (Bloom *et al.*, 1984). Such skills require that students *engage* with the subject matter, a factor that has been identified as the key to successful learning in tertiary education (Pascarella & Terenzini, 1991).

We can situate active learning strategies within the constructivist approach to student learning. Proponents of this approach believe that knowledge does not exist independently of the knower (Prosser & Trigwell, 1999). In other words, if a student is to learn something, there must be an interaction between the student's internal knowledge structures and the outside world. This interaction can be supported by requiring the student to both participate in an activity and then reflect on his/her experience with the activity. This process of engagement with learning enables students to internalize key concepts and make linkages between theory and practice (Charman & Fullerton, 1995). For example, when students are encouraged to relate what they are learning to their previous experiences, they are more likely to absorb new ideas. Other related approaches include activated learning (the specific relation of experiences of current learning activities with experiences of prior activities, described in van Hoven & de Boer, 2001), and Vygotsky's (1978) construct of the zone of proximal development, in which he argues that students will learn most efficiently when teachers can make connections with what students already know.

Active learning strategies require more than simple activity. As Gibbs (1988, p. 9) suggests: "It is not enough just to do, and neither is it enough just to think. Nor is it enough to simply do and think. Learning from experience must involve linking the doing and the thinking." It is this process of reflection that creates the critical link between the student's internal knowledge structures and the outside world (i.e. his/her experience of an activity). Toohey (1999) presents a generic model of learning that is composed of five stages, the latter four of which can be iterative: (1) be introduced to it (a topic, concept, method, etc.), (2) get to know it, (3) try it out, (4) get feedback and (5) reflect and adjust. She notes that, in many university courses, lecturers place too little emphasis on the last three stages of her learning model and that, furthermore, this imbalance is a key factor in explaining why students fail to learn. Active learning strategies can help rectify this imbalance by explicitly asking students to reflect on their experience and their learning.

If we accept that reflection is a necessary component of successful active learning strategies, we can look to theories of experiential learning to guide us in how we might incorporate reflection into our classroom activities. Although many others have since proposed minor extensions of or changes to his theory, Kolb's (1984) theory of experiential learning provides a starting point for considering how to integrate activity, reflection, conceptualization, and experimentation. Kolb theorized that learning is cyclical and occurs in four stages: concrete experience, reflective observation, abstract conceptualization, and active experimentation. In his theory, we can consider the active part of active learning to encompass both the concrete experience (an event) and active experimentation (planning for an experience) stages of learning, while reflection requires both reflective observation (thinking about what happened) and abstract conceptualization (thinking about what was learned and implications of what was learned). Finally, active learning strategies that aim to utilize and develop all four of these stages of learning can help to produce more balanced learners with a richer range of learning capabilities (Healey *et al.*, 2005).

Implementing Active Learning

Reports from the Literature

The geography education literature contains a number of descriptions of the implementation of active learning strategies (some examples are provided in Table 1).

Table 1 List of resources for finding out more about how active learning strategies have been implemented in geography courses

General resources

Centre for Active Learning in Geography, Environment and Related Disciplines, University of Gloucestershire, England. Available at http://www.glos.ac.uk/ceal/index.cfm (accessed September 2006).

Healey, M. & Jenkins, A. (2000) Kolb's experiential learning theory and its application in geography in higher education, *Journal of Geography*, 99, pp. 185–195.

Healey, M. & Roberts, J. (Eds) (2004) *Engaging Students in Active Learning: Case Studies in Geography, Environment and Related Disciplines* (Cheltenham: Geography Discipline Network and School of Environment, University of Gloucestershire).

Human geography

Association of American Geographers. (2003) *ARGWorld: Activities and Resources for the Geography of the World* (Austin, TX: Holt, Reinhart & Winston).

Association of American Geographers (n.d.) *ARGUS: Activities and Readings in the Geography of the United States* (Austin, TX: Holt, Reinhart & Winston).

Buckley, G. L., Bain N.R. & Luginbuhl A.M. (2004) Adding an active learning component to a large lecture course, *Journal of Geography,* 103 (6), pp. 231–237.

Chacko, E. (2005) Exploring youth cultures geographically through active learning, *Journal of Geography*, 104 (1), pp. 9–16.

Elwood, S. (2004) Experiential learning, spatial practice and critical urban geographies, *Journal of Geography*, 103 (2), pp. 55–63.

Hanson, S. & Moser, S. (2003) Reflections on a discipline-wide project: developing active learning modules on the human dimensions of global change, *Journal of Geography in Higher Education*, 27 (1), pp. 17–38.

Hooey, C. A. & Bailey, T. J. (2005) Journal writing and the development of spatial thinking skills, *Journal of Geography*, 104 (6), pp. 257–261.

Klein, P. (2003) Active learning strategies and assessment in world geography classes, *Journal of Geography*, 102 (4), pp. 146–157.

Kuby, M., Harner, H. & Gober, P. (2003) *Human Geography in Action*, 3rd edn (Hoboken, NJ: Wiley).

Kurtz, H. (2004) Reflecting on role play in geographic education: The case of the banana war, *Journal of Geography*, 103 (1), pp. 16–27.

Newnham, R. M. (1997) Lecture reviews by students in groups, *Journal of Geography in Higher Education*, 21 (1), pp. 57–64.

Oberle, A. P. (2004) Understanding public land management through role-playing, *Journal of Geography*, 103 (5), pp. 199–210.

Pandit, K. & Alderman, D. (2004) Border crossings in the classroom: the international student interview as a strategy for promoting intercultural understanding, *Journal of Geography*, 103 (3), pp. 127–136.

Physical geography

Carbone, G. J. & Power, H. C. (2005) Interactive exercises for an introductory weather and climate course, *Journal of Geography*, 104 (1), pp. 3–7.

Haigh, M. J. & Revill, G. (1995) The landscape assay: exploring pluralism in environmental interpretation, *Journal of Geography in Higher Education*, 19 (1), pp. 41–55.

Taylor, A. (2005) Lab instructions and data. Introduction to physical geography. Available at http://www.geog.psu.edu/courses/geog10/taylor/ (accessed May 2006).

Tschakert, P. (2006) Syllabus. Participatory research and methods. Available at http://www.geog.psu.edu/courses/ (accessed May 2006).

Geographic methods and techniques

Livingstone, D. & Lynch, K. (2002) Group project work and student-centred active learning: two different experiences, *Journal of Geography in Higher Education*, 26 (2), pp. 217–237.

These examples range in scope from single-class period active learning exercises to whole-of-course active learning implementations. Some of the descriptions explicitly reference Kolb's theory of experiential learning or other methods of integrating action with reflection, although most do not.

We can also discern differences in the way in which active learning is applied in physical geography, techniques-based and human geography courses. Courses in physical geography, methods, and geospatial technologies (cartography, GIS, and remote sensing) traditionally include activities such as conducting experiments, collecting and analyzing data, observing and mapping phenomena, and using computer software. In these contexts, activity is systematically incorporated into the design of the course, including the time schedule and credit allocation (that is, time is split between lecture and laboratory sections and students receive more credit for the additional course meetings). In contrast, human geography courses traditionally follow the lecture model and time schedule, such that it is up to the lecturer to incorporate active learning strategies. In these contexts, active learning may not be systematically incorporated, but used occasionally. It is important, however, to distinguish between merely providing opportunities for activity and activities that are successful in promoting learning. Here, we can take the example of field trips, an activity that is commonly used in both human and physical geography courses. As Lonergan and Andresen (1988, p. 70) note: "Effective learning cannot be expected just because we take students into the field." Kent *et al.* (1997) document the changing nature of activity in field trips over time, which started out as 'look-see' tours, but have more recently taken on a problem-orientated, project-based character.

For effective learning, whether in physical geography laboratory exercises or human geography student discussions, students must be encouraged to reflect on and articulate the ways in which the activity promoted their own learning (i.e. they should be able to identify the purpose of the activity and what they learned from it).

Case Studies of Practice

In this section, we describe some of our own experiences in using active learning strategies at various levels of the curriculum, ranging from occasional implementations in individual class sessions to active learning as a major component of a course. We start with an example from a first-year course, and finish with an upper level undergraduate course. Later we reflect on the outcomes of these different approaches to utilizing active learning with geography students.

(1) Using Problem-Based Learning in a 'Techniques in Geography' course

One of the geography courses, Techniques in Geography, taught by Yan Liu at the National Institute of Education, Singapore, includes some significant problem-based learning activities. This is a first-year course which typically attracts 20–30 students. The course is designed to equip students with various practical skills in geographical studies, including basic computer skills, geographical sampling, map reading and interpretation, geographical data collection, processing and presentation using GPS and GIS technologies. Using a problem-based learning (PBL) approach,[1] students encounter a real-world problem first in the learning process. One of the problems they have is to update an old campus map using GPS and GIS technologies. They are assigned to work in groups to critique the existing map, hence developing critical map-reading skills. They then draw up an 'action plan' to decide what they need to do, how they would like to do it, what data they require, where and how to collect the data, how to integrate data from difference sources and present the data effectively in digital map form. Students thus learn various geographical techniques throughout the problem-solving process. They are assessed continuously through various hands-on activities, fieldwork and project presentations.

While many PBL practitioners do not use lectures to transmit knowledge to students (Aspy *et al.*, 1993; Spronken-Smith, 2005), the lecturer in this course combines some lectures with practical and group work. The lectures cover the theoretical background of geographical technologies, which is considered to be necessary for the first-year students as most of them have no prior knowledge in the subject area. However, as the students are exposed to the problems before lectures commence, they bring questions to the class and are also more active in participating in class discussions.

Yan assessed student learning in this course via a questionnaire which included both short-answer questions and a Likert scale. Feedback shows that 82 per cent of the students agree or strongly agree that the course stimulated them to think critically. One student wrote that "problem-based learning enabled the class to learn together, but more effort is needed by some students to make the contribution more even. However, discussions do stimulate thinking and clarify doubts for all." Regarding the usefulness of lectures offered in the course, 36 per cent of the students think that lectures are not necessary. One student said: "while it is important to know some theories behind the techniques, ultimately it is the application of the technologies that would prove vital and most relevant." However, the majority (64 per cent) felt the lectures enabled them to understand the technologies better and therefore they could apply their GIS and GPS skills in practice with more flexibility.

(2) Use of Online Discussions in a 'World Regional Geography' Course

Christine Jocoy sought to facilitate active learning through student discussion in World Regional Geography at California State University, Long Beach, in the United States. Class enrolment ranges from 40 to 200 students. For most students in the course, it is their first engagement with geography. In 2005 and 2006 course offerings, students completed two discussions outside class through an online course-management system. They discussed videos shown in class and supplemental readings. The assignment required students to respond to at least one of two questions posed by the lecturer and to at least one answer, comment, or question posted by one of their classmates. Additional participation was rewarded. A rubric including descriptions of appropriate postings was provided to guide the students because many students in introductory courses have had limited exposure to discussion-based learning.[2] Jocoy found that students needed explicit direction, especially on how to respond to other students.

The online forum is especially useful for incorporating discussion into classes with large enrolments. Student can be divided into smaller online groups. The discussions are asynchronous and can last for several days. When everyone is required to participate, shy students have as much opportunity to contribute as extrovert ones. Assessing the quality of the discussion is challenging, as less motivated students will simply repeat what others have said. However, the insightfulness of postings is less important than the main goals of encouraging students to (1) think about what they learned from the videos and readings, (2) articulate what they learned in writing and apply it in a discussion forum, and (3) learn from, respond to, and discuss geography with other students.

Student learning was assessed using a questionnaire which asked: 'How useful was the video and online discussion in helping you understand the interaction of human and physical geography?', and 'To what extent do you feel the online discussion improved your understanding of the video?'. Feedback of one of the online discussions in 2006 revealed that 35 out of 38 students (92 per cent) found the exercise useful or very useful in helping them understand the interaction of human and physical geography. Fifteen out of 38 (37.5 per cent) said the online discussion improved their understanding of the video a lot, while half said it somewhat improved their understanding.

(3) Use of Reading Journals in a 'Development and Inequality' Course

Regina Scheyvens also wanted to encourage active engagement with course readings, lectures, and videos among her second-year Development and Inequality students at Massey University in New Zealand. This class typically attracts 30–40 students. In 2002 students were asked to complete a questionnaire which asked about their expectations of the course, study habits and what classroom activities they like to participate in. This revealed that many students would only read the set readings if an essay was due, while those who were more diligent might have a 'quick flick' through the study guide each week. As a result of this exercise, reading journals were introduced as a new means of assessment, replacing one 20 per cent essay, in order to encourage more reading and reflection on course materials. The reading journals required students to write one-paragraph summaries of two articles they read that week (three readings were assigned per week, so some choice was accommodated), as well as one-paragraph reflections on these articles in which they were asked to express their feelings about the content of the article, and to consider how it related to other material presented in lectures, videos shown in class, or to real-life events they were aware of.

Evidence of students engaging with the readings and developing critical thinking skills can be found in the following excerpts drawn from their journals:

> This reading was a little disturbing...
> This makes me wonder...
> It has changed my thinking...
> I was *captivated* by the dialogue at the beginning of the piece...
> I had started to think that the notion of development was pretty much mastered,

but I can see [author's] reason for suggesting we need to unlearn many preconceived notions.

The reading journal exercise was evaluated at the end of semester utilizing a short questionnaire with a mix of open and closed questions. Most students noted that they had learned a great deal from their reading journals and thus 25 out of 27 students who completed the evaluation exercise recommended that journals be retained as a method of assessment. The one common complaint was that they had been required to work harder than usual. By providing a focus for reading, a choice of articles to read, and a chance for reflection, one student found it "helped me to understand issues involved in a topic from several viewpoints". Another noted it was "A really useful exercise in organising my thoughts". Students thus developed skills that would assist their learning in future courses.

(4) Use of e-portfolios in an 'Environmental Hazards' Course

Amy Griffin designed her final-year Environmental Hazards course at the University of New South Wales-Australian Defence Force Academy around a series of active learning exercises in which students are encouraged to operationalize and further explore theoretical constructs that are developed in lectures and tutorials. This class typically attracts 30–40 students, and is further broken up into groups of 10 students in each tutorial/discussion section. Students develop an electronic portfolio (e-portfolio) within the online course management system by completing 10 entries related to a set of exercises that prompt them to think more deeply or broadly about a particular topic (Figure 1). They are provided with an empty HTML shell of the 10 entries and required to populate this shell (using the HTML editor contained within the course management system) with content based on the 10 exercises. Some examples of the exercises include: describing an environmental hazard that the student or someone close to the student has experienced; comparing how different levels of privilege and poverty had an impact on how Australian communities experienced Cyclone Larry and the US Gulf Coast experienced Hurricane Katrina; in small groups, constructing and exploring the utility of social and environmental indicators for profiling the vulnerability of different countries to environmental hazards; and performing a small survey with individuals with different personal characteristics to identify differences in the perception of risk involved with nuclear power plants.

At the end of the course, students chose five of the 10 entries to submit for assessment, and submitted a short essay which discussed the impact that participating in the e-portfolio exercise had on how they learned during the course. They were explicitly asked to consider the following questions:

- How did I choose which pieces to submit for assessment?
- Did completing the learning activities change how I thought about concepts discussed in this course?
- Did completing the learning activities change the way I studied in this course?
- How did I go about the process of reflecting?
- Do I think reflection is a useful technique for facilitating learning?

Griffin designed this e-portfolio exercise in part to prompt her students to engage regularly with the course concepts. She had noticed that previously most students coasted through the semester until the week before an exam or an assessment was due, and were not putting

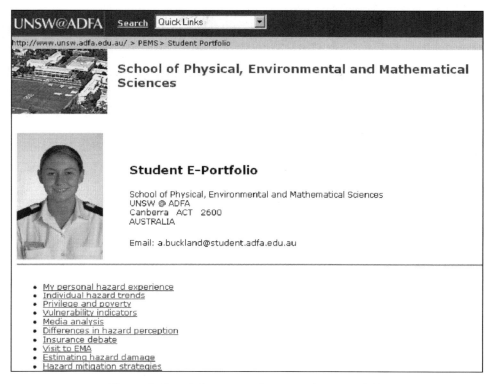

Figure 1. Sample home-page from a student e-portfolio

in a sustained effort towards thinking about the course concepts. The 10 exercises that make up the e-portfolio are spread throughout the semester, and are designed to get students to further engage with concepts that were recently discussed in a lecture or tutorial.

Most of the students on the course had a very positive reaction to working on the e-portfolio. For example, in a survey about the course, one student remarked:

> [It] allowed me to participate more in the tutorials whilst providing me with an understanding of the issues that surround hazards. I believe that reflection is a good method for facilitating learning, as it allows the student to participate in independent learning and develop a better understanding of the concepts presented in the course.

Other students have commented on the assessment's ability to prompt them to develop and use higher-level thinking skills:

> Compared to many other courses I have taken throughout my degree, this course has actually required me to make my own judgments and theories on certain environmental situations. Most lecturers tend to tell students what they believe is right, and then they ask students to interpret information given to them, that agree with the lecturer's opinions. The way that this course was structured forced me to

find my own information, while leaving it completely open for me to come to my own conclusions rather than someone else's.

Other students, however, resent having to engage regularly with course material, as is evidenced by this student's quote:

For me, however, I found that the goal became to write something down and submit it, and it did not really succeed in making me reflect. I was just writing down what I already thought, as opposed to coming to new insights.

A key lesson that Griffin learned from utilizing the e-portfolio assessment in her course (and that may help minimize student reactions such as the one above in the future) was the importance of carefully considering the weighting of assessment pieces, as this is the primary signal that students read in determining how much effort they should put into completing the task. In 2006, the e-portfolio was worth 25 per cent of the course marks, but given its effectiveness in developing both students' generic skills in independent learning and their understanding of course concepts, the lecturer decided to raise this to 60 per cent in 2007.

Active Learning: Dispelling the Myths

The above examples are varied in terms of the subject matter, the level at which they are directed and the extent to which active learning is integrated into the course, yet all show that active learning methods have considerable value. But despite the apparent benefits, there is still confusion about active learning and resistance to it, partly because of several myths which prevail concerning this approach. In this section we will draw further on the experiences of the lecturers of the above courses in order to dispel these myths.

Myth 1: Just 'Doing' is Active Learning

While active learning does involve a lot of 'doing' or activities, such as group discussions, field investigations, data collection, or lab work, active learning does not happen just because students are engaged in 'doing'. Thus in a techniques-based course, while students may be busy learning to work with new GIS software, they might be simply following instructions to press certain buttons without even thinking why they need to do so. This is surface learning, rather than deep learning.

Biggs (2003) elaborates on the effects of activity on learning by arguing that although the student arousal that is produced by participating in an activity is important, activities that are relevant to achieving the educational objectives are far more powerful than those that are irrelevant. This argument then leads to the question of how students develop a perception that an activity that they undertake is relevant to an educational objective. In other words, how do they link the doing and the thinking in active learning?

A principal method through which students can make this connection between the activity and the objectives of the activity is through reflection on what they have done or what they are doing. In Griffin's e-portfolio exercise, students had to engage in reflection by adding a caption that described the importance of each entry (to their own learning, to the study of hazards generally, or to developing their understanding of the particular concept(s) the entry addressed). At the end of the semester, one student noted:

> I believe that by reflecting on the concepts, highlighted by the e-portfolio, my knowledge of them improved and became far greater than it would be if no reflection occurred. The reflection encouraged me to examine the concepts and how they related to me, particularly as an officer in the ADF [Australian Defence Force]. By developing an understanding of how the concepts relate to me, they became important, making my learning appear more valuable for my future.

Myth 2: Active Learning Doesn't Suit Students Taking Their First Geography Class

It has been suggested that less experienced learners often require more direction and structure in their classes, so there are concerns that this may make active learning less appropriate for beginning undergraduate students (Hanson & Moser, 2003; Elliott, 2005). It is assumed that these students lack the prior knowledge which is necessary for active learning. However, we suggest that often lecturers underestimate what students know and understand. As long as their curiosity is aroused and they have a framework to work within as well as some investigative skills, they can proceed successfully with some specific active learning methods. Thus Jocoy found that the online discussions in her World Regional Geography course encouraged novice geography students to reach the last three stages of Toohey's (1999) model of learning by (1) trying out their knowledge of what geographers study, (2) getting feedback by reading other students' postings, and (3) reflecting on and adjusting their responses to other students. The following exchange illustrates one of the more successful student online interactions.

> Student 1: One of the physical geographies of north east Australia (Queensland) is its tropical climates [*sic*], which is very humid and wet; ideal features for cane toads to thrive in.
> Student 2: I agree with [student 1] on this claim. In the extra research I did it stated, "Cane Toads are found in habitats ranging from sand dunes and coastal heath to..." This was in an article titled... Australia obviously meets these standards.
> Student 3: In addition to [student 1], over time, the cane toads are adapting to the environment. According to the video...
> Student 4: I agree with [student 3] that the cane toads are definitely adapting to all of Australia's environments. In an article I read... it states that cane toads are not limited to traditional toad food sources. In fact...
> Student 1: Moreover, we learn from the video that cane toads can live in almost any habitat as long as there is water, for they have rapidly adapted to things that could have previously restricted them from spreading.

Myth 3: There is No Place for Lecturing within an Active Learning Approach

Lecturing is the major method of instruction used in most undergraduate geography courses. While lecturing may be overused, it is still a useful and necessary teaching method in many cases. Lectures can deliver essential information about a subject, and this may be particularly important in institutional contexts (such as in the United States, or in New Zealand BA or BSc degrees) where there is not one core group of students moving through the geography programme from one level to the next. Where students taking different majors enrol in geography courses, it is difficult to assume that the whole group has adequate prior knowledge to be able to engage in active learning methods such as PBL straight away. In Liu's techniques-based course discussed above, it was important to transmit theoretical knowledge to students through lectures while they were practising their problem-solving activities.

Because lectures are effective in transmitting information, there is no reason why they cannot be used in meeting that objective or be used in combination with active learning methods to meet other objectives (Bligh, 2000). The lecture theatre does not preclude the inclusion of active learning methods (Jenkins, 1992). In Scheyvens' Development and Inequality course, for example, a single teaching session may include use of lecturing, along with buzz groups, discussion of a video, and role play. Official course evaluations for this and other courses in which Scheyvens utilizes active learning tools within the lecture context demonstrate that students (a) are learning actively, and (b) appreciate this experience. For example:

> Videos and class exercises are very beneficial. An innovative and effective way of learning.
> I feel the interactive lectures and tutorials provide a fun and informative learning experience.
> She encourages the class to think for ourselves, not just listing things we are taught, but own thinking as well.

Myth 4: Active Learning Requires Too Much Work of Students and Lecturers

Hanson & Moser (2003, p. 33) stress that active learning requires a greater commitment from both the teaching staff and students: "more preparation, more engagement with the material and each other; in short, more work". However, in our experience this is not necessarily the case. When a lecturer is preparing to teach any new material it will always take some time, regardless of the method of instruction: active learning methods do not necessarily require more preparation time.

For students active learning may seem to involve more work if they are used to revising superficially for exams. For students who try to achieve deep learning from their revision, however, it is unlikely to. It might actually reduce their workload at the end of the course when they would otherwise feel the need to 'cram' for an exam. Instead, they may learn things and understand them earlier in a course, as one of Griffin's e-portfolio students showed:

> This reflection has given me the chance ... to revise most, if not all, of the concepts and the work that has been in this course. The type of revision would normally be associated with the work I do for an end-of-session test, just without the heartache of a three-hour exam!

In addition, provided that there is assessment of the active learning components so that students have the opportunity to be rewarded for their participation in active learning activities, resistance is minimized. Thus although students completing Scheyvens's reading journal activity felt it required them to work quite hard, they were willing to do this because the activity was worth 20 per cent of their final grade and thus the majority recommended that the activity be continued in future years. Griffins's use of e-portfolios provides students with considerable choice so that while they were required to work on 10 activities during the semester, they only needed to present polished submissions of five pieces of work for their portfolios. Such choice can both be a way of motivating students to focus on learning activities which they are most interested in, as well as ensuring that the overall workload is not too onerous when utilizing active learning methods.

While we do not think that active learning requires too much work of students, we do acknowledge that it requires students who are mature enough to see that they are in part responsible for their own learning. There are always some students who will resist being asked to learn more than the minimum they need to get through the course with a passing grade. However, if using active learning strategies helps at least some students to become more self-aware, responsible learners, then we contend that it is worth doing. In our own classes, we have found evidence that active learning can provoke this response:

> As I initially approached the first few e-portfolio submissions with irritation, I didn't really change my initial perspective on the course concepts as I wasn't thinking about them ... as I began approaching them with a willingness to learn and to complete them, I began to get more from each submission.

There are ways of minimizing the additional workload that may arise for lecturers utilizing active learning methods. First, it is important that assessment of learning from active learning methods is substituting, rather than additional to, existing forms of assessment. Second, it may be possible to build in peer assessment. Thus, for example, Scheyvens found the marking of reading journals three times during the semester to be quite arduous, but in 2006 she trialled peer review as a method of assessing around half of the journal entries. Peer assessment can also help students to reflect more critically on the quality of their own work.

Myth 5: There are Significant Institutional Constraints to Promoting Active Learning

Institutional constraints are department-, university-, and/or profession-wide directives that proscribe particular teaching practices or orientations. For example, some universities or departments may not allow instructors to run field schools due to liability issues and/or budgetary limits. Other institutional constraints include: a lack of physical teaching spaces that support group work, requirements on the type of assessment instructors ask students to complete, and the length and structure of degrees. Often, however, all that is needed is the willingness to implement change; for example, from 'look-see' fieldwork to skills-based and project-based work, involving learning by doing with associated thinking and reflection.

More generally, however, it is easier to implement change if there is an institutional culture of encouraging experimentation, accepting that some innovations will fail, and learning from failures. If the institution exhibits a blame culture then some lecturers will hesitate to experiment. This may be particularly so if student evaluations are treated in a way that inhibits innovation.

There may be other institutional constraints involving guidelines on assessment and plagiarism. For example, some institutions require a minimum amount of work under examination conditions in students' overall assessment to ensure that it is the students' own work. This is not a problem if there is an identifiable degree programme to which units contribute. Then a mix of assessments can be included within the programme, so that some courses have no work under examination conditions, allowing all types of active learning. In a recently devised second-year unit on the geographies of children at the University of Manchester, for example, Bradford included a portfolio of exercises that drew on students' experiences as children, a short piece that related the literature and one of their reflections, and a team project on a topic not directly covered in lectures. One of the learning outcomes of the unit was to improve the ability to reflect. On the other hand, if each course has to include work under examination conditions, some lecturers may see this as inhibiting active learning, and restricting their teaching only to knowledge transmission. One way around this is to include a short, but carefully constructed objective test that promotes deep learning and understanding and meets the requirements of assessing the broad range of learning outcomes, while a piece of project work allows some of the learning outcomes to be assessed in depth. Of course, project work can be open to plagiarism. Careful setting of the task and changing the tasks from year to year can limit this (Brown *et al.*, 1996).

It is certainly important not to overemphasize institutional constraints to active learning, because the reality is that in many institutions there is now direct *support* for active learning in courses for new academics. There are also often courses available through the staff development or educational development unit for more experienced lecturers to learn new methods, for example in interactive teaching, and more about the ways students learn. One Californian university offers a 'Summer Institute on Teaching and Learning', while in a number of countries universities provide active learning modules in their tertiary teaching certificates which are open to all academic staff. Kenneth Foote at the University of Colorado has a five-year project funded by the National Science Foundation to provide summer workshops "to strengthen support and training for new faculty in geography in two and four-year institutions of higher education across the United States" (http://www.colorado.edu/geography/gfda/gfda.html). The Centre for Active Learning at the University of Gloucestershire, England, is a more general source of support for geography and related disciplines.

Myth 6: Active Learning Can Detract from the Transmission of Fundamental Knowledge in a Degree Programme

Some argue that active learning can be very time consuming and may "detract from the transmission of fundamental knowledge that is required for academic achievement" (Elliott, 2005, p. 54). As Liu's example of her 'Techniques in Geography' course shows, active learning may accompany some transmission of basic knowledge and help to reinforce it. Elliott's comment seems to make a number of assumptions which include that: knowledge is transmitted in a way that leads to understanding and deep learning and not just short-term memory for repetition in exams; and there is a given set of knowledge that is fundamental to academic achievement. Both of these assumptions can be contested. As Ramsden (2003, pp. 114–115) noted: "Transmission of existing knowledge is at best a half-true description of education; all knowledge is new and requires to be decoded if you have not met it before; all facts must be interpreted imaginatively." Hence, teaching strategies that promote active engagement by students should be more effective in promoting student learning than strategies that allow students to passively let the class pass them by. A quote from one of Griffin's Environmental Hazards students reinforces the value of a deeper approach to learning:

> As the portfolio required me to actually go away and do work rather than just sit in a lecture theatre and tune out, I found that I retained the information much better and believe that I will actually remember the different aspects of environmental hazards.

Guidelines for Successful Integration of Active Learning

It has been important to dispel a number of myths about active learning in the section above, but what is essential now is to consider ways forward. What steps should be taken by advocates of active learning, or those wanting to try it for the first time, in their courses? Five suggestions are provided below.

(1) Active Learning Should Be Written into Course Objectives and Learning Outcomes

Active learning is most effective when it is used to achieve course and programme objectives and learning goals (Mathews, 1999), rather than simply being conceived as a type of toolbox of classroom methods which can be dipped into from time to time. Thus if active learning is to be a key approach used in a course it should be written into the course objectives and learning outcomes, informing overall expectations of the course, and it should from the start be part of the routine of course meetings whether they be lectures, tutorials, or labs. Integrating active learning comprehensively into a course or programme is more likely to facilitate a sustained deep learning experience.

(2) Students Should Be Introduced to Active Learning from the Start of their Degree Programme

We need to acknowledge that other lecturers in our geography degree programmes play an important part in setting students' expectations about what they should do at university and even how they should be taught. If a routine of lecturing is established, it may be hard to motivate students to view active participation as equally important. There is thus considerable merit in utilizing active learning methods from year one, semester one, day one, in a range of geography courses. As with all innovations it is better to introduce them early in a student's degree programme when he/she is more likely to become an accepted part of higher education. Later introduction can lead to more resistance. Early introduction of active learning helps students to normalize this method of learning rather than seeing it as 'strange' compared with lectures, or feeling uncomfortable about being asked to participate in class after the apparent anonymity of the lecture theatre. It may also lead to better engagement of students in both the course and programme and, where it is closely related to assessment activities, can help to spread students' workload.

(3) Students May Need Guidance on How They Can Actively Participate in Courses and Why this is of Value

While some students are introduced to active learning strategies at high school, many are not. Lecturers need to spend time teaching students how to learn actively, and explaining what value engaging in active learning strategies holds for them. Examples provided in this paper show how electronic communication such as online discussion boards can provide innovative means for students to collaborate and reflect on their learning. However, clear guidance on how often and to what extent they must contribute to the boards is important if such methods are to encourage wide participation and be a successful learning tool. Jocoy, for example, found that students needed explicit direction on appropriate ways of responding to other students in her online discussion group on World Regional Geography.

In addition, students may require repetition of active learning activities before they understand how to participate effectively in an active manner, as is evidenced by this quote from a student in Griffin's Environmental Hazards course:

> At first, I found it difficult to understand the point of the portfolios, but realized after the first three that their point was not to simply be a fill in for time with a write up of the information, but rather a requirement for me to actually study a subject in more depth and therefore get more understanding about a certain hazard or aspects of hazards.

It can be valuable to have some courses in which active learning has been institutionalized as the 'learning culture' of that particular course.

(4) Appropriate Assessment Activities are Critical to Promoting Active Learning

The nature, timing and weighting of assessment are key to the successful introduction of active learning. As the above examples show, a variety of inquiry-type methods of assessment, whether individual or team based, work well in encouraging active learning. Using peer assessment not only produces more timely feedback to students and saves lecturers' time, which is why Scheyvens is trialling this in her Development and Inequality course, but also helps students to understand assessment criteria, match their expectations to those of the course and programme, and, most importantly, improve their performance. The active learning element of the assessment needs to have a substantial weighting, subject to institutional constraints, partly so that students take it seriously and partly because it is fundamentally 'assessment for learning'. Hence the increase in weighting of the e-portfolios in Griffin's course.

(5) Students Should Regularly Be Asked to Reflect on Learning Activities

Even when students are familiar with active learning strategies and they are largely happy to participate in a range of classroom activities, for optimal learning outcomes lecturers will still need to encourage them to *reflect on* what they are learning and how they are learning it. Unfortunately, as Brookfield (1990) notes, our implementation of active learning strategies in the classroom often emphasizes the activity at the expense of reflection. This may be a particular danger for lecturers who only occasionally dip into the active learning toolbox, in that they may not be able to socialize students enough to overcome resistance to active learning. This resistance may in part stem from students' lack of appreciation of the relevance of what they are learning, which may in turn come about because of a lack of 'abstract conceptualization' (drawing on Kolb, 1984), whereby lecturers encourage students to think about what was learned and the implications of what was learned.

Conclusion

This paper has discussed a number of ways in which active learning methods are being applied in geography courses in different institutional settings, showing the continued importance of an active learning approach. Geography is often considered a 'hands on' subject, yet the educational literature aptly demonstrates that activity alone will not lead to deep learning; rather, thinking about and reflecting on learning activities is what is important. This is how students can begin to explore concepts and theorize about various fields of geographical knowledge:

> This process of continuous reflection greatly enhances my ability to absorb information rather than trying to memorize facts and other people's theories. Because these are my own ideas, I actually understand what I am writing about, and thus have a greater understanding of the themes and aims of the course. (Third-year Environmental Hazards student commenting on the e-portfolio exercise)

Thus, confirming the results of earlier studies, our classroom experiences revealed a wide range of benefits to students from engaging in active learning including the development of critical thinking skills, deep as opposed to surface learning, and generic skills such as collaboration and team work. Importantly, use of active learning methods is motivating for many students, encouraging them to be more interested in their own learning.

One question posed at the start of this paper was whether it was appropriate for lecturers to dip into the active learning methods toolbox from time to time, or whether they needed to fully embrace this approach to learning if they wanted to ensure improved learning outcomes. While fully embracing active learning is ideal, we want to encourage all geography lecturers to introduce some component of active learning into their courses. You may already utilize some interesting activities, such as videos and field trips, but you could try restructuring the experience so that students are required not only to 'do' the activities but to reflect on their participation in relation to course objectives. It is also useful to note that lecture-based courses can effectively inspire active learning. In the five courses described in this paper all of us still deliver regular lectures and we recognize the value of this style of teaching, but lectures are no longer necessarily our main means of instruction. It has taken some time and thought to introduce more active learning into our courses but it has also been stimulating and inspiring: we have all experienced significant satisfaction from seeing students' curiosity aroused and their active engagement with course concepts and materials.

For those who do decide to experiment with active learning, we have a few recommendations. Students' learning will be enhanced if they are encouraged to reflect on the relevance of various activities—be they fieldtrips, lab exercises, discussion forums, essays, GIS mapping, journals, or others—to what they are learning in our courses. Related to this point, active learning should be closely tied into the learning outcomes for the course. Furthermore, if we start with active learning from day one and provide appropriately weighted assessment exercises, students are likely to come to view it as a 'normal' way of learning and will not regard it as excessively time intensive. We also need to build on students' prior knowledge of a subject area, even if this involves exposing and challenging their assumed knowledge and stereotypes. Finally, in order to overcome potential resistance to active learning we need to explain to students the rationale behind it and to offer instruction, where necessary, on how to actively involve themselves in new learning activities. Much can be achieved when we recognize that it is what *students* do, rather than just what we as lecturers deliver, that can really enhance learning outcomes.

Notes

[1] PBL is an instructional approach that uses problems as a context for students to develop content knowledge and problem-solving skills. It is a particular type of active learning which requires students to work together in small groups to find solutions to real-world problems. This approach originated in medical schools to teach students about clinical cases (Vernon & Blake, 1993). However, it has now been widely adopted in many different areas, including engineering, law, architecture, business, education and geography (Uden & Beaumont, 2006).

[2] The online discussion instructions and rubric can be accessed from Jocoy's homepage: http://www.csulb.edu/ ~ cjocoy/

References

Aspy, D. N., Aspy, C. B. & Quimby, P. M. (1993) What doctors can teach teachers about problem-based learning, *Educational Leadership*, 50(7), pp. 22–24.

Biggs, J. (2003) *Teaching for Quality Learning at University*, 2nd edn (Buckingham: Society for Research into Higher Education & Open University Press).

Bligh, D. A. (2000) *What's the Use of Lectures?* (San Francisco: Jossey-Bass).

Bloom, B. S., Krathwohl, D. R. & Masia, B. B. (1984) *Taxonomy of Educational Objectives: The Classification of Educational Goals* (New York: Longman).

Bonwell, C. C. & Eison, J. A. (1991) Active learning: creating excitement in the classroom. *ERIC Digest*, Available at http://www.ericdigests.org/1992–4/active.htm. (accessed September 2006).

Brookfield, S. D. (1990) *The Skillful Teacher: On Technique, Trust and Responsiveness in the Classroom* (San Francisco: Jossey-Bass).

Brown, S., Race, P. & Smith, B. (1996) *500 Tips on Assessment* (London: Kogan Paul).

Charman, D. & Fullerton, J. (1995) Interactive lectures: a case study in a geographical concepts course, *Journal of Geography in Higher Education*, 19(1), pp. 57–68.

Elliott, D. (2005) Early mornings and apprehension: active learning in lectures, *Journal of Leisure, Sport and Tourism Education*, 4(1), pp. 53–58.

Gibbs, G. (1988) *Learning by Doing: A Guide to Teaching and Learning Methods* (London, UK: Further Education Unit).

Gibbs, G. (1992) *Improving the Quality of Student Learning* (Oxford: Oxford Centre for Staff Development).

Hanson, S. & Moser, S. (2003) Reflections on a discipline-wide project: developing active learning modules on the human dimensions of global change, *Journal of Geography in Higher Education*, 27(1), pp. 17–38.

Healey, M. & Jenkins, A. (2000) Kolb's experiential learning theory and its application in geography in higher education, *Journal of Geography*, 99, pp. 185–195.

Healey, M., Kneale, P. & Bradbeer, J. (2005) Learning styles among geography undergraduates: an international comparison, *Area*, 37(1), pp. 30–42.

Houghton, R. S. (2003) Applying higher order (Bloom's taxonomy) thinking skills. Available at http://www.ceap.wcu.edu/HOughton/Learner/think/thinkhigherorder.html (accessed September 2006).

Jenkins, A. (1992) Active learning in structured lectures, in: G. Gibbs & A. Jenkins (Eds) *Teaching Large Classes in Higher Education*, pp. 63–77 (London: Kogan Page).

Kent, M., Gilbertson, D. D. & Hunt, C. O. (1997) Fieldwork in geography teaching: a critical review of the literature and approaches, *Journal of Geography in Higher Education*, 21(3), pp. 313–332.

Kolb, D. A. (1984) *Experiential Learning: Experience as the Source of Learning and Development* (Englewood Cliffs, NJ: Prentice-Hall).

Lonergan, N. & Andresen, L. W. (1988) Field-based education: some theoretical considerations, *Higher Education Research and Development*, 7, pp. 63–77.

Marton, F. & Säljö, R. (1976) On qualitative differences in learning, I: Outcome and process, *British Journal of Educational Psychology*, 46, pp. 4–11.

Mathews, L. K. (1999) Strategies and ideas for active learning. Available at http://www2.una.edu/geography/Active/strategi.htm (accessed September 2006).

Pascarella, E. T. & Terenzini, P. T. (1991) *How College Affects Students: Findings and Insights from Twenty Years of Research* (San Francisco: Jossey-Bass).

Prosser, M. & Trigwell, K. (1999) *Understanding Learning and Teaching: The Experience in Higher Education* (Buckingham: Open University Press).

Ramsden, P. (2003) *Learning to Teach in Higher Education*, 2nd edn (London: Routledge).

Spronken-Smith, R. (2005) Implementing a problem-based learning approach for teaching research methods in geography, *Journal of Geography in Higher Education*, 29(2), pp. 203–221.

Toohey, S. (1999) *Designing Courses for Higher Education* (Buckingham, UK: Society for Research in Higher Education & Open University Press).

Uden, L. & Beaumont, C. (2006) *Technology and Problem-Based Learning* (Hershey, PA: Information Science Publishing).

Van Hoven, B. & De Boer, E. (2001) Student empowerment through 'area analysis', *Journal of Geography in Higher Education*, 25(1), pp. 83–93.

Vernon, D. T. & Blake, R. L. (1993) Does problem-based learning work? A meta-analysis of evaluative research, *Academic Medicine*, 68(7), pp. 550–563.

Vygotsky, L. S. (1978) *Mind and Society: The Development of Higher Mental Processes* (Cambridge, MA: Harvard University Press).

Problem-based Learning in Geography: Towards a Critical Assessment of its Purposes, Benefits and Risks

ERIC PAWSON*, ERIC FOURNIER**, MARTIN HAIGH[†],
OSVALDO MUNIZ[‡], JULIE TRAFFORD[§] & SUSAN VAJOCZKI[^]

*Department of Geography, University of Canterbury, New Zealand, **Department of Geography, Samford University, USA, [†]Department of Anthropology and Geography, Oxford Brookes University, UK, [‡]Department of Geography, Texas State University–San Marcos, USA, [§]Student Learning Centre, University of Auckland, New Zealand, [^]School of Geography and Earth Sciences, McMaster University, Canada

ABSTRACT *This paper makes a critical assessment of problem-based learning (PBL) in geography. It assesses what PBL is, in terms of the range of definitions in use and in light of its origins in specific disciplines such as medicine. It considers experiences of PBL from the standpoint of students, instructors and managers (e.g. deans), and asks how well suited this method of learning is for use in geography curricula, courses and assignments. It identifies some 'best practices in PBL', as well as some useful sources for those seeking to adopt PBL in geography. It concludes that PBL is not a teaching and learning method to be adopted lightly, and that if the chances of successful implementation are to be maximized, careful attention to course preparation and scenario design is essential. More needs to be known about the circumstances in which applications of PBL have not worked well and also about the nature of the inputs needed from students, teachers and others to reap its benefits.*

Introduction

This article provides an overview of the nature and development of problem-based learning (PBL) as well as its applications in and potential for the teaching of geography. PBL is one of a cluster of recent innovations in active learning for which a wide range of positive outcomes for students is claimed. An editorial in an earlier issue of this journal noted that supporters of such innovations generally declare that they promote deep learning through greater understanding of concepts and the development of skills, as well as fostering student participation and motivating and enthusing classes (Agnew, 2001). Proponents of

PBL go further, arguing that it brings benefits not only for assignments or for courses, but for part or all of disciplinary curricula as well as for lifelong learning. They see PBL both as an instructional strategy or method and as a curricular philosophy (Maudsley, 1999).

What then is PBL, and what are its purposes and alleged benefits? What are the experiences of PBL amongst students, instructors and managers (such as deans), factors which Agnew (2001) observes are rarely assessed for new learning methods? How extensively has PBL been adopted in geography, a discipline some distance from those in which it first flourished, such as medicine and engineering? Can a geography curriculum be delivered with extensive or exclusive use of PBL? This paper explores such matters as a preparatory step to establishing an international research project that will evaluate the issues in greater depth.

We consider this a timely intervention, as increasing numbers of younger faculty with qualifications in higher or tertiary education teaching practice are coming into direct contact with PBL, and may wish to develop or are developing its use in geography courses and curricula. Nonetheless to date it has been claimed that "very little critical evaluation of problem-based learning has emerged" (Fenwick, 1998, p. 1). The article proceeds by posing a series of questions, or problems, whose formulation enables us to get to grips with the epistemology of PBL using the spirit of the method itself.

What is Problem-based Learning?

It has been suggested that PBL "has almost as many forms as places where it is used" (Macdonald, 2001, p. 1). Published definitions of PBL, however, share an emphasis on learning rather than instruction and a belief that PBL is a mould-breaking means to this end. Beyond this, PBL definitions emphasize different aspects of structure, process or goals (Figure 1). It may therefore be useful to attempt an understanding from a number of perspectives. One is in terms of 'the vital distinction' between problem-based learning and problem-solving and inquiry-based approaches (Savin-Baden, 2001, p. 5). Another concerns the emergence and development of PBL: in what contexts and for what purposes did it originate? These first two perspectives are considered in this section. The third, an attempt to characterize not only the methods but also the distribution of both benefits and risks of PBL, is undertaken in the next section.

Analytically, a useful starting point is to distinguish between, on the one hand, PBL and, on the other, the problem-solving and inquiry-based approaches. All three are active learning approaches, predicated on the constructivist belief that to involve the student is to enhance understanding. Each offers explicit although differing opportunities for co-learning amongst students (Le Heron *et al.*, 2006). However, in problem-solving and inquiry-based approaches, the knowledge to be developed must often be acquired in advance of participation in the problem-solving process. Examples would include experience in the field following in-class learning, or laboratory group work designed to explore concepts introduced in the lecture room. In other words, students attempt to inquire or to resolve problems from bounded curricula content (Savin-Baden, 2001; Lamb, 2004).

In contrast, problem-based learning is 'problem first learning' (Spencer & Jordan, 1999). It is the problem, usually set by an instructor, which defines what is to be learned. Curriculum content (in what is sometimes called 'pure PBL'), or course or assignment content (in 'hybrid' forms of PBL), is organized around problem scenarios, rather than subjects or topics (Dahlgren & Oberg, 2001; King, 2001). Students, normally working in groups, then engage with the problem scenarios and decide for themselves what

- PBL is both a curriculum and a process. The curriculum consists of carefully selected and designed problems that demand from the learner acquisition of critical knowledge, problem-solving efficiency, self-directed learning strategies and team participation skills. The process replicates the commonly used systemic approach to resolving problems or meeting challenges that are encountered in life and career.
- PBL is an approach to structuring the curriculum that involves confronting students with problems from practice, which provides a stimulus for learning.
- PBL is an instructional method that challenges students to 'learn to learn', working cooperatively in groups to seek solutions to real-world problems. These problems are used to engage students' curiosity and initiate learning the subject matter. PBL prepares students to think critically and analytically, and to find and use appropriate learning resources.
- PBL is a development and instructional approach built around an ill-structured problem that is a mess and complex in nature; requires inquiry, information-gathering and reflection; is changing and tentative; and has no simple, fixed, formulaic, 'right' solution.
- PBL is an instructional strategy that promotes active learning. PBL can be used as a framework for modules, courses, programmes, or curricula.

Figure 1. Definitions of PBL, *Source*: 'PBL background: definitions', Problem-based learning at Samford University (http://www.samford.edu/pbl/definitions.html).

information and skills they need to resolve the situation, or questions, effectively. The onus is on students determining their own learning needs and on independence of enquiry. Faculty maintain a distance, keeping a watching brief on group dynamics, direction, and progress. This requires an active, aware and respectful form of co-learning, breaking down the usual dichotomy between students and faculty (Le Heron *et al.*, 2006).

Since problems do not respect disciplinary boundaries, PBL often involves collaboration between disciplines. It is certainly likely to require students to integrate knowledge from different fields within disciplines. Such experiences are said to enhance means of managing—or synthesizing—knowledge, or of learning how to learn, rather than attempting to assimilate content before entering employment. Jenkins (1985) drew attention to this distinction as the difference between 'drawing out' and 'filling up'. However, in the first major international survey of good teaching practices in geography (Gold *et al.*, 1991), problem-based learning was not featured (although 'problem-solving' was).

PBL was initially developed for learning in the applied disciplines of medicine and engineering in countries such as Canada and New Zealand because doctors and engineers spend their professional lives toying with problem scenarios. In so doing, they need the ability to draw together the insights from different chapters of the textbook, because organ systems, for example, are not independent but are all part of the one human body. PBL grew from research in the 1960s into the reasoning abilities of medical students and a desire to improve their capacity to relate knowledge learned to the problems with which patients presented (Schwartz *et al.*, 2001). In other words, medical students need both knowledge and the ability to integrate it, needs exacerbated by the speed of change in that knowledge. They are now routinely told that "half of what they learn will be obsolete in ten years' time" (A. Hornblow, personal communication, University of Canterbury, 17 May 2004).

Much the same can be said of the education of geography students, many of whom will enter careers that are not related to their first degree expertise. For these students, the ability to learn as self-starters in new situations is clearly vital, and they have "little need for content-driven instruction" in geography (Wu & Fournier, 2000, p. 112). Even those who do make careers drawing directly on their degrees, such as in geographic information systems and in environmental management, face a similar pace of knowledge renewal to those in medicine. Core competences are vital, but need to be understood sufficiently well to be applied in different situations, and adapted as knowledge and the methods used to construct it evolve. What matters, then, is the ability to 'learn to learn' (Duch, 1995), rather than what is actually learned or taught (Healey, 2005).

Experiences of PBL

The bulk of the literature on PBL focuses on examples of practical applications "rather than on the examination of the complexities and challenges involved in its application" (Savin-Baden, 2001, p. 4). It also relies on assumptions, often untested, regarding the ways in which students learn, let alone regarding the ability or willingness of instructors to relinquish the role of 'instructing' in favour of something more facilitative. Less emphasis is usually given to discussion of disadvantages alongside claims of significant benefits (although in recent geographical writing on PBL, Lee (2001) and Beringer (2005) are exceptions). What are the effects, for example, on the time commitments of instructors and of students (Agnew, 2001), and the resource implications for managers? What differences do students' prior learning and teaching experiences make in PBL situations (Schwartz *et al.*, 2001)? Overall, do the gains match that of the PBL rhetoric?

Claims that PBL experiences are overwhelmingly positive abound in the literature. In the top part of Table 1, the benefits that are commonly identified for students and instructors (and less commonly for managers) are listed. The method is supposed to produce "creative, independent problem-solvers able to harness their creativity through organization and planning" (Casey & Howson, 1993, p. 361). It aims to orient learners towards meaning-making over information storage, fostering learning strategies and skills that are geared to rapid adaptation to new situations and problem domains. Through new arrays of knowledge-forming skills, it is said that learners achieve higher levels of comprehension (Rhem, 1998). PBL students may feel that they are learning less in content terms but, in Lieux's (1996) study, their final results as measured through multiple-choice test scores showed no significant difference from those taught through lectures. Other studies emphasize that less knowledge is compensated for with greater retention of that

Table 1. Benefits and risks of PBL relative to traditional learning methods: for students, instructors and managers (e.g. deans)

	Students	Instructors	Managers
Benefits	I. Student-centred approach	I. Increases class attendance	I. Prioritizes student learning
	II. Perceived by students as more enjoyable and satisfying	II. Intrinsically rewarding	II. May assist with student retention
	III. Encourages greater understanding	III. Higher level of student comprehension	III. Links to real-world pedagogical focus
	IV. Students graduate with a high perceived concept of their abilities	IV. Encourages students to spend more time studying	IV. Provides evidence that the institution values teaching
	V. Focuses on skill development needed for lifelong learning	V. Promotes interdisciplinarity	V. Provides public relations benefits, branding distinctiveness and innovation
	The benefits of lifelong learning may not be immediately apparent and must be taken on trust	Making students responsible for their learning requires a 'paradigm shift' that the lecture is not necessarily the best way to learn	The benefits are difficult to quantify whereas the costs are tangible
Risks	I. Prior learning experiences may not have prepared students adequately	I. Creating suitable problem scenarios	I. Necessitates a 'paradigm shift' for people taught predominantly in a lecture format
	II. Increases time commitment; this may impinge negatively on other studies	II. Increases time necessary for preparation	II. Requires more instructors and instructor contact time
	III. Loss of security for students because of 'messiness' of PBL over traditional lecture	III. Requires commitment to resolve student queries	III Requires staff development
	IV. Failures may occur with group dynamics	IV. Moderating failures in group dynamics	IV Dependent on flexible classroom space and relevant library resources
	V. Less knowledge of content gained	V. What to assess and how to assess it?	V. Willingness to adopt may be limited by lack of robust evidence of its effectiveness

Note: This table is based on benefits and risks identified in: Coulson (1983); Woodward and Ferrier (1983); Martinsen *et al.* (1985); Saunders *et al.* (1985); West and West (1987); Heale *et al.* (1988); Nolte *et al.* (1988); Eisenstaedt *et al.* (1990); Post and Drop (1990); Rangachari (1991); Albanese and Mitchell (1993); Vernon and Blake (1993); Bligh (1995); Lieux (1996); Rhem (1998); Burch (2000); Agnew (2001); Benbow and McMahon (2001); Schwarz *et al.* (2001); Dochy *et al.* (2003); Beringer (2005); Spronken-Smith (2005).

learned, laying the groundwork for lifelong learning (Dochy *et al.*, 2003). Students may find PBL more nurturing, enjoyable, challenging and satisfying (Albanese & Mitchell, 1993; Bligh, 1995), so that class attendance can be significantly higher than for conventional teaching (Lieux, 1996).

To others, such statements should be more openly problematized. As the summary statements in the centre of Table 1 indicate, benefits are accompanied by risks. The more commonly identified risks are listed in the lower part of the table. How, for example, are those faculty who consider that the lecture is the most efficient means of teaching (although there are many ways of seeking active engagement of students in lectures) to be persuaded that there are benefits from a less structured, more time-consuming process of PBL facilitation, in which the results at any one time may not be particularly tangible (Prideaux *et al.*, 2001)? How are problems of group dynamics to be resolved, when it is quite likely that some students may dominate and others withdraw, or not pull their weight? Mature students may take over, demoralizing those whose life experiences have so far yielded less opportunity to become articulate (Benbow & McMahon, 2001).

Such situations may be exacerbated in highly competitive geography departments, as in medical schools, where entry has been gained through the individual attainment of high grades. A switch to group work may then be anathema to certain students. Furthermore, high school systems in many countries do not produce students practised in cooperative learning styles. Against this background, the introduction of, or a high level of, course fees in countries such as Australia, New Zealand, the United States and Britain may lead both students and parents to expect that they will be taught, rather than having to invest in the effort of learning. This may be particularly so given the most commonly held conceptions of teaching and of learning amongst new geography undergraduates in those countries: that teaching is 'information transfer' and learning is 'increase in knowledge' (Bradbeer *et al.*, 2004).

Such conceptions are a challenge for the proponents of PBL, where the focus is much more towards 'learning to learn, not learning to imitate' (Chappell, 2006). Many would urge that this is all the more reason to introduce it to both students and instructors. Even so, students may react against the messiness of real-world PBL scenarios, preferring the security that comes from the structure lent by more traditional learning situations (Beringer, 2005). It has also been argued that in conceiving of life as fundamentally problem-governed, PBL prioritizes the instrumental, the doing, ahead of the thinking, reflection and accommodation. Fenwick (1998, p. 2) sees such an approach as consistent with "the modernist pursuit of efficiency, predictability, productivity, measurable concrete outcomes, and unitary meaning subordinated to instrumentality".

Many would disagree, claiming that PBL gives instructors an approach to the encouragement of learning that can be used in flexible and diverse ways. Indeed, a central tenet of the approach is that of developing meta-cognitive skills through reflection (Barrows & Tamblyn, 1980). At the same time, if applied with some courage, it is a method with which students can pursue many avenues, some of which will be inappropriate, thereby giving them the freedom to make mistakes and to learn from these (King, 2001).

Problem-based Learning and Geography Curricula

How suitable is PBL for adoption in geography curricula? How widely has it been adopted? It arrived in the discipline long after its development in medicine and engineering, its absence from the Gold *et al.* (1991) survey of innovative practice in the geography having been noted.

It also did not feature by name in the one national-level survey of teaching practice that is readily available, that of the Higher Education Funding Council of England's Quality Assessment of Geography undertaken in 1994–1995. HEFCE (1995, p.1) nonetheless found that geography "is characterized by a wide diversity of provision; students have a wide choice [of course types] ... [and] there has been a growing commitment to providing students with transferable skills". Despite lectures still playing 'a central role in the delivery of the geography curriculum', there is much in this report such as catholic approaches, interest in a range of teaching and learning methods, and 'high quality pastoral support' that should make geography in England a fertile ground for PBL experiments.

More recently it has been suggested in a New Zealand-based study that "although it is relatively new in geography, one could argue that the technique is ideally suited to this discipline since, by its very nature, geography is already interdisciplinary — one of the main ingredients of a PBL approach" (Spronken-Smith, 2005, p. 206). For example, physical geography texts often deal with topics in a set sequence. Tropical cyclones and coastal erosion occur in probably widely separated chapters. Tourism processes will often be dealt with in another course, and book, altogether. A multi-dimensional PBL scenario, centred on the development of a resort complex on a barrier island, would enable students to explore the range of interconnections between these topics, at the same time as making the deeper point that life is not neatly divided into discrete chapters.

In addition, geography has a long tradition of group work, which underlies most practices of PBL. It has also been argued by Bradbeer (1996) that there are sufficient similarities between fieldwork traditions and the purposes of PBL to warrant exploring this relationship. However, he points to the problems in taking a PBL approach to fieldwork very far, given the commitments to changes in practice that need to be made by colleagues. This comment focuses attention on the extent to which PBL is consistent with geography curricula. Parts of such curricula are, after all, as applied in nature as medicine or engineering. Large parts, however, are not, being more in the mould of traditional arts or science-based subjects where the emphasis is on an understanding of such features as concept and context.

How suitable is PBL for use in such differing fields of knowledge? Or is any distinction more apparent than real? A recent article in the magazine *Nature*, entitled 'Mapping Opportunities,' is of interest in this regard. It quoted the US Department of Labor as identifying geotechnologies as "one of the three most important emerging and evolving fields, along with biotechnology and nanotechnology" (Gewin, 2004, p. 376). It drew attention to the need to strengthen and expand geography departments to help prepare students for the resulting job opportunities. But it also emphasized that students will require a deep understanding of underlying geographical concepts to work effectively in growing geotechnologies fields.

So can GIS or environmental remote sensing, as geotechnologies, be taught using PBL? The proceedings from a recent European conference on GIS in higher education suggest that the dominant concerns remain the technology itself and its value for the description and analysis of spatial distributions (Donert, 2005). However, there is some use of active learning methods, including engagement with participatory planning and strategic environmental assessment in GIS learning at the University of Padova, Italy (De Marchi, 2005), and specific use of PBL in GIS 'taster' courses at Exeter University (Fraser, 2005). The Exeter approach is in the spirit of Solem's (2001, p. 3) caution that PBL will work well in collaborative group activities once "students have gained hands-on practice with GIS in the lab and are beginning to learn basic spatial analysis techniques". He deploys a hybrid form of PBL as a small component of a larger course.

But what of the need to learn and understand the underlying geographical concepts? Are these best taught using PBL? There are undoubtedly ways in which such outcomes could be achieved but, for many departments, PBL is more likely to be part of rather than the means by which the whole curriculum is delivered. PBL modules can be effectively integrated into a lecture-based course, and have been shown to help to resolve the time-content dilemma with something as wide ranging as 'world regional geography' (Fournier, 2002).

Figure 2 gives a specific example of how PBL is used in a world regional geography course in Chile. In this case, the aim of the exercise is to gain understanding of a many-sided 'problem'—how to contain population growth in developing countries, and in addition to explore the underlying concepts: the dynamics of demographic change, and the socioeconomic context within which a grasp of these must be situated. The two stories would be given to the class at the start of the assignment, along with a carefully mapped process for students to follow through to completion of the task and its assessment.

Practising PBL in Geography

There is little information available on the extent of use of PBL and PBL hybrids in geography courses and curricula. Even specific examples of its use are not common in the geographical literature; Beringer (2005), reporting from Australia about PBL in a subject called Earth Systems Interactions, found only Bradbeer's (1996) paper from the UK on fieldwork as an earlier example in the discipline. To these can be added at least Spronken-Smith (2005), on a New Zealand-based research methods course, as well as the special issue of *Planet* in 2001, which is devoted to case studies in PBL from geography and the earth and environmental sciences (King, 2001). This collection from the UK-based Learning and Teaching Support Network considers the risks as well as benefits of PBL. It includes Perkins and colleagues' (2001) field-study programme, which is based on the Van der Vleuten and Wijnen (1990) 'Maastricht 7-Jump Model' of PBL but, curiously, this paper does not define the problems they sought to address. Gabrys Alexson and Kemnitz (2001) report details of a classroom exercise devoted to solving the problem of which nation should receive a World Bank loan.

PBL websites, some of the most useful of which are listed in Table 2, tend to contain no, or only passing, reference to geographical applications. For example, the UK-based PBL on-line discussion board (www.jiscmail.ac.uk/lists/pbl.html) has only two geographical contributions in its searchable archive. Universiteit Maastricht's online PBL bibliography (www.unimaas.nl/pbl/default.htm) contains details of 3393 articles, with only seven including the word 'geography' in the tag line. The Post Conference Proceedings of the 2nd Asia Pacific Conference on PBL, held in Singapore in 2000 (www.tp.edu.sg/pblconference/3.htm), has papers on a range of topics, including cross-cultural issues, ethics and obstacles to implementation, with a range of disciplines being represented but not geography.

There is undoubtedly more PBL use and experimentation going on in geography than these sources indicate. Just how much, and where, and in what form is not clear. Are there any 'pure PBL' curricula? Or is geography only suited to hybrid forms? Such matters require more investigation. The first issue to be tackled, in the follow-up project to this paper, will be the compilation of an inventory of the uses, in different parts of the world, of PBL in geography. The second will be to uncover what students, instructors and managers, from their different perspectives, consider to be the benefits and risks of the use of PBL.

The first story is about a rural family in Africa:

Mary, a Kenyan farmer, has just had her third son. The father of Mary's children works in a distant city and visits the family only several weeks a year. He supports himself with his earnings and buys occasional nonessentials for the family. Mary tells an interviewer that three children are enough for happiness and so today, at age 29, she is having surgery that will prevent conception. She owns only one cow and a small piece of land that can't be further divided, so all she can provide for her children is an education. Mary says that she can afford to educate only three children.

Such attitudes are spreading in Kenya, where food, health care, and jobs are in short supply. Mary plans to augment her farm income by starting a sanitary pit toilet business. She has applied for a small loan (U.S. $150) for this purpose. The success of her business could mean that her children will become well educated and that she herself will gain prestige. If Mary accomplishes her goals, she could become a role model for other women seeking to limit their families so that they become self-sufficient owners of small businesses.

Source: Adapted from Jeffrey Goldberg, *The New York Times Magazine*, March 2, 1997: 39; and *World Resources, 1996-1997* (New York: Oxford University Press, 1996). In Pulsipher & Pulsipher (2002).

The second story is about a rural family in Brazil:

Jair is a *fazendero*, known in Brazil as the owner of a ranching system. As southern agriculturalists or *gauchos*, Jair, his wife Marilena, and their three children came to Uberlandia and the *Triangulo Mineiro* in the state of Minas Gerais, migrating from Rio Grande do Sul. They found new land that they were able to rent and then buy, after five years of intensive work to create pasture areas. However, they started to shift to sugarcane and soybean production in their 350 hectares due to special incentives offered by the state government. This change brought about more work and economic development. They eventually had two more children during those good years.

Jair and Marilena learned about family planning through local agencies, but did not pay as much attention to contraceptive methods as the majority of couples in this rural area. Both of them believe that life should be fully enjoyed and no restrictions must obscure this sentiment. They say that children are God's blessing. Besides, they add, our children will look after us once we get very old.

Source: Adapted from Osvaldo A. Muniz, *Rural Electrification and Innovation of Electrical Equipment in Minas Gerais, Brazil.* Report submitted to the World Bank, 1992.

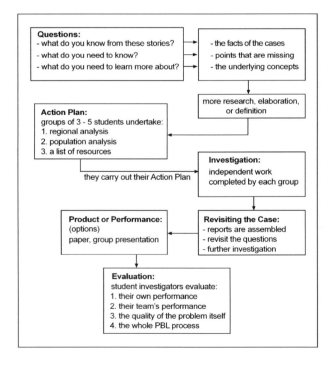

Figure 2. PBL Case Study: A comparison of two stories.

Table 2. Some Web-based resources on PBL (accessed August 2004)

Introductions to PBL		
Carleton University, Canada	Introduction, including a bibliography of French language resources	http://www.carleton.ca/(jchevali/PBLFOLDER/PBLNOTE/PBL.html
Adelaide University, Australia	Aimed at the novice lecturer	http://www.adelaide.edu.au/ltdu/leap/leapinto/prob_based_lrng.pdf
California State University	Introducing PBL good practice to CSU faculty	http://edweb.sdsu.edu/clrit/learningtree/Ltree.html
Hong Kong Polytechnic University	Overview of PBL in Hong Kong	http://www.hku.hk/pblhk/pblhk.htm
Articles, case studies, course portfolios		
University of Delaware, USA	Influential multidisciplinary site	http://www.udel.edu/pbl/ Online discussion listserv: http://www.udel.edu/pbl/ud-pbl-undergrad.html
Universiteit Maastricht, The Netherlands	Includes bibliography of nearly 4000 articles	http://www.unimaas.nl/pbl/default.htm
Samford University, USA	Supports major inter disciplinary adoption of PBL at Samford	http://www.samford.edu/pbl/ Insight Newsletter with reports on PBL from around the world: http://www.samford.edu/pbl/articlelist.html
Brighton University, UK	PBL course directory, by subject and institution	http://interact.bton.ac.uk/pbl/index.php
Higher Education Academy, UK	Problem Based Learning Project Network	http://www.heacademy.ac.uk/709.htm
PBL in Geography		
Geography, Earth and Environmental Subject Centre (GEES)	Resource Database	http://www.gees.ac.uk/search.htm; including GEES magazine *Planet*, with PBL issue: http://www.gees.ac.uk/planet/PBL.pdf

Table 3. Best practices in PBL

Preparation
- Prepare well in advance and, if possible, negotiate teaching release time
- Search for similar courses or assignments, and share ideas with colleagues, including those outside the discipline and academy
- Assemble resources for student use: access to pertinent library and online resources is necessary
- Consider level and training of students. Are they first years or students in a seminar or non-traditional students?

Scenario design
- The scenario should reflect reality as closely as possible and be contemporary in tone
- The scenario should be compelling, so as to draw students in and generate self-directed learning
- The scenario should be complex enough to involve multi-dimensional problems and solutions, requiring students to work as a team
- The scenario should be focused enough to be resolvable in the time available

Implementation
- The PBL experience should begin at or near the beginning of a term. Ideally this type of work will be infused into the class culture, not dropped in at random
- Students should be formed into instructor-assigned, permanent groups of 4–6; Permanent groups allow students to develop team-building skills. Reduce barriers to participation by assigning specific roles to students (leader, recorder, sceptic, etc.)
- Instructors should work with groups to provide clear guidelines for conduct and expectations; they should facilitate by asking probing questions, and help guide student inquiry (depending on student level)
- There should be a clear product or outcome for the problem. Students must know what is expected of them. A report? A poster? An oral presentation? A decision supported by references?

Assessment
- Develop authentic assessment mechanisms that mirror problem-solving process
- Instructors should have clearly established marking criteria that are transparent to students
- Work accountability into the assessment process. Consider both individual and group components to marks
- Students may be asked to do a self-assessment of their learning process, and be assessed by peers both for their problem-solving abilities and for contribution to team effort

Note: The above comments are synthesized from: Barrows (1988); Cuseo (1992); Wilkerson and Gijselaers (1996); Clark & Wareham (1998); Rhem (1998); Duch (1999); Leckman *et al.* (1999); Boud (2000); Savin-Baden (2000); Duch *et al.* (2001); Chapman *et al.* (2002).

Having constructed inventory and assessment, our current compilation, from the literature, of best practices in PBL (Table 3) may then be augmented and modified.

PBL is not a teaching/learning method to be adopted lightly, and if the chances of successful implementation are to be maximized, then careful attention to course preparation and scenario design is essential. Clear guidance must be given to students and instructors about what is expected, and an assessment method that aligns with objectives and intended learning outcomes has to be in place (Macdonald & Savin-Baden 2004). Table 3, therefore, represents an initial guide to instructors, based on a wide range of largely non-geographical sources, of essential matters for new PBL users to consider.

Conclusion

This article has explored a range of perspectives on PBL. To its supporters, PBL poses the fundamental challenge for higher education of "how do colleagues teach and how do students learn?" (Lee, 2001, p. 10), or, in the words of a faculty member from Sherbrooke's PBL-oriented engineering school in Canada: "what are we about at the university, and how can we do it better?" (K. Johns, personal communication, University of Canterbury, 18 March 2004). PBL is an active learning method that leads to greater understanding and achievement of competences, rather than retention of knowledge for its own sake. It usually takes place in group environments where the focus is on attempting to resolve problems, or to work through scenarios, with the aim of developing lifelong learning skills that are transferable to career situations. However, while the literature is full of examples of applications (albeit few from geography) that claim to achieve these ends, rather less has been written about the circumstances in which PBL is or, as important, is not successful. The same is true of the inputs required from students, teachers, and often administrators as well, in order to gain the benefits claimed for PBL. Our conclusion from this review is that these themes all deserve more exposure in the evaluation of PBL as a viable project for delivery of all or parts of geography curricula.

References

Agnew, C. (2001) Editorial: Evaluating changes in learning and teaching, *Journal of Geography in Higher Education*, 25(3), pp. 293–298.
Albanese, M. A. & Mitchell, S. (1993) Problem-based learning—a review of literature on its outcomes and implementation issues, *Academic Medicine*, 68(1), p. 615.
Barrows, H. (1988) *The Tutorial Process* (Springfield: Southern Illinois University School of Medicine).
Barrows, H. (1998) The essentials of problem-based learning, *Journal of Dental Education*, 62(9), pp. 630–633.
Barrows, H. & Tamblyn, R. M. (1980) *Problem-based Learning: An Approach to Medical Education* (New York: Springer).
Benbow, E. W. & McMahon, R. F. T. (2001) Mature students?, in: P. Schwartz, S. Mennin & G. Webb (Eds) *Problem-based Learning: Case Studies, Experience and Practice*, pp. 119–125 (London: Kogan Page).
Beringer, J. (2005) Application of problem-based learning through investigation of a real-world research problem, Unpublished paper.
Bligh, J. (1995) Problem-based small group learning, *British Medical Journal*, 311, pp. 342–343.
Boud, D. (2000) Assessment: tethinking assessment for the learning society, *Studies in Continuing Education*, 22(2), pp. 151–167.
Bradbeer, J. (1996) Problem-based learning and fieldwork: a better method of preparation, *Journal of Geography in Higher Education*, 20(1), pp. 11–18.
Bradbeer, J., Healey, M. & Kneale, P. (2004) Undergraduate geographers' understandings of geography, learning and teaching: a phenomenographic study, *Journal of Geography in Higher Education*, 28(1), pp. 17–34.
Burch, K. (2000) A primer on problem-based learning for international relations courses, *International Studies Perspectives*, 1, pp. 31–44.
Casey, M. B. & Howson, P. (1993) Educating pre-service students based on a problem-centered approach to teaching, *Journal of Teacher Education*, 44(5), pp. 361–369.
Chapman, D., Keller, G. & Fournier, E. (2002) *Implementing Problem-based Learning in the Arts and Sciences* (Birmingham, AL: Samford University Press).
Chappell, A. (2006) Using the 'grieving' process and learning journals to evaluate students' responses to problem-based learning in an undergraduate geography curriculum, *Journal of Geography in Higher Education*, 30(1), pp. 15–31.
Clark, G. & Wareham, T. (1998) *Small-group Teaching in Geography* (Cheltenham: Geography Discipline Network).
Coulson, R. L. (1983) Problem-based student-centred learning of the cardiovascular system using the problem-based learning module (P.B.L.M.), *The Physiologist*, 26(4), pp. 220–224.
Cuseo, J. (1992) Cooperative learning vs. small group discussions and group projects: the critical differences, *Cooperative Learning and College Teaching*, 2(3), pp. 5–10.
Dahlgren, M. & Oberg, G. (2001) Questioning to learn and learning to question: structure and function of problem-based learning scenarios in environmental science education, *Higher Education*, 41(3), pp. 263–282.

De Marchi, M. (2005) GIS at Department of Geography University of Padova: state of the art, in: K. Donert (Ed.) *Higher Education GIS in Geography: A European Perspective*, pp. 68–74 (Liverpool: Liverpool Hope University; HERODOT Network).

Dochy, F., Segers, M., Van den Bossche, P. & Gijbels, D. (2003) Effects of problem-based learning: a meta-analysis, *Learning and Instruction*, 13(5), pp. 533–568.

Donert, K. (Ed.) (2005) *Higher Education GIS in Geography: A European Perspective* (Liverpool: Liverpool Hope University; HERODOT Network).

Duch, B. (1995) What is problem-based learning? *About Teaching 47*. Available at www.udel.edu/pbl/cte/jan95–what.html (accessed November 2004).

Duch, B. (Ed.) (1999) *Problem-based Learning in Undergraduate Education* (Newark: University of Delaware Center for Teaching Effectiveness).

Duch, B., Groh, S. & Allen, D. (2001) *The Power of Problem-based Learning* (Sterling: Styles Publishing).

Eisenstaedt, R. S., Barry, W. E. & Glanz, K. (1990) Problem-based learning: cognitive retention and cohort traits of randomly selected participants and decliners, *Academic Medicine*, 65(9) Supplement pp. S11–S12.

Fenwick, T. J. (1998) Fixing' the world? Problem-based learning in professional education, *Studies in the Education of Adults*, 30(1), pp. 53–66. Extract available at http://www.ualberta.ca/~tfenwick/ext/pubs/pbl.htm (accessed May 2004).

Fournier, E. J. (2002) World regional geography and problem-based learning: using collaborative learning groups in an introductory-level world geography course, *Journal of General Education*, 51(4), pp. 293–305.

Fraser, D. (2005) Teaching GIS taster courses at Exeter University, in: K. Donert (Ed.) *Higher Education GIS in Geography: a European Perspective*, pp. 110–116 (Liverpool: Liverpool Hope University; HERODOT Network).

Gabrys Alexson, R. & Kemnitz, C. (2001) The World Bank scenario—a problem-based learning activity in human geography and environmental science, *Planet*, Special Issue 2, pp. 25–26.

Gewin, V. (2004) Mapping opportunities, *Nature*, 427, pp. 376–377.

Gold, J. R., Jenkins, A., Lee, R., Monk, J., Riley, J., Shepperd, I. & Unwin, D. (1991) *Teaching Geography in Higher Education: A Manual of Good Practice* (Oxford: Blackwell).

Heale, J. D., Davis, G., Norman, C., Woodward, V., Neufeld, V. & Dodd, P. (1988) A randomized controlled trial assessing the impact of problem-based versus didactic teaching methods in CME, *Proceedings of the Twenty-Seventh Annual Conference on Research in Medical Education*, pp. 72–77 (Washington, DC: Association of American Medical Education).

Healey, M. (2005) Linking research and teaching to benefit student learning, *Journal of Geography in Higher Education*, 29(2), pp 183–201.

HEFCE (1995) Quality Assessment of Geography, Higher Education Funding Council for England. Available at: http://www.qaa.ac.uk/revreps/subj_level/qo11_95_textonly.htm (accessed May 2004)

Jenkins, A. (1985) Peace education and the geography curriculum, in: D. Pepper & A. Jenkins (Eds) *The Geography of Peace and War*, pp. 202–213 (Oxford: Blackwell).

King, H. (2001) Editorial: Case studies in problem-based learning from geography, earth and environmental sciences, *Planet*, Special Issue 2, pp. 3–4.

Lamb, A. (2004) Project, problem and inquiry-based learning (Toledo, University of Toledo Teacher Tap), Available at: http://www.eduscapes.com/tap/ (accessed August 2005)

Leckman, A. -M., Levesque, K. & Audet, G. (1999) Assessment of a problem-based learning program in biology at the University of Quebec at Montreal by the first year cohort, in: J. Conway & A. Williams (Eds) *Themes and Variations in PBL*, pp. 159–168 (Newcastle: Australian Problem-based Learning Network).

Lee, C. (2001) Problem-based learning: a personal view, *Planet*, Special Issue 2, pp. 10.

Le Heron, R., Baker, R. & McEwen, L. (2006) Co-learning: re-linking research and teaching in geography, *Journal of Geography in Higher Education*, 30(1) pp. 77–87.

Lieux, E. M. (1996) A comparative study of learning in lecture vs. problem-based format, *About Teaching: Newsletter of the Center for Teaching Effectiveness* (University of Delaware). Available at: http://www.udel.edu/pbl/cte/spr96–geol.html) (accessed April 2004).

Macdonald, R. (2001) Problem-based learning: implications for educational developers, *Educational Developments*, 2(2), pp. 1–5.

Macdonald, R. & Savin-Baden, M. (2004) *A Briefing on Assessment in Problem-based Learning*, LTSN Generic Centre Assessment Series, no.13 (York: LTSN Generic Centre). Available at: http://www.ltsn.ac.uk/application.asp?app=resources.asp&process=full_record&section=generic&id=349 (accessed November 2004).

Martinsen, D., Eriksson, H. & Ingelman-Sundberg, M. (1985) Medical chemistry: an evaluation of active and problem-oriented teaching methods, *Medical Education*, 30(3), pp. 22–28.

Maudsley, G. (1999) Do we all mean the same thing by 'Problem-based learning'? A review of the concepts and a formulation of the ground rules, *Academic Medicine*, 74, pp. 178–185.

Nolte, J., Eller, P. & Ringel, S. (1988) Shifting toward problem-based learning in a medical school neurobiology course, *Proceedings of the Twenty-Seventh Annual Conference on Research in Medical Education*, pp. 66–71 (Washington, DC: Association of American Medical Colleges).

Perkins, C., Evans, M., Gavin, H., Johns, J. & Moore, J. (2001) Fieldwork and problem-based learning, *Planet*, Special Issue 2, pp. 27–28.

Post, G. J. & Drop, M. J. (1990) Perceptions of the content of the medical curriculum at the medical faculty in Maastricht: a comparison with traditional curricula in The Netherlands, in: M. Zohair, H. Nooman, G. Schmidt & E. Ezzat (Eds) *Innovation in Medical Education: An Evaluation of Its Present Status*, pp. 64–75 (New York: Springer Verlag).

Prideaux, D., Gannon, B., Farmer, E., Runciman, S. & Rolfe, I. (2001) Come and see the real thing, in: P. Schwartz, S. Mennin & G. Webb (Eds) *Problem-based Learning: Case Studies, Experience and Practice*, pp. 13–19 (London: Kogan Page).

Pulsipher, L. & Pulsipher, A. (2002) *World Regional Geography: Global Patterns, Local Issues* (New York: W.H. Freeman).

Rangachari, P. K. (1991) Design of a problem-based undergraduate course in pharmacology: implications for the teaching of physiology, *American Journal of Physiology*, 260(6), Part 3, pp. S14–S21.

Rhem, J. (1998) Problem-based learning: an introduction, *National Teaching & Learning Forum*, 8(1), pp. 1–4.

Saunders, K., Northrup, D. E. & Mennin, S. P. (1985) The library in a problem-based curriculum, in: A. Kaufman (Ed.) *Implementing Problem-based Medical Education: Lessons from Successful Innovations*, pp. 71–88 (New York: Springer Verlag).

Savin-Baden, M. (2000) Facilitating problem-based learning: the impact of the tutor's pedagogical stances, *Journal on Excellence in College Teaching*, 11((2/3)), pp. 97–111.

Savin-Baden, M. (2001) The problem-based learning landscape, *Planet*, Special Issue 2, pp. 4–6.

Schwartz, P., Mennin, S. & Webb, G. (Eds) (2001) *Problem-based Learning: Case Studies, Experience and Practice* (London: Kogan Page).

Solem, M. (2001) Using Geographic Information Systems and the internet to support problem-based learning, *Planet*, Special Issue 2, pp. 22–24.

Spencer, J. A. & Jordan, R. K. (1999) Learner centred approaches in medical education, *British Medical Journal*, 318, pp. 1280–1283.

Spronken-Smith, R. (2005) Implementing a problem-based learning approach for teaching research methods in geography, *Journal of Geography in Higher Education*, 29(2), pp. 203–221.

Van der Vleuten, C. & Wijnen, W. (1990) *Problem-based Learning: Perspectives from the Maastricht Experience* (Amsterdam: Thesis Publishers).

Vernon, D. T. A. & Blake, R. L. (1993) Does problem-based learning work? A meta-analysis of evaluative research, *Academic Medicine*, 68(7), pp. 550–563.

West, D. A. & West, M. M. (1987) Problem-based learning of psychopathology in a traditional curriculum using multiple conceptual models, *Medical Education*, 21, pp. 151–156.

Wilkerson, L. & Gijselaers, W. (Eds) (1996) *Bringing Problem-based Learning to Higher Education: Theory and Practice* (San Francisco: Jossey-Bass).

Woodward, C. A. & Ferrier, B. M. (1983) The content of the medical curriculum at McMaster University: graduates' evaluation of their preparation for postgraduate training, *Medical Education*, 17, pp. 54–60.

Wu, C. V. & Fournier, E. J. (2000) Coping with course content demands in a problem-based learning environment, *Journal of the Alabama Academy of Science*, 71(3), pp. 110–119.

Where Might Sand Dunes be on Mars? Engaging Students through Inquiry-based Learning in Geography

RACHEL SPRONKEN-SMITH*, JO BULLARD**, WAVERLY RAY†, CAROLYN ROBERTS‡ & ARTIMUS KEIFFER^

*Higher Education Development Centre, University of Otago, New Zealand, **Department of Geography, Loughborough University, UK, †MiraCosta College, Oceanside, California, USA, ‡Environmental Knowledge Transfer Network, University of Oxford, UK, ^Department of Geography, Wittenberg University, Ohio, USA

ABSTRACT *This paper encourages readers to experiment with inquiry-based learning (IBL) in their courses in the interest of identifying more diverse styles of instruction, and developing a wider understanding of the advantages and disadvantages of the methodology. The aims of the paper are to unpack the meanings of IBL, describe some uses of IBL in geography, and discuss their benefits and challenges for students and teachers. IBL is essentially a question-driven, philosophical approach to teaching that involves active, student-centred learning. The teacher acts principally as a facilitator or mentor, guiding and encouraging students through the inquiry process. Examples of IBL are presented, ranging from questioning exercises embedded in the class, through to entire courses or degrees using an inquiry-based approach. Students can benefit greatly from IBL since they are active in the learning process, can have improved understanding, more enjoyable learning, develop valuable research skills, achieve higher-order learning outcomes and perform better academically. Teachers can also benefit through a strengthening of teaching–research links and the clear gains in student engagement and learning. However, in order for IBL to be effective, teachers must be encouraged and supported to take on this facilitating role. When IBL elements are embedded in a more traditional curriculum, particular care needs to be taken so that students and teachers are carefully oriented to the expectations regarding the outcome of learning and teaching in this mode.*

Introduction

Inquiry-(or enquiry) based learning (IBL) is premised on stimulating curiosity and wonder in students. The purpose of this approach is to create a "state of perplexity by presenting information that conflicts with prior knowledge and experiences of the learner"

(Ciardiello, 2003, p. 229). Ciardiello argues that students are prompted to search for questions that guide them in their quest to resolve any discrepancy, and that will aid them in their development of important skills—such as critical inquiry. The value of inquiry in education has long been recognized. Its early development has been attributed to the American philosopher and educator John Dewey (1859–1952). He wrote widely on the links between thinking, reflection and experience and promoted 'learning by doing' or active learning (Dewey, 1933), but its early origins precede even Confucius. Inquiry-based learning is thus an approach to teaching that is question-driven, rather than topic-driven, and aims to build research skills in students (McMaster University, 2007). The approach has been relatively widely adopted in some disciplines, such as medical training, and in more recent years has become more extensively used in the sciences (Prince & Felder, 2006) and geography (e.g. Pawson *et al.*, 2006). This is, in part, because the inquisitive and flexible characteristics of the learning process are akin to the research process engaged in by academic staff. Hence IBL is research oriented and can facilitate closer links between teaching and research in higher education than traditional lecture formats may achieve (e.g. Jenkins *et al.*, 2003; Healey, 2005). Such synergy is often attractive to academic staff. It is also probable that the traditional field and laboratory emphasis of many geography programmes has provided a longstanding and convenient platform for the development of IBL exercises, particularly where student numbers are not excessive.

Our paper explores contested landscapes of IBL to explain the core theoretical underpinnings of this teaching approach. Second, it gives a range of geographical and environmental examples, from embedded class activities to degrees based on an inquiry approach. Third, the paper discusses the benefits and challenges of using IBL for students and staff. Based on the evidence, the authors believe it appropriate to encourage readers to experiment with IBL in their own courses, and to circulate the outcomes widely to allow others to share their experiences.

Contested Landscapes of Inquiry-based Learning

Inquiry-based learning is challenging to define. Meanings articulated in previous academic literature (e.g. Brew, 2003; Kahn & O'Rourke, 2004; Sandoval & Reiser, 2004) are plural and contested, and even amongst the five authors of this paper there was considerable difference of opinion as to what the essential constituents of IBL might be. We do not use IBL to refer to a narrowly defined style of learning. Rather, we see it as a more philosophical approach to learning and teaching which must have certain attributes, but

Table 1 Essential and optional attributes of IBL

Essential	Optional
Active approach to learning	Collaborative/group learning
Question-driven or research-focused	Individual learning
Inductive approach to teaching	University-focused
Student/learner-centred with teacher as a facilitator	Community involvement
Facilitated/scaffolded learning	Field-based activity
Constructivist	Resource-based learning (resources provided)
	Multi- or inter-disciplinary focus

may incorporate a range of additional characteristics where appropriate (see Table 1). Specifically, IBL must constitute 'active' learning (Healey & Roberts, 2004) and must be question-driven or research-focused (in the broadest sense of the term). IBL is 'student- or learner-centred' (Kember, 1997) and the lecturer, demonstrator or module leader acts as a facilitator of learning. Furthermore, it is an 'inductive approach' (Prince & Felder, 2006) to teaching in which learning is driven through the student's inquiry and his/her need for facts, procedures and guiding principles in order to explore possible answers. This is in contrast to deductive approaches in which the teacher begins with theories and principles and progresses to applications. The inductive process of IBL is illustrated by Figure 1. This model involves a cycle in which students become engaged with a topic, develop a question to explore, determine what information needs to be found, gather data, synthesize findings, communicate these and then evaluate success. The process is circular since the inquiry can lead to further questions and an attitude of self-reflection and evaluation are central to the process (Justice *et al.*, 2002).

Facilitated, or scaffolded, learning is also a requirement for IBL—specifically, following the initiation of inquiry, learners are provided with guidance, resources or feedback when and where appropriate. The balance between giving students the freedom to explore, and the amount of guidance provided by the facilitator is a delicate one that varies according to the experience and confidence of both the facilitator and the learner in relation to the subject matter (e.g. Savin-Baden, 2003; Crabtree, 2004). In IBL, understanding is chiefly created by what the learner actually does; it is a constructivist approach to learning (e.g. Bruner, 1990).

The range of additional attributes that may characterize IBL varies and is driven by intended learning outcomes along with factors external to the specific course, module or programme on which it is being used. For example, whilst IBL on geographical themes is often a collaborative exercise undertaken by groups of learners, we do not consider this an essential feature since assessment requirements, class size or resource availability may make individual IBL more appropriate. Early users of IBL tended to be restricted to the on-campus learning environment; however, raised awareness of the importance and role of universities in the wider community may increase community-based or employer-based IBL. Setting up the inquiry is vitally important—the question needs to be broad to allow for multiple perspectives and scope for exploration (McMaster University, 2007.) However, unlike some authors

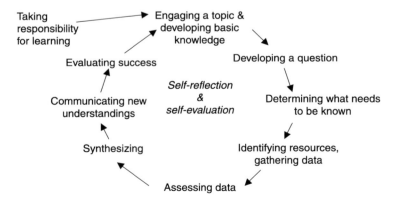

Figure 1. Model of the inquiry process. *Source*: After Justice *et al.* (2002, p.19).

(e.g. Kahn & O'Rourke, 2004) we do not consider it necessary for the inquiry to have multiple possible answers. What is necessary is for learners to have the space or opportunity to work through multiple possibilities. In mathematical notation this is akin to exploring the relationship between x and y as opposed to asking the question 'what is $x + y$?'

Table 1 shows that the contemporary scope of IBL is broad and covers a range of learning approaches that are student-centred, active, and driven by a process of inquiry. Kahn & O'Rourke (2004) attempted to classify inquiry approaches to learning and included a range of activities—problem-based learning (PBL), small-scale investigations and project work—within the scope of IBL. Spronken-Smith *et al.* (2007) argued that the relationship between IBL and PBL is not well defined. PBL is a better known pedagogy with a more fully developed literature base. Both IBL and PBL are inductive approaches in which learning is driven by student engagement in an inquiry process. However, PBL usually focuses on questions to which the answers are already known (particularly in a medical context), while IBL often involves students in the production of knowledge; that is their teachers may not know the answers. PBL often has a shorter timescale (one class to a few weeks) while IBL can be for a sustained period. PBL is usually done in collaborative groups while IBL can be done in groups, but not always. Thus it appears that PBL is a more prescriptive form of IBL, and thus PBL is seen to be a subset of IBL, with both IBL and PBL being subsets of active learning (Figure 2).

Examples of IBL in Geography

Documented use of IBL in geography is limited when compared with other disciplines; however, it is likely that IBL in its broadest sense is, in fact, widely used. In the more

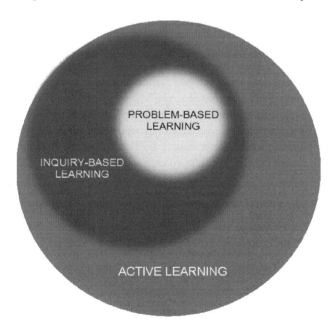

Figure 2. The relations between inquiry-based learning, problem-based learning and active learning. Both IBL and PBL fall in the realm of active learning and PBL is a subset of IBL

traditionally taught (i.e. lecture-based) degrees (particularly in science subjects), a stronger commitment to IBL often takes place at more advanced levels. This is due to the perceived need for students to become familiar with a base of knowledge and to learn the associated language and concepts of the discipline. Once they have this knowledge base, the challenge is for students to develop their research skills. IBL can provide a multitude of ways which progressively develop these research skills. Initially this could be through field work and case studies that are focused on students applying their knowledge in a practical, hands-on environment. At more advanced levels, students are ready to tackle the challenges of pure IBL courses, where they are fully involved in research tackling professional problems. By developing a natural progression strategy early on, students could then be prepared to ask more relevant questions for a senior or master's thesis or a doctoral dissertation. Since learning is a cumulative process, a strategy that cumulates in the best possible scenario for the learner should be employed. This is especially true for the multi-faceted discipline of geography.

IBL can be adopted at range of scales, from within-class activities to an entire degree programme. At smaller scales, a tutorial in which the discussion follows Socratic modes of dialogue could be seen as IBL, although our examples involve larger groups and timescales. The range of examples from the following different geography programmes illustrates how IBL can be used with an increasing level of commitment to engage and challenge staff and students.

IBL as a Short In-class Activity

Earth Surface Processes and Landforms, Loughborough University, UK. Part of this second year course (*c.*150 students) requires students to think about the variables governing geomorphological processes on Earth and then, when given basic information about another planet, to consider whether similar processes could operate elsewhere. The ways any consequent landforms might differ from those on Earth are explored. Students work in groups of two or three in a lecture theatre, with each group having an infra-red transmitting handset. The tutor outlines the differences between Earth and, for example, Mars, in terms of gravity, atmospheric density and similar concepts. Through questioning, the students are then required to apply their knowledge of Earth's surface processes to the Martian situation. For example: "If you controlled the Mars Orbital Camera, where on the planet would you look for linear or star type dunes?" The groups have up to three minutes (depending on the complexity of the question) to discuss the question and choose one of three or four possible scenarios by pressing the appropriate button on their handset and transmitting the answer to a central receiver in the lecture room. When each group has selected an answer, a graph is displayed showing what percentage chose each response and the tutor discusses the validity of each. Up to 10 questions might be posed and discussed in a 90-minute session. Assessment of understanding is through a traditional essay-style question in a timed exam at the end of the course.

IBL as a Component of a Field Course

Social and Cultural Field Course, Loughborough University, UK. This is an optional field course in which up to 20 students visit the volcanic island of Montserrat in the Caribbean. The intended learning outcomes include developing an understanding of the complexities evident in responses (social, cultural, economic, and political) to natural disasters. One assessment component (15 per cent) requires groups of four students to produce social/cultural maps of one of the communities on the island to explore the question "How has living under the influence of an active volcanic hazard shaped the community?" After their first visit to the area the students are asked to reflect as a group on the meaning of their map and historical and contemporary factors contributing to the character of the area. The groups are given the opportunity to revisit the location a few days later to refine and finalize their ideas before giving a short oral presentation to their peers and producing a poster. In the process of making the maps, students use a variety of sources of information including conversations with local residents, library resources, and photographs. The geographical focus of the cultural map is determined by the group, giving students considerable flexibility to shape their own learning processes.

IBL Assignment as Part of a Course

Geography in the News, Wittenberg University, USA. The idea for this IBL assignment has been used for 20 years to introductory classes in Human/Cultural/World Regional Geography ranging in size from 15 to 200 at several institutions. The assignment, usually given early on in the course, requires students to follow a major news story that is being carried by national media, or a local story that occurred in their hometown. At least 25 newspaper articles or 50 web-based reports need to be identified in journals or newspapers held in the university and local libraries; web sources have traditionally been found to be less suitable, since they usually have no illustrations or related stories around them. Students are encouraged to read newspapers for this reason. The story is then synthesized in a series of questions (e.g. what is the descriptive nature, what are the geographic implications, how does it affect those in the area or those removed, what are your personal perceptions?). After reading about a particular incident, students perceive themselves to be 'expert' and can see the spatial connections inherent in human activities. Based on the data that they accumulate in their stories, students trace over a base map and construct a thematic map illustrating an effective display of national or global connections based on their topic. The overall purpose of this assignment is to make students 'aware of their place in time and space'. This is important as we examine various geographic concepts in class, such as movement, globalization, social stratification and diffusion. It helps to know that what happens in one part of the world usually does have an effect on others that are distant. This assignment has potential to be adapted to other geography courses. It constitutes 10 per cent of the final grade in the class.

IBL Incorporating International Collaboration and e-Learning as Modules of a Course

Population, Global Economy, and Nationalism, Association of American Geographers' online Center for Global Geography Education (CGGE), USA. The Association of American Geographers' online Center for Global Geography Education (CGGE) offers three inquiry-based e-learning modules supporting international student collaborations at the introductory and advanced level. Multinational teams of students collaborate on geographic problems using an e-learning software platform. The 'Population', 'Global Economy', and 'Nationalism' modules are designed to support tutors who are interested in promoting the understanding of geographic concepts in their courses through expanding their students' awareness of international perspectives (CGGE, 2006). The key learning objectives are to examine global issues using the information, methods, and concepts of geography, and to formulate and carry out strategies for asking and answering geographic questions in an international team (CGGE, 2006). Instructor Guides provide scoring and collaborative work rubrics for the assessment of student work, which may be adapted to fit the needs of the particular course.

IBL Course

Field Research Studies, University of Otago, New Zealand. This is a full-year physical geography research methods course for third-year students entailing group-based inquiry into research topics closely aligned with staff interests. Topics in 2006 included assessing the frost risk in a vineyard, determining slope instability hazards in alpine environments, the processes of marram grass seed production and dispersal in a transgressive dune system, heavy metal leaching in vineyards, and the influence of weather and climate on air pollution in the city of Dunedin.

Up to 60 students enrol forming about 10 groups, with tutors typically supervising one or two groups. The course outcomes include the ability to design, conduct and report on a research project, effective communication, team-work skills, organizational and project management skills. Weekly group meetings are held with the tutor, together with 12 seminars covering aspects of the research process and development of communication skills (e.g. oral presentations, report writing). The research involves collection of field data and students take a lead role in organizing the fieldtrips (ranging from a weekend to five days in the field). Assessment consists of individual elements (80 per cent: literature critique, a report based on group work and an individual critique on their learning) and group work (20 per cent: research proposal presentation, 'conference' presentation, and a self- and peer assessment of contribution to the group).

Degree Programmes

Geography and Related Disciplines, University of Gloucestershire, UK. A suite of related degree programmes at the University of Gloucestershire was developed in 1998 with a principal emphasis on investigative styles of learning (Roberts, 2001). The programmes include human and physical geography, pure and applied environmental and geo-sciences, applied humanities disciplines such as heritage management, and environmental design subjects such as landscape architecture. Many of the 160 or more modules are interdisciplinary, including collaborative student activity in a variety of settings: classroom, library, field, laboratory and studio, community and employer-based. Students work both on-campus, and at a distance using electronic platforms. In some modules, distance learners and campus-based students collaborate on writing tasks. IBL begins in Level I with simple projects, often involving short classroom activities and field investigations, building through more extended investigations in the UK and overseas in Level II, expanding to extended independent projects in Level III. All students in the relevant disciplines undertake a common element of study on sustainable development, which introduces a set of real issues, and focuses on personal development of capability to undertake IBL. Students also participate in an induction activity introducing collaborative learning thus providing opportunities to reflect on individual learning styles.

Modules in Levels II and III tend to emphasize students undertaking 'live' projects in real settings, with genuine stakeholders, requiring students to develop high-level skills in research and effective communication, including the determining of fact from opinion. Examples include undertaking community development projects in the UK and elsewhere, a development aid partnership in Africa, undertaking industry-standard environmental audits and green business plans for local companies, and pollution investigations in former industrial sites or sites of alleged contamination incidents (Healey & Roberts, 2004). Assessment tasks of a wide variety are viewed as integral to the classroom activity with a high level of external involvement from people in professional practice, often drawn in from staff research and consultancy work. The success of the approach in developing students' capabilities was recognized in January 2005 by the award of a UK University Centre for Excellence in Teaching and Learning, and £5 million for further development.

Benefits and Challenges of IBL for Students and Teachers

For Students

It is widely recognized that students who actively engage with the learning process gain more from their experience than those who receive information transmitted passively to them (e.g. Gibbs, 1992; Race, 1993). While additional rigorous studies are still needed to track the quantitative and qualitative changes in student learning that result from IBL, there is increasing evidence that IBL is more effective than traditional teaching for achieving a variety of student learning outcomes. Such outcomes include an improvement in academic achievement, student perceptions, process skills, analytic abilities, critical thinking and creativity (e.g. see studies cited by Prince & Felder, 2006). Berg *et al.* (2003) compared the learning outcomes of an open inquiry versus an expository version of a first-year chemistry laboratory class and found that students in the IBL stream were more motivated, developed a deeper understanding, had a higher degree of reflection, and achieved higher-order learning. Justice *et al.* (2007) did a comparative study using five years of data to determine whether taking a first-year inquiry course improved student performance. They found that those who took the inquiry course had statistically positive gains in passing grades, achieving Honours and remaining in the university. Students can become more engaged by IBL and develop an enthusiasm for IBL courses (e.g. Kennedy & Navey-Davis, 2004) and indeed they may become apprentice researchers in the field (e.g. Slatta, 2004).

Given our argument that IBL is an umbrella term that encompasses, for example, problem-based learning (see Figure 2), we can draw on the better developed literature base for PBL to examine the impact of this approach on student learning. Pawson *et al.* (2006) suggested the benefits for students who engage in PBL include improved understanding, more enjoyable learning, a greater sense of achievement and improved preparation for lifelong learning. An enduring challenge of PBL is convincing and encouraging students that this more demanding and apparently more time-consuming approach is worthwhile (Spronken-Smith, 2005; Chappell, 2006; Pawson *et al.*, 2006). Perhaps the key is to view the total student study time—whether in or out of the classroom—as the relevant period, and blur the distinction between the settings of 'classroom contact' or 'other learning'. In our experience there is no particular difference in the total study time involved—although students may often drive themselves, and their colleagues, harder on IBL projects.

Spronken-Smith (2006) examined how students' initial struggle with PBL transformed into a 'new awareness of learning'. Whilst occasional use of IBL—for example, intermittent exercises over the course of a degree—is unlikely to facilitate major changes in student approaches to learning (e.g. Fuller *et al.*, 2000), more extensive use of IBL does enable students to develop more than just their cognitive abilities. Through closer interaction with peers and a reflective approach to learning, they can also develop physical (dexterity and personal presentation), emotional, psychological and social skills (Chappell, 2006).

The potential disadvantages, or risks, associated with PBL include a perception of the increased time commitment required, some lack of security (of both format and content) and problems associated with group work. Spronken-Smith (2006) suggested ways in which instructors can mediate student risks in PBL, such as explaining the rationale for PBL to students and providing specific opportunities for groups to discuss how they will function effectively. Another concern regarding PBL based on work with students at pre-higher education levels (ages 15–17) suggested that PBL in particular may be less suitable for disabled students than more traditional forms of learning (e.g. Könings *et al.*, 2005), although there is also evidence that inclusive approaches to curriculum design, playing to the strengths and talents of every student, will also yield benefits to all (Healey *et al.*, 2002).

Based on their research of Kolb learning styles from a sample of geography students in Australia, New Zealand, the United Kingdom, and the United States, Healey *et al.* (2005) note the importance of considering the diversity of student learning styles when planning and implementing curriculum and assessment. A special concern may exist since IBL is well matched with some learning styles and not others. Differing student learning styles need not pose an insurmountable barrier for implementing IBL in geography since student exposure to different modes of teaching ultimately enhances student learning (Kolb, 1984). Practitioners of IBL should be aware of the impact of student learning styles on student achievement to ensure that their curricula hold true to the constructivist tradition.

Most types of IBL, not only PBL, are ideally suited to students working as teams or groups. Group work is often considered to be a 'good thing' in terms of skills development and is often highly valued by employers (in terms of students developing skills of working with others, sharing resources, pooling ideas, working as part of a team, stimulating creativity) and by academic staff (encourages active engagement of topics through discussion, enables range of assessment modes, may reduce assessment load). While group work may be viewed with suspicion by both students and staff (e.g. Parsons & Drew, 1996; Healey *et al.*, 1996), the difficulties can be resolved in a range of ways (e.g. Livingstone & Lynch, 2000; Spronken-Smith, 2006).

For Teaching Staff

One of the main benefits teachers can gain from using IBL is a strengthening of teaching–research links. Many prominent higher education specialists (e.g. the Boyer Commission, 1998; Rowland, 2000; Brew, 2003) including geographers (Jenkins *et al.*, 2003; Healey, 2005) have called for a strengthening of these links. According to these researchers, one of the key ways to strengthen the links, and one which is of particular value for students, is to engage them in the research process. IBL, with its focus on answering questions, stimulates curiosity and allows the development of research skills. Scheduled activities and assignments, within and beyond the class contact time, start the process to help develop research skills such as finding, interpreting and analysing information and ideas. But the benefits do not just occur for the students. The Boyer Commission (1998, p. 15) stated that "inherent in inquiry-based learning is an element of reciprocity: faculty can learn from students as students are learning from faculty". Certainly, as the level of IBL increases to that of a whole course or indeed a degree, students can gain higher research and metacognitive skills, and staff act as co-learners in the process. French & Russell (2002) found that postgraduate students who were tutors for inquiry-based laboratories benefited by gaining valuable scientific training. This externality stems from teaching inquiry-based labs that involved critiquing experimental design, evaluating arguments and interpreting and solving problems, all skills essential to researchers. When students and staff both engage on research problems with unknown outcomes, there is the potential for staff to co-learn in the process.

Another significant benefit of IBL for teachers derives from the clear gains in other aspects of student engagement such as improved understanding, more enjoyable learning, a greater sense of achievement and an improved preparation for lifelong learning. To recognize these outcomes as benefits, though, requires a teacher who is focused on the needs of learners. Such teachers are known as being 'student-centred, learning-oriented' (Kember, 1997) or 'student-focused' (Trigwell & Prosser, 1996). Those with this teaching philosophy aim to facilitate understanding, intellectual development and conceptual change in their students (see also work by Ramsden, 2003). In contrast, teachers may be 'teacher-centred, content-oriented', emphasizing the imparting of information or transmitting structured knowledge (Kember, 1997). However, Bond *et al.* (2006) are critical of the focus on knowledge as being equated with teacher-centred and argue that, particularly in the sciences (including subjects such as physical geography), teachers can have a student-centred approach by using their experience of discipline knowledge to bring students in relation with it. While this approach is knowledge-centred, it is very much focused on student needs. Kember and others (e.g. Entwistle & Walker, 2000; Bond *et al.*, 2006) moreover suggested that the continuum from teacher-centred to student-centred is developmental, i.e. that over time a teacher might progress from a teacher-centred to a student-centred approach, if the environment was appropriately supportive. IBL is congruent with a student-centred approach, and thus can be a challenge for teachers, particularly if they have a teaching philosophy that is teacher-centred.

As with student experiences of IBL, most research on staff experiences reports on PBL, rather than IBL in its entirety. Many researchers have shown that teaching in PBL is perceived to be enjoyable and rewarding (e.g. Bernstein *et al.*, 1995; Kaufman & Holmes, 1996; King, 2004; Spronken-Smith & Harland, 2008). King (2004, p. 114) reports the views of a lecturer who was initially quite resistant to the notion of PBL:

> I think it is, for me so far, being involved in teaching for six years, the most enjoyable way of teaching. After experiencing the whole process [of facilitation] I find that I enjoy working with the tutorial group... I like to bring the best out of the students, guiding them without giving them the answers... it's been good.

Similarly, Spronken-Smith & Harland (2008) reported that the teachers in their PBL course on research methods in geography found the teaching fun, easy and "wonderfully relaxing".

However, IBL can be challenging and can involve emotional turmoil. The main problem is frustration or difficulty knowing when to intervene (e.g. Khoo et al., 2001; Maudsley, 2002; King, 2004; Spronken-Smith & Harland, 2008) and anxiety over the lack of structure and unpredictable nature of the course (Bernstein et al., 1995; Azer, 2001; Spronken-Smith & Harland, 2008). Spronken-Smith & Harland (2008) also raise the issue of disparate levels of intervention by tutors in a teaching team, and the impact on student learning and grades. Some tutors, who were more interventionist, ultimately helped students to produce higher-quality work and thus achieve better grades, while other tutors were willing to let students make more mistakes and perhaps produce final products (conference presentations and consultancy reports) that were of lesser quality. However, it may be that students in the groups with more autonomy are actually learning more than those students in groups with tutors who are giving more direction.

Implications for Teaching

This section draws out the practical implications for teaching IBL from the preceding discussion. First the type of IBL to use is discussed, followed by managing the teaching team and finally some guidance is given on facilitating learning in this mode.

Which Type of IBL to Use?

This paper has provided a range of examples that illustrate how IBL can be used at varying levels—from Level I through to advanced undergraduates—and at varying scales (from within-class activities through to whole degree programmes based on inquiry). The authors believe that students will benefit the most from more prolonged exposure to IBL, so ideally teachers should aim to build in IBL activities or courses throughout the degree programme. The activities should build upon one another so that the students are progressively given more autonomy and responsibility in determining the nature and method of the inquiry. For example, at Level I activities such as the "Where might sand dunes be on Mars" exercise encourage students to work collaboratively through the possibilities and draw on their collective knowledge to put forward a feasible answer. Project work within courses is also a valuable way to develop research skills in students. Perhaps the most benefit comes, though, when the course takes a fully IBL approach and engages students directly in the research process. It is hoped that, by the end of their degree, students will have had the opportunity to engage in an IBL course which required them to work either collaboratively or independently on a research project. In order to increase motivation and commitment to the research project, students should be able to self-select topics that are of personal interest or relevance. However, workload issues must be kept in mind since IBL courses can result in anxiety for students as they tend to get fully engaged in these courses at the expense of other study.

How to Manage the Teaching Team?

The sparse research to date on teacher experiences of IBL has implications for course coordinators. Initially, the teacher or teaching team should consider published research on student learning theory and on IBL in particular. Ideally, they should be fully involved in all stages of planning the IBL course, module or programme, so that they develop ownership of the resulting approach. If the course is premised entirely on an IBL approach, and a number of teachers are involved, then it is crucial to develop opportunities for supporting teachers as they teach in this mode. This is particularly important for new tutors who may have a tendency to dominate group processes and may be reluctant to relinquish control to the students (Spronken-Smith & Harland, 2008). If the teaching team can develop a 'community of practice' (Lave & Wenger, 1991), in which the teachers share experiences of their teaching both formally (in team teaching meetings) and informally (through corridor conversations), then new teachers (or those more experienced but with a teacher-centred philosophy) can learn from their peers and develop the confidence and skills to take on this new role (Spronken-Smith & Harland, 2008). Thus, experience suggests that once the course is running there should be regular meetings of the teaching team at which tutors share feelings about how the group work and the group dynamics are progressing. This open forum can be of immense help to tutors who are struggling with this approach to teaching.

How to Facilitate IBL?

If students are new to IBL, it is important to orient them to the expectations of this type of learning environment, especially regarding the contact time and requirements of self-directed learning outside the classroom. This is particularly important for geography students since many may be uncomfortable with this experiential style of learning (Healey *et al.*, 2005) and thus require appropriate support to learn in this mode. The rationale for the approach should be described and, if group work is required, there should be specific opportunities for groups to discuss how they will function effectively. In terms of facilitating an inquiring approach, Kahn & O'Rourke (2004, p. 6) provide several practical suggestions for teaching staff. These include:

(a) asking open-ended questions that provoke further discussion and stimulate deeper exploration (McMaster University (2007) provides some excellent guidelines for developing effective inquiry questions);
(b) supporting students, motivating them to engage with the task and valuing their ideas and contributions;
(c) encouraging students to reflect on their experiences—a requirement for keeping a reflective diary, together with an assessment item that requires students to draw on their diary, is a useful mechanism to aid reflection;
(d) monitoring progress and ensuring that students understand where they are in the process;
(e) challenging student thinking, encouraging them to extend their boundaries and to seek new ways to work with problems and situations;
(f) developing an atmosphere of trust in which students are willing to share and exchange ideas or work cooperatively.

Further to these suggestions, Kahn & O'Rourke (2004) add that the key to a successful IBL experience lies in the questioning techniques used by the facilitator. These should stimulate the generation of ideas, demonstrate support and genuine interest in what students have to say, and give clues as to whether the students are 'on track'.

As with any educational innovation it is vital that feedback is gained from both students and teachers to inform further development of the IBL activity or course. Teachers using an IBL approach are strongly encouraged to publish case studies that can add to the sparse literature.

Conclusion

Inquiry-based learning is a philosophical approach to teaching that is question-driven, and involves active, student-centred learning. The role of the teacher is one of a facilitator or mentor, who seeks to guide the students through the inquiry process. IBL can be used at all scales and levels from within-class activities through to whole degree programmes. This paper has presented a series of cases of the use of IBL in geography. At a minimal, but nevertheless valuable, scale, teachers can use puzzling questions (such as where are sand dunes on Mars?) to spark debate and discussion amongst students in lectures or laboratories. As the level of engagement with IBL increases, teachers can use inquiry-based assignments where students have to work either individually or in groups, researching a particular question. We suspect this use of IBL is probably widespread in the geography curriculum, although teachers may not term it as such. Entire modules, as part of a course, can be based on a further emphasis on IBL. Examples were given of three modules on population, global economy and nationalism from the CGGE. These module examples are an excellent demonstration of international collaboration enabled through e-learning. Less common perhaps are IBL courses in geography whereby students focus on researching a problem or set of problems for the entire course. Yet these courses offer the possibility of students engaging in authentic problems that they may meet in the workplace and so can provide strong stimulation and motivation for students, as well as more fully developing research skills. IBL can also be used to teach fundamental concepts to beginning students—a systematic approach they can use in all their classes, not just geography. Finally, entire degrees (e.g. Gloucestershire) or institutions (e.g. McMaster University) can be premised on an inquiry approach, with consequent benefits for students and staff.

Students can greatly benefit from IBL as they are active in the learning process, can have improved understanding, more enjoyable learning, a greater sense of achievement and improved preparation for lifelong learning. Furthermore they can achieve higher-order learning outcomes and perform better academically. However, as the level of IBL increases to that of a whole course, particularly in a more traditional degree programme, there can be concerns over the time commitment required, a lack of security, and, if involving group work, issues with group dynamics. Teachers using IBL can benefit from a strengthening of teaching–research links and take pride in the clear gains in student engagement and learning. IBL teaching is often perceived to be fun and enjoyable. As the level of IBL increases to that of a whole course, it is vital that teachers are comfortable acting as facilitators, rather than as experts transmitting knowledge. Inexperienced tutors may need particular support to make this transition in teaching approach. However, it is in this fuller engagement with IBL (at the scale of course or degree dominance) that teachers can benefit as co-learners in the research process.

This paper has highlighted the lack of published research on IBL—in geography and elsewhere. There is a growing literature on the use of PBL, but few descriptive or analytical studies of other types of IBL. Further research is therefore required to determine the extent and nature of IBL courses in geography curricula. Also more empirical evidence is required to determine the benefits and challenges of this approach for both students and teachers, and how best teachers can be supported when using IBL.

Acknowledgements

Thanks are due to the constructive criticism on the developing paper from colleagues at the INLT workshop in Brisbane, July 2006, and to the anonymous referees.

References

Azer, S. A. (2001) Problem-based learning: challenges, barriers and outcome issues, *Saudi Medical Journal*, 22, pp. 389–397.

Berg, C. A., Bergendahl, V. C. B. & Lundberg, B. K. S. (2003) Benefiting from an open-ended experiment? A comparison of attitudes to, and outcomes of, an expository versus an open-inquiry version of the same experiment, *International Journal of Science Education*, 25(3), pp. 351–372.

Bernstein, P., Tipping, J., Bercovitz, K. & Skinner, H. A. (1995) Shifting students and faculty to a PBL curriculum: attitudes changed and lessons learned, *Academic Medicine*, 70, pp. 245–247.

Bond, C. B., Ross, E. & Madill, B. (2007) The development of tertiary teachers' experiences of teaching. Proceedings of the 31st Improving University Teaching Conference, Dunedin, NZ, 3–6 July. Available at: http://www.iutconference.org/2006/schedule.htm (accessed March 2007).

Boyer Commission (1998) Reinventing undergraduate education: a blueprint for America's research universities. Available at: http://naples.cc.sunysb.edu/Pres/boyer.nsf (accessed March 2007).

Brew, A. (2003) Teaching and research: new relationships and their implications for inquiry-based teaching and learning in higher education, *Higher Education Research and Development*, 22(1), pp. 3–18.

Bruner, J. (1990) *Acts of Meaning* (Cambridge, MA: Harvard University Press).

Ciardiello, A. V. (2003) "To wander and wonder": pathways to literacy and inquiry through question-finding, *Journal of Adolescent and Adult Literacy*, 47(3), pp. 228–239.

CGGE (2006) The online Center for Global Geography Education. Available at: http://www.aag.org/Education/center/cgge–aag%20site/index.html (accessed March 2007)

Chappell, A. (2006) Using the 'grieving' process and learning journals to evaluate students' responses to problem-based learning in an undergraduate geography curriculum, *Journal of Geography in Higher Education*, 30(1), pp. 15–32.

Crabtree, H. (2004) Improving student learning using an enquiry based approach, *Learning Based on the Process of Enquiry*, Conference Proceedings, September 2003, Curriculum Innovation, University of Manchester, pp. 77–84. Available at: http://www.intranet.man.ac.uk/rsd/ci/ebl/cproceed.pdf (accessed March 2007).

Dewey, J. (1933) *How We Think: A Restatement of the Relation of Reflective Thinking to the Educative Process* (Boston, MA: D.C. Heath).

Entwistle, N. & Walker, P. (2000) Strategic alertness and expanded awareness within sophisticated conceptions of teaching, *Instructional Science*, 28, pp. 335–361.

French, D. & Russell, C. (2002) Do graduate teaching assistants benefit from teaching inquiry-based laboratories?, *Bioscience*, 52(11), pp. 1036–1041.

Fuller, I., Rawlinson, S. & Bevan, R. (2000) Evaluation of student learning experiences in physical geography fieldwork: paddling or pedagogy? *Journal of Geography in Higher Education*, 24(2), pp. 199–215.

Gibbs, G. (Ed.) (1992) *Teaching More Students Projects* (Oxford: Polytechnics and Colleges Funding Council and Oxford Polytechnic).

Healey, M. (2005) Linking research and teaching to benefit student learning, *Journal of Geography in Higher Education*, 29(2), pp. 183–201.

Healey, M., Kneale, P. & Bradbeer, J. (2005) Learning styles among geography undergraduates: an international comparison, *Area*, 37, pp. 30–42.

Healey, M., Matthews, H., Livingstone, I. & Foster, I. (1996) Learning in small groups in university geography courses: designing a core module around group projects, *Journal of Geography in Higher Education*, 20, pp. 167–180.

Healey, M. & Roberts, J. (Eds) (2004) *Engaging Students in Active Learning: Case Studies in Geography, Environment and Related Disciplines* (Cheltenham: Geography Discipline Network).

Healey, M., Roberts, C., Jenkins, A. & Leach, J. (2002) Towards inclusion: disabled students and fieldwork, *Planet* 3, 9–10, reprinted in *Planet Special Edition* 3: Special Educational Needs and Disabilities—Learning and Teaching Guidance for Geography, Earth and Environmental Sciences, pp. 24–26

Jenkins, A., Breen, R., Lindsay, R. & Brew, A. (2003) *Reshaping Teaching in Higher Education—Linking Teaching with Research* (London: Kogan Page).

Justice, C., Rice, J., Warry, W. & Laurie, I. (2007) Taking inquiry makes a difference—a comparative analysis of student learning, *Journal on Excellence in College Teaching* (inpress).

Justice, C., Warry, W., Cuneo, C., Inglis, S., Miller, S., Rice, J. & Sammon, S. (2002) *A Grammar for Inquiry: Linking Goals and Methods in a Collaboratively Taught Social Sciences Inquiry Course. The Alan Blizzard Award Paper: The Award Winning Papers,* Special Publication (Windsor: The Society for Teaching and Learning in Higher Education and McGraw-Hill Ryerson).

Kahn, P. & O'Rourke, K. (2004) *Guide to Curriculum Design: Enquiry-Based Learning.* Available at: http://www.heacademy.ac.uk/resources.asp?id = 359&process = full_record&section = generic (accessed March 2007).

Kaufman, D. M. & Holmes, D. B. (1996) Tutoring in problem-based learning: Perceptions of teachers and students, *Medical Education*, 30, pp. 371–377.

Kember, D. (1997) A reconceptualisation of the research into university academics' conceptions of teaching, *Learning and Instruction*, 7(3), pp. 255–275.

Kennedy, A. & Navey-Davis, S. (2004) Inquiry-guided learning and the foreign language classroom, in: V. S. Lee (Ed.) *Teaching and Learning Through Inquiry: A Guidebook for Institutions and Instructors,* pp. 71–80 (Sterling, VA: Stylus).

Khoo, H. E., Chhem, R. K., Gwee, M. C. E. & Balasubramaniam, P. (2001) Introduction of problem-based learning in a traditional medical curriculum in Singapore—Students' and tutors' perspectives, *Annals Academy of Medicine Singapore*, 30, pp. 371–374.

King, S. (2004) The emotional dimension of collaborative exchange to problem-based learning: the staff experience, in: M. Savin-Baden & K. Wilkie (Eds) *Challenging Research in Problem-based Learning* (Maidenhead: Society for Research into Higher Education and Open University Press).

Kolb, D. A. (1984) *Experiential Learning: Experience as the Source of Learning and Development* (Englewood Cliffs, NJ: Prentice-Hall).

Könings, K. D., Wiers, R. W., ven de Wiel, M. W. J. & Schmidt, H. G. (2005) Problem-based learning as a valuable educational method for physically disabled teenagers? The discrepancy between theory and practice, *Journal of Developmental and Physical Disabilities*, 17(2), pp. 107–117.

Lave, J. & Wenger, E. (1991) *Situated Learning: Legitimate Peripheral Participation* (New York: Cambridge University Press).

Livingstone, D. & Lynch, K. (2000) Group project work and student-centred active learning: two different approaches, *Studies in Higher Education*, 25(3), pp. 325–345.

Maudsley, G. (2002) Making sense of trying to teach: an interview study of tutors' ideas of problem-based learning, *Academic Medicine*, 77, pp. 162–172.

McMaster University (2007) What is inquiry? Available at: http://www.mcmaster.ca/cll/inquiry/whats.unique.about.inquiry.htm (accessed March 2007).

Parsons, D. E. & Drew, S. K. (1996) Designing group project work to enhance learning: key elements, *Teaching in Higher Education*, 1, pp. 65–80.

Pawson, E., Fournier, E., Haigh, M., Muniz, O., Trafford, J. & Vajoczki, S. (2006) Problem-based learning in geography: towards a critical assessment of its purposes, benefits and risks, *Journal of Geography in Higher Education*, 30(1), pp. 103–116.

Prince, M. J. & Felder, R. M. (2006) Inductive teaching and learning methods: definitions, comparisons, and research bases, *Journal of Engineering Education*, 95(2), pp. 123–138.

Race, P. (1993) *Never Mind the Teaching, Feel the Learning,* Paper 80 (London: SEDA).

Ramsden, P. (2003) *Learning to Teach in Higher Education*, 2nd edn (London: Routledge/Falmer).

Roberts, C. R. (2001) Mapping the territory at Cheltenham and Gloucester, *Planet*, 2, pp. 15–16.

Rowland, S. (2000) *The Enquiring University Teacher* (Buckingham: Society for Research into Higher Education and Open University Press).

Sandoval, W. A. & Resier, B. J. (2004) Explanation-driven inquiry: integrating conceptual and epistemic scaffolds for scientific inquiry, *Science Education*, 88(3), pp. 345–372.

Savin-Baden, M. (2003) Disciplinary differences or modes of curriculum practice? Who promised to deliver what in problem-based learning? *Biochemistry and Molecular Biology Education*, 31(5), pp. 338–343.

Slatta, R. W. (2004) Enhancing inquiry-guided learning with technology in history courses, in: V. S. Lee (Ed.) *Teaching and Learning Through Inquiry: A Guidebook for Institutions and Instructors,* pp. 93–102 (Sterling, VA: Stylus).

Spronken-Smith, R. (2005) Implementing a problem-based learning approach for teaching research methods in geography, *Journal of Geography in Higher Education*, 29(2), pp. 203–221.

Spronken-Smith, R. (2006) Problem-based learning: challenging but empowering. In: *Proceedings of the 31st Improving University Teaching Conference, 3–6 July, Dunedin, New Zealand*. Available at: http://www.iutconference.org/schedule.htm (accessed March 2007).

Spronken-Smith, R., Angelo, T., Matthews, H., O'Steen, B. & Robertson, J. (2007) How effective is inquiry-based learning in linking teaching and research? Paper presented at International Colloquium on International Policies and Practices for Academic Enquiry, Marwell, Winchester, UK, 19–21 April. Available at: http://portal-live.solent.ac.uk/university/rtconference/colloquium_papers.aspx (accessed September 2007).

Spronken-Smith, R. A. & Harland, T. (2008) Learning to teach with problem-based learning, *Active Learning* (in press).

Trigwell, K. & Prosser, M. (1996) Congruence between intention and strategy in science teachers' approach to teaching, *Higher Education*, 32, pp. 77–87.

International Perspectives on the Effectiveness of Geography Fieldwork for Learning

IAN FULLER*, SALLY EDMONDSON**, DEREK FRANCE[†], DAVID HIGGITT[‡] & ILKKA RATINEN[§]

*School of People, Environment & Planning, Massey University, New Zealand, **Department of Geography, Liverpool Hope University, UK, [†]Department of Geography & Development Studies, University of Chester, UK, [‡]Department of Geography, National University of Singapore, Singapore, [§]Department of Teacher Education, University of Jyväskylä, Finland

ABSTRACT *This paper seeks to address assumptions on the effectiveness of fieldwork as a mode of learning in geography. This is approached from an international perspective, both in review of available evidence, which demonstrates a need for rigorous research into the issue, and in providing preliminary findings of research into the value of fieldwork from universities across three continents. Common themes to emerge concern the effectiveness of fieldwork in terms of learning and understanding of the subject: providing first-hand experience of the real world, whichever part of the world the students are in; skills development (transferable and technical); and social benefits. The extent to which fieldwork develops transferable skills depends on the context in which the fieldwork is undertaken. The paper points to avenues of future research to be investigated to deepen our understanding of the role fieldwork plays in student learning and to address the question, 'how effective is fieldwork in improving learning?'*

Introduction: Definitions and Form of Fieldwork in Geography

The UK Quality Assurance Agency (QAA) benchmark statement provides a definition of fieldwork as being "active engagement with the external world" (QAA, 2002), and as such the geography fieldtrip should not be confused with picnics, outings or class excursions (Lewis, 1968). Whether every activity described as fieldwork fits the criteria of 'active engagement' is debatable. Defined 'fieldwork' may include field teaching, field trips, field research or field camps (Dando & Wiedel, 1971), or indeed "any arena or zone within a subject where, outside the constraints of the four walls classroom setting, supervised learning can take place via first hand experience" (Lonergan & Andreson, 1988 p. 64). This latter definition was adopted by Gold *et al.* (1991), who go on to categorize fieldwork into five types of activity:

1. Short field excursion: limited travel in limited time;
2. Cook's Tour: limited activity in extended travel;
3. Residential course: extended travel and time;
4. Study tour: multi-location activity;
5. Project work: (i) learner-practitioner and (ii) participant observation.

A single fieldwork component of a degree programme, such as a residential course, could comprise a range of these activities.

Much has been written on the use of fieldwork (in all its guises) in undergraduate geography degree programmes (see the annotated bibliography by Cottingham *et al.*, 2002). This reflects the high regard for fieldwork by practitioners of the subject: fieldwork is perceived by many geographers as being at the heart of geography (Gold *et al.*, 1991), an essential component of undergraduate education in geography (Haigh & Gold, 1993; Kent *et al.*, 1997), and as intrinsic to the discipline as clinical practice is to medicine (Bligh, 1975). Not only is it considered essential, but it is considered by both academics and students to be an extremely effective and enjoyable learning and teaching method (Kent *et al.*, 1997; Fuller *et al.*, 2003). Stoddart & Adams (2004, p.46) suggest that, "the field is central to the way we have experienced Geography, both as a discipline within which we have lived and worked since our first degree, and as a context within which to think about the way the world works". Sauer's presidential address to the American Association of Geographers in 1956 stated: "the principal training of geographers should come, wherever possible, by doing fieldwork" (Sauer, 1956, p. 296). Nearly 50 years later, this view remains prominent, reinforced by the UK QAA (2002) and 10 years earlier the UK's teaching inspectorate (HMI) recognized that "fieldwork gives opportunities for learning which cannot be duplicated in the classroom. It greatly enhances students' understanding of geographical features and concepts, and allows students to develop specific as well as general skills" (HMI, 1992, p. 1). Stoddart & Adams (2004) suggest that the field reveals the complexity of geographical problems, but that in the field this complexity then becomes amenable to comprehension. Fieldwork is thus viewed by many as a ubiquitous element of geographical higher education (Rynne, 1998), although there are some within the discipline who have become philosophically (poststructuralist) opposed to the notion of 'expert-led' student fieldwork (Roche, personal communication), and the structuring of some degree schemes may still allow students to graduate with a geography major without having completed any field training.

This paper goes on to provide a brief review of the development of fieldwork before considering how effective fieldwork is as a mode of learning. We seek to address this issue from an international perspective drawing on four case studies from three continents, identifying common and contrasting themes and providing a set of recommendations for implementing effective fieldwork practice. We conclude by raising a series of research questions that we anticipate will take the effectiveness of fieldwork to new levels. The appendix provides four case studies that explore the effectiveness of fieldwork.

History of Fieldwork

Since Sauer's address, fieldwork has generally evolved from its traditional, observational-based origins to a diversity of learning and teaching processes that, since the 1960s and 1970s, have been characterized by increased orientation around (i) study of geographical processes compared with observation and description of form (e.g. Finlayson, 1981; Burt, 1988) and (ii) research and problem-solving approaches (e.g. Bradbeer, 1996; Fuller *et al.*, 2000). Such approaches have necessarily demanded development of subject-specific technical skills, but also transferable skills (for example teamwork, leadership) and student employability, the latter being recognized in the 1980s when such skills became explicit learning objectives of fieldwork (Kent *et al.*, 1997). This is not to suggest that research and problem-based fieldwork is superior in learning benefits to critical thinking associated with observation-based fieldwork; the aims and consequent outcomes are explicitly different. In Southeast Asia there remains a strong tradition of observation-based fieldwork, though of a form that incorporates not just observation of form but also process, and furthermore develops key technical skills (Goh & Wong, 2000). In addition, in contrast to developments in many British and Australasian universities, Southeast Asian fieldwork often integrates both physical and human geography, providing a much more holistic approach to the students' experience of the field (Goh & Wong, 2000).

The precise role of technology in fieldwork teaching remains subject to debate. It is almost 20 years since Gardiner & Unwin (1986) used computers on fieldtrips to analyse results. They identified difficulties in rekindling student enthusiasm on return from a field trip, analysis and debriefing being best done while fresh in students' minds. This integrated approach gives student ownership of the data, analysis and subsequent presentation of results. Thus technology may play a useful role in enhancing effectiveness of fieldwork, used as an integral part of all stages of fieldwork: preparation, practice and debriefing (Kent *et al.*, 1997). The further advantage of integrating computer and information technology (C&IT) with fieldwork is that, as a by-product, it provides enhanced IT key skills training. In an interesting innovation, France & Ribchester (2004) have inverted the conventional roles of fieldwork and IT by adopting fieldwork as a specific strategy to develop skills in web design and construction, providing a new stage for skills development. Recent research on UK geography, earth and environmental science (GEES) practitioners by Fletcher *et al.* (submitted) provides a first insight into how the GEES practitioners' use of C&IT is driven by technological developments, rather than pedagogical developments generating novel ways of teaching in the field.

Significant changes have therefore occurred in the delivery of fieldwork. In New Zealand, Welch and Panelli (2003) suggest that a tendency towards passive rather than active learning resulted in a re-evaluation of the efficacy of fieldwork as a learning tool in the 1990s (Gold *et al.*, 1991; Higgitt, 1996; Clark & Higgitt, 1997). Consequently, some fieldwork has been adjusted for important pedagogic reasons and reorientated toward small-group learning and small-scale problem-solving, as used by Simm & David (2002). Geography fieldwork in many New Zealand universities may be less prominent because it is integrated and embedded as a learning tool within taught courses (Pawson, personal communication), rather than run as a separate entity in its own right. Such a refocus on active learning will improve the affective domain and enhance the value of fieldwork (Kern & Carpenter, 1984, 1986). Is this shift from passive to active learning using fieldwork a global trend amongst a pedagogically responsive community? The phrasing of the UK QAA benchmark statement in terms of 'active engagement' (QAA, 2002) would certainly suggest so in terms of the UK scene. The extent to which this *is* the case is worth researching.

Fieldwork Effectiveness: What Works?

Having defined and recognized diversity in the categorization of fieldwork, as well as its development over the last 50 years, how effective is fieldwork as a tool for learning in geography? Does fieldwork *improve* student learning? Given the range of activities into which fieldwork may be categorized, this is a supremely difficult question to address. What is certain, however, is that "effective learning cannot be expected just because we take students into the field" (Lonergan & Andreson, 1988, p. 70). Fuller *et al.* (2000) suggest that a 'descriptive-explanation' approach to field teaching of first-year undergraduates was more effective than an 'analytical-prediction' approach, although both styles involved active learning 'by doing' (Race, 1993; Healey & Roberts, 2004).

Effective field teaching therefore requires careful design, and alignment of the activity within the wider course/module or degree programme structure (Biggs, 2003). The principle of alignment is one whereby all components of teaching support one another (Biggs, 2003). In fieldwork the teaching method, assessment procedure and climate created by staff–student interaction, as well as institutional and curriculum issues, all ought to be balanced if the activity is to be aligned. Gold *et al.* (1991) identify a series of guidelines aimed at improving the effectiveness of a field course through careful consideration of course design, location, curriculum, preparation, themes, staff supervision, skills development, data analysis and post-fieldwork activity. The need for carefully integrated preparation, debriefing and feedback is also emphasized by Kent *et al.* (1997). Nairn *et al.* (2000) noted that fieldwork delivered as a discrete 'field week' (common in the UK and at times in New Zealand) often lacked integration between the fieldwork and the remainder of the curriculum. There is a sense in which well-integrated fieldwork contributes to the notion of a spiral curriculum (Bruner, 1960). Students can revisit concepts covered in class during fieldwork, when they are also expected to acquire and display deeper levels of understanding.

Fletcher & Dodds (2004) have identified negative perceptions of fieldwork relating to costs of residential work and time, perceptions that were also reported by Fuller *et al.* (2003). In addition, students felt some trepidation over housekeeping arrangements and expectations in terms of learning. This emphasizes the importance of providing advance warning of fieldwork to allow students to plan for both financial and time commitments, as well as stating learning objectives clearly and recognizing the importance attached to housekeeping arrangements by some students. However, does carefully prepared and integrated fieldwork (even down to domestics) provide an effective learning opportunity? Careful preparation is necessary for fieldwork to successfully engage all participants.

Kern & Carpenter (1984) found that the affective (attitude (enjoyment), value (importance) and interest) responses of students engaged in an Earth Science course were 'significantly enhanced' by local (on-site) field activities. Students engaged in fieldwork left the course feeling much higher levels of importance, interest and enjoyment. Kern & Carpenter (1986) also found that fieldwork enhanced student learning; although lower levels of learning (information recall) were not affected, deeper learning (comprehension, application, analysis and synthesis) was significantly improved. This improvement was attributed to the enhanced affective responses of the student group (Kern & Carpenter, 1984) and the nature of the field activities, which "encouraged perception of the natural environment as an integrated whole" (Kern & Carpenter, 1986, p. 180). This research goes a long way to demonstrate the effectiveness of fieldwork as a learning tool, where it is integrated into a course, and demonstrates that fieldwork does not have to be exotic to be effective in enhancing learning. Similar results were found in local fieldwork conducted by Pawson & Teather (2002), where the pedagogical significance of fieldwork improved when students actively engaged in a field methodology ('streetwork'). Students tend to perceive fieldwork positively (where it is well executed), providing opportunity for experiential, holistic learning, and developing subject knowledge and technical skills within a non-threatening environment (Fuller *et al.*, 2003).

Positive views were also held by lecturers who taught these student cohorts (Scott *et al.*, 2006) and similar results have been reported by Fletcher & Dodds (2004) in their international review of fieldwork as part of integrated coastal management programmes. This research was far broader than that of Fuller *et al.* (2003) or Scott *et al.* (2006), drawing responses from nine countries distributed across four continents, but the positive perceptions of fieldwork, from both staff (international representation) and student (single institute) perspectives, were reinforced for the same reasons. In all three of Fletcher & Dodds's (2004), Fuller *et al.*'s (2003) and Scott *et al.*'s (2006) research, the positive perceptions of fieldwork as an effective learning tool outweighed the negative misgivings surrounding time, financial and domestic issues. Nevertheless, there are potential drawbacks to fieldwork, as have been identified by Nairn *et al.* (2000). However, Fink (1977) suggested that fieldwork positively affected students' attitudes to study and what they remembered subsequently, even into postgraduate employment. Given the link between students' affective response and learning (Fink, 1977; Kern & Carpenter, 1986), such positive perceptions support the notion that fieldwork does achieve its stated objectives (Gold *et al.*, 1991; Fuller *et al.*, 2003). However, there remains a need for more extensive research on the generic value of fieldwork. Nevertheless, it is no longer fair to state that there is virtually nothing in the public domain that could be recommended to a new lecturer to justify a field-based course or component (Lonergan & Andreson, 1988). The pedagogy of fieldwork has moved on, but needs to move further.

One way forward would be to link fieldwork more explicitly into an inquiry or problem-based curriculum as advocated by Pawson *et al.* (2006) and to adopt a co-learning model as suggested by Le Heron *et al.* (2006).

An International Case for the Effectiveness of Fieldwork?

In seeking to address the issue of international perspectives on the effectiveness of fieldwork, we summarize the findings of four preliminary surveys of field provision from the UK (Chester and Liverpool), Singapore and New Zealand. Details on these surveys are given in Appendix 1, from which we provide illustrations on how fieldwork is perceived in these differing contexts and countries and whether the range of fieldwork experience offered improves student learning.

The results from these preliminary investigations drawn from three continents strongly suggest that fieldwork *is* an effective means of learning as part of study for a geography degree. Just *how* effective it is compared with other methods of learning remains in need of investigation. Nevertheless, there are common themes that emerge from these preliminary results, namely the perception that fieldwork provides an unparalleled opportunity to study the real world, with all the benefits this brings. In each of the preliminary studies, fieldwork is perceived overwhelmingly positively by the students who offered their opinions. Whether conducting independent, field-based research in Europe, or spending half a day in the vicinity of the institution in New Zealand, or reflecting on accumulated experience throughout their degree programme in Singapore, fieldwork is perceived as an effective learning tool. Fieldwork is effective because it reinforces what the students have learnt in class, or via texts (Appendix 1). As such the effectiveness of the fieldwork reported here is in part due to its integration within the wider degree programme or course structure, in effect reinforcing the spiral curriculum model of learning. This, together with the opportunity to study in more detail a facet of the subject, means that fieldwork increases students' knowledge, skills and subject understanding (breadth, depth and recognition of complexity). The range of skills developed by fieldwork depends on the nature of the study, but may include use of technical instrumentation, development of research/observation skills, enhancing time management and/or critical thinking. These preliminary results also concur with Kern & Carpenter's (1984, 1986) observation that fieldwork stimulates learning in the affective domain, quite simply because students find it an enjoyable experience. Furthermore, one of the reasons students tend to enjoy fieldwork is the opportunity to work more closely with staff, often (although not always) with smaller staff:student ratios, which increases the students' feeling of importance, especially when working on an authentic problem, as part of a genuine research expedition.

These themes are common amongst students in every institution, across cultures, academic structures, academic levels, type and context of fieldwork. In the Caucasian-dominated institutions fieldwork is also valued as a means of improving social skills and developing group identity/teamwork, but this is not the case in an Asian university, implying that the wider benefits of fieldwork may be culturally constrained. In addition, this group of students did not articulate the effectiveness of fieldwork in terms of learning research techniques or developing research design, as is emphasized in project-based fieldwork in the UK, but focused on issues of observation and critical thinking. There remains a need to explore these issues in further depth to build up a more detailed, international perspective on the role of fieldwork and its effectiveness across cultures, in different modes/levels and in contrasting academic structures. However, on the basis of these preliminary findings, we offer the following interim recommendations for maximizing the effectiveness of fieldwork:

- Fieldwork should be clearly integrated with the course/programme/module of study, thus providing opportunities for deeper learning in which students are building upon a foundation of previously acquired theory (be it from the class, texts or study guide), as per the spiral curriculum model of learning (Bruner, 1960) and concept of alignment (Biggs, 2003).
- Deeper learning (knowledge and understanding) will be facilitated where fieldwork enhances student interest, enjoyment and recognition of importance (Kern & Carpenter, 1984, 1986).
- Residential fieldwork provides opportunity for learning to be reinforced during 'evening conversation' and in less formal lecturer–student and student–student interactions.
- Students respond positively to 'hands-on' data acquisition. Field use of technical instrumentation, and research design and data analysis are valued.

Effectiveness of Fieldwork Beyond Learning: Research Questions

Besides the key issue of whether or not fieldwork enhances student learning (and, if so, how and why) as discussed above, are wider issues related to the role of fieldwork in geography. These issues go beyond subject learning per se, but are important to address in an increasingly market-driven academy.

Cohort Identity and Engagement

An often stated objective of fieldwork is the development of social skills, breaking down barriers between staff and students and strengthening group identity (e.g. Gold *et al.*, 1991).

These issues have certainly been identified as strong perceptions amongst the student community (e.g. Fuller *et al.*, 2003; Fletcher & Dodds, 2004). However, the extent to which fieldwork achieves this depends on the nature of the fieldwork and, we suggest, cultural constraints (Singapore). Group-based field exercises incorporating project work may do much to develop such skills (e.g. Simm & David, 2002), whereas whole-class exercises may do less to break down barriers between peer groups, although our research suggests that even when teaching a whole class, social interaction is facilitated (New Zealand). Research is therefore needed on different modes of fieldwork in order to assess the impacts these modes of delivery have in terms of enhancing (or diminishing) student engagement and strengthening (or weakening) cohort identity. Furthermore, this question needs to be asked in the context of different academic cultures. For example, in the UK geography degree courses tend to comprise a fairly coherent group of students who will study more or less the same papers intensively during three years. In contrast, in Singapore and New Zealand, the degree structure is much more open, and group coherence is low, with students taking geography papers (course/unit/module) being drawn from a very wide variety of disciplines. In addition, there are cultural differences between countries that may also impact on the extent of cohort identity and engagement, as our results in this paper have suggested.

Employability, Skills and Lifelong Learning

Gerber (2000, p. 197) suggests that "fieldwork as one of life's experiences should not be underestimated". Increasingly attention has been turned towards life after the degree. In the UK this has been formalized with the introduction of student reflective journals (progress files), aimed at plotting the development of defined key skills (QAA, 2002) developed during the course of the degree. This moves the student beyond looking at performance as an academic qualification, and addresses the acquisition of key transferable skills (these are listed in the QAA benchmark statement for Geography, QAA, 2002). What is the role of fieldwork in development of these skills? Once again, Gold *et al.* (1991) and McEwen (1996) have identified as key objectives the development of certain key skills acquisition (e.g. observation skills and analytical skills), and student perception is that these skills are addressed by fieldwork (Fuller *et al.*, 2003) but, specifically, what skills are developed, by what type of fieldwork, and in what educational context (level and location)? Furthermore, what is the longer term impact of fieldwork on students post-graduation? Higgitt (unpublished) contacted students some years after graduation to ask about perceived benefits of fieldwork and its usefulness in the workplace. Recent graduates tried to equate usefulness to particular techniques or methodologies that they picked up during field classes. The students who have 3–4 years' experience in employment recognize the group-building skills as paramount. Stoddart and Adams (2004, p. 48) identify the importance of who they were with on fieldwork (either tutors or peers) and allude to influential field teachers, commenting, "being in places, and being there with people, has punctuated our lived experiences and provided the engine for geographical writing", clearly suggesting that, in their experience, fieldwork was vital and the effects long-lasting but this is the perception of one small proportion of geography graduates: the academics. There remains a need to investigate the longer-term impacts of a range of fieldwork types and contexts to elucidate the effectiveness of fieldwork in preparing students for the workplace, and the extent to which fieldwork is one of 'life's experiences' (Gerber, 2000).

Recruitment and Image

Given that "Geography without fieldwork is [perceived as being] like science without experiments" (Bland *et al.*, 1996, p. 165), the image of geography outside the academy is closely bound with fieldwork. UK universities with an overseas fieldwork component always find places on such trips easy to fill, no matter how far the destination (e.g. University of Plymouth to Australia, Gaskin personal communication; University of Wales, Aberystwyth, to New Zealand, Brewer, personal communication). Whether such trips are justifiable, or good for coherence of a year group (given issues of financial exclusion), remains unknown. Nevertheless, it is common practice, for example in UK and Finnish geography degrees, to engage in a residential overseas fieldtrip of some kind, and these are marketed as a draw to students, who perhaps see the opportunity for a potentially cheap trip to an exotic location. Clearly in such circumstances fieldwork is or may be used for recruitment purposes. Massey University and Victoria University, Wellington also offer fieldtrips to 'exotic' locations in the South Island of New Zealand, although the geographic isolation of New Zealand generally precludes overseas fieldtrips on grounds of expense. Certainly at Massey this is part of a recruitment drive, to encourage students to take the necessary geography papers and consider majoring in the subject, thus bringing income to the programme, and potentially 'growing the business'. Stoddart & Adams (2004) suggest that field courses to exotic locations are an important feature of competition between university departments of geography for students (and student fees). A recent study of courses in Kenya, Zimbabwe and Gambia by Robson (2002) concluded that they were highly effective in terms of both teaching and learning and also good for student recruitment, thus "the field has become an important terrain for corporate competition with the academy" (Stoddart & Adams, 2004, p. 56). A commentary on the pre-workshop discussion draft of the paper, based on recent experience as a geography undergraduate, noted that members of the cohort chose geography because of the fieldwork (one week residential).[1] The extent to which fieldwork (again the type and context) succeeds as a means of recruitment and lives up to the image in students' minds is thus a further question worth asking as part of an evaluation of the wider effectiveness of fieldwork in geography degrees.

Care needs to be taken in promoting the role of fieldwork not to portray a masculine, able-bodied image as does occur in some prospectuses (Hall *et al.*, 2002) and to consider inclusiveness as part of the social transformation agenda (Wellens *et al.*, 2006).

Conclusions

This paper begins to go some of the way towards addressing the effectiveness of fieldwork from an international perspective, having drawn on preliminary research into fieldwork practised on three continents. Impacts on the effectiveness of learning in the field may vary from the mundane (e.g. weather or domestic arrangements) to the deep seated (cultural) through to the pedagogic practice employed before, during and after the fieldwork. This paper suggests that there are a number of common themes that make fieldwork effective from the students' perspective, the strongest of which is the hands-on experience of the real world that fieldwork provides across cultures and continents.

There remains a need for rigorous research into just *how* effective fieldwork is compared with other means of learning, and what factors impact upon this effectiveness.

Research is particularly needed on:

- the impacts different modes of fieldwork have in terms of enhancing (or diminishing) student engagement and strengthening (or weakening) cohort identity;
- the longer-term impacts of a range of different types and contexts of fieldwork to elucidate the effectiveness of fieldwork in preparing students for the workplace;
- the extent to which fieldwork recruits students to a degree programme and why.

In the meantime we would encourage the use of carefully integrated, enjoyable fieldwork at any and every opportunity to facilitate and deepen our students' learning experience.

Acknowledgements

The authors would like to thank those colleagues who contributed to discussion of an earlier draft of this paper at the post IGC workshop in Glasgow (August 2004), both at the event and prior to it via web discussion. Thanks are also due to those student groups whose views have contributed to this paper and to three anonymous referees, whose helpful comments have improved the manuscript.

Note

[1] Comments received from Ruth Healey on the pre-workshop version of the draft discussion paper (Edmondson, S. *et al.* (2004) Fieldwork in geography in higher education: international perspectives. Discussion paper, available at: http://www.gees.ac.uk/pigupapa.rtf)

References

Biggs, J. (2003) *Teaching for Quality Learning at University*, 2nd edn (Buckingham: Society for Research in Higher Education & Open University Press).

Bland, K., Chambers, B., Donert, K. & Thomas, T. (1996) Fieldwork, in: P. Bailey & P. Fox (Eds) *Geography Teachers' Handbook*, pp. 165–175 (Sheffield: Geographical Association).

Bligh, D. A. (1975) *Teaching Students* (Exeter: Exeter University Teaching Services).

Bradbeer, J. (1996) Problem-based learning and fieldwork, a better method of preparation, *Journal of Geography in Higher Education*, 20(1), pp. 11–18.

Bruner, J. S. (1960) *The Process of Education* (Cambridge: Harvard University Press).

Burt, T. (1988) A practical exercise to demonstrate the variable source area model, *Journal of Geography in Higher Education*, 12(2), pp. 177–186.

Clark, G. & Higgitt, M. (1997) Geography and lifelong learning: a report on a survey of geography graduates, *Journal of Geography in Higher Education*, 21(2), pp. 199–213.

Cottingham, C., Healey, M. & Gravestock, P. (2002) Fieldwork in the Geography, Earth and Environmental Sciences Higher Education curriculum: an annotated bibliography. Available at http://www2.glos.ac.uk/gdn/disabil/fieldwk.htm (accessed September 2005).

Dando, W. A. & Wiedel, J. W. (1971) A two-week field course with deferred papers: a possible solution to the problem of undergraduate fieldwork, *Journal of Geography*, 70, pp. 289–293.

Finlayson, B. (1981) The analysis of stream suspended loads as a geomorphological teaching exercise, *Journal of Geography in Higher Education*, 5(1), pp. 23–35.

Fink, L. D. (1977) *Listening to the Learner: An Exploratory Study of Personal Meaning in College Geography Courses*, Research Paper 184 (Chicago: Department of Geography, University of Chicago).

Fletcher, S. & Dodds, W. (2004) Dipping toes in the water: an international survey of residential fieldwork within ICM Degree Course Curricula, *Littoral 2004: 7th International Symposium; Delivering Sustainable Coasts: Connecting Science and Policy*, Aberdeen Scotland, UK, Volume 1, pp. 305–309 (Cambridge: Cambridge Publications).

Fletcher, S., France, D., Moore, K. & Robinson, G. (2003) Fieldwork, education and technology: A GEES perspective, *Planet*, 4, pp. 17–19.

Fletcher, S., France, D., Moore, K. & Robinson, G. (in submission) Putting technology into fieldwork education: a pedagogic evaluation, *Journal of Geography in Higher Education*.

France, D. & Ribchester, C. (2004) Producing web sites for assessment: a case study from a level 1 fieldwork module, *Journal of Geography in Higher Education*, 28(1), pp. 49–62.

Fuller, I. C., Rawlinson, S. R. & Bevan, J. R. (2000) Evaluation of student learning experiences in physical geography fieldwork: paddling or pedagogy?, *Journal of Geography in Higher Education*, 24(2), pp. 199–215.

Fuller, I. C., Gaskin, S. & Scott, I. (2003) Student perceptions of geography and environmental science fieldwork in the light of restricted access to the field, caused by foot and mouth disease in the UK in 2001, *Journal of Geography in Higher Education*, 27(1), pp. 79–102.

Gardiner, V. & Unwin, D. (1986) Computers and the field class, *Journal of Geography in Higher Education*, 10, pp. 169–179.

Gerber, R. (2000) The contribution of fieldwork to lifelong learning, in: R. Gerber & K. C. Goh (Eds) *Fieldwork in Geography: Reflections, Perspectives and Actions*, pp. 195–210 (Dordrecht: Kluwer).

Goh, K. C. & Wong, P. P. (2000) Status of fieldwork in the geography curriculum in Southeast Asia, in: R. Gerber & K. C. Goh (Eds) *Fieldwork in Geography: Reflections, Perspectives and Actions*, pp. 99–117 (Dordrecht: Kluwer).

Gold, J. R., Jenkins, A., Lee, R., Monk, J., Riley, J., Shepherd, I. D. H. & Unwin, D. J. (1991) *Teaching Geography in Higher Education* (Oxford: Blackwell).

Haigh, M. & Gold, J. R. (1993) The problems with fieldwork: a group based approach towards integrating fieldwork into the undergraduate geography curriculum, *Journal of Geography in Higher Education*, 17, pp. 21–32.

Hall, T., Healey, M. & Harrison, M. (2002) Fieldwork and disabled students: discourses of exclusion and inclusion, *Transactions of the Institute of British Geographers*, 27(2), pp. 213–231.

Healey, M. & Roberts, J. (Eds) (2004) *Engaging Students in Active Learning: Case Studies in Geography, Environment and Related Disciplines* (Cheltenham: University of Gloucestershire, Geography Discipline Network and School of Environment).

Higgitt, M. (1996) Addressing the new agenda for fieldwork in higher education, *Journal of Geography in Higher Education*, 20(3), pp. 391–398.

HMI (Her Majesty's Inspectorate) (1992) *A Survey of Geography Fieldwork in Degree Courses, Summer 1990–Summer 1991: a Report by HMI*, Report 9/92/NS (Stanmore: Her Majesty's Inspectorate, Department of Education and Science).

Kent, M., Gilbertson, D. D. & Hunt, C. O. (1997) Fieldwork in geography teaching: a critical review of the literature and approaches, *Journal of Geography in Higher Education*, 21(3), pp. 313–332.

Kern, E. & Carpenter, J. (1984) Enhancement of student values, interests and attitudes in earth science through a field-orientated approach, *Journal of Geological Education*, 32, pp. 299–305.

Kern, E. & Carpenter, J. (1986) Effect of field activities on student learning, *Journal of Geological Education*, 34, pp. 180–183.

Le Heron, R., Baker, R. & McEwen, L. (2006) Co-learning: Re-linking Research and Teaching in Geography, *Journal of Geography in Higher Education*, 30(1), pp. 77–87.

Lewis, P. F. (1968) On field trips in geography, in: Association of American Geographers (Ed.) *Field Training in Geography*, Technical Paper 1, Commission on College Geography (Washington, DC: Association of American Geographers).

Lonergan, N. & Andreson, L. W. (1988) Field-based education: some theoretical considerations, *Higher Education Research and Development*, 7, pp. 63–77.

McEwen, L. (1996) Fieldwork in the undergraduate geography programme: challenges and changes, *Journal of Geography in Higher Education*, 20(3), pp. 379–384.

Nairn, K., Higgitt, D. & Vanneste, D. (2000) International perspectives on fieldcourses, *Journal of Geography in Higher Education*, 24, pp. 246–254.

Pawson, E. & Teather, E. K. (2002) 'Geographical expeditions': assessing the benefits of a student-driven fieldwork method, *Journal of Geography in Higher Education*, 26(3), pp. 275–289.

Pawson, E., Fournier, E., Haigh, M., Muniz, O., Trafford, J. & Vajoczki, S. (2006) Problem-based learning in geography: towards a critical assessment of its purposes, benefits and risks, *Journal of Geography in Higher Education*, 30(1), pp. 103–116.

QAA (2002) http://www.qaa.ac.uk/crntwork/benchmark/benchmarking.htm.

Race, P. (1993) *Never Mind the Teaching, Feel the Learning*, SEDA Paper 80 (Birmingham: SEDA).

Robson, E. (2002) 'An unbelievable academic and personal experience': issues around teaching undergraduate field courses in Africa, *Journal of Geography in Higher Education*, 26(1), pp. 36–59.

Rynne, E. (1998) Utilitarian approaches to fieldwork: a critique, *Geography*, 83(3), pp. 205–213.

Sauer, C. O. (1956) The Education of a Geographer, *Annals of the Association of American Geographers*, 46, pp. 287–299.

Scott, I., Fuller, I. C. & Gaskin, S. (2006) Life without fieldwork: some staff perceptions of geography and environmental science fieldwork, *Journal of Geography in Higher Education*, 30(1), pp. 161–171.

Simm, D. J. & David, C. A. (2002) Effective teaching of research design in physical geography, *Journal of Geography in Higher Education*, 26(2), pp. 169–180.

Stoddart, D. R. & Adams, W. M. (2004) Fieldwork and unity in Geography, in: J. A. Matthews & D. T. Herbert (Eds) *Unifying Geography: Common Heritage, Shared Future*, pp. 46–61 (London: Routledge).

Welch, R. V. & Panelli, R. (2003) Teaching research methodology to geography undergraduates: rationale and practice in a human geography programme, *Journal of Geography in Higher Education*, 27(3), pp. 255–277.

Wellens, J., Bernardi, A., Chalkley, B., Chambers, W., Healey, R., Monk, J. & Vender, J. (2006) Teaching geography for social transformation, *Journal of Geography in Higher Education*, 30(1), pp. 117–131.

Appendix: Four Case Studies Exploring the Effectiveness of Fieldwork

UK: University College Chester

Summary: final-year students, project-based fieldwork, residential, method—questionnaire

University College Chester (UCC), like many UK institutions, enables undergraduates to develop researcher skills by undertaking a final-year dissertation, which allows students to design and execute a major independent geographical research project. However, an option within the UCC geography programme is to undertake a group expedition to Norway to obtain primary data. An ongoing research project in association with the Department of Psychology & Therapeutic Studies at Roehampton University is evaluating student perceptions of the expedition learning experience. Preliminary research findings suggest a significant difference between expedition and non-expedition (locally-based) dissertation students with regards to knowledge- and perception-based identifiers. The expedition students score higher and are more positive overall towards (1) fieldwork increasing their knowledge and skills and (2) fieldwork contributing to their subject understanding and future career opportunities. In 'pre-' and 'post-' fieldwork measures the expedition students experienced a significant increase in confidence in using technical equipment and accurately and systematically recording data. Their views and experiences of fieldwork in general (both pre and post) were overwhelmingly positive.

UK: Liverpool Hope University

Summary: final-year students, project-based fieldwork, residential, method—questionnaire

This fieldwork at the very start of the honours year (3rd year undergraduate in the UK) was part of a course on Alpine Glacial Environments in which students prepared by reading and assignment preparation (but no teaching) prior to the trip. They were taught on a guided walk where they were challenged to ask questions for two days, and then spent two days on a short research topic. In addition, Master's students attended this trip as part of a Field Methods course in which they develop fieldwork research protocols and are encouraged to think very carefully about all stages of their research design then trial it. They join the early stages of the undergraduate 'questioning' sessions.

This fieldwork positively affected learning by teaching new skills and making theory much clearer: "*Hands on experience, practical learning works very well*". The residential component was also perceived to enhance learning by providing opportunity for conversation to "*include what we've experienced geographically*". The fieldwork also challenged the Master's students in terms of the mode of learning: "*although I have been on field trips before I have never had to think so much for myself before*". The fieldwork provided "*valuable first hand experience*" that enhanced students' understanding of geography, in terms of both depth and breadth. The skills this fieldwork developed focused on the use of technical equipment and research methodology. All students responded positively, as they did in identifying transferable skills development, which was expressed in terms of time management, group work and independent work and a recognition of increased confidence in their study and social interaction. Some students were concerned about unhelpful group dynamics, although most indicated that the fieldwork developed mutually supportive relationships.

Singapore: National University of Singapore (NUS)

Summary: final-year students, range of fieldwork experiences accumulated during 3 years of study, residential and non-residential, method—questionnaire

The fieldwork experience of these students is varied with some not having undertaken any modules with fieldwork. The survey was conducted at the beginning of the fourth year (Honours year) at a stage when students have completed 30 modules (about half of which have been in geography). Some 30 per cent of students claim to have only done fieldwork on one module or not all, while 45 per cent claim to have done some fieldwork activity on four or more modules. In terms of the effects on learning, fieldwork is perceived to enable conceptual and theoretical ideas to be grounded in the real world, and it provides hands-on activity and engagement, and research skills and opportunity for data collection: "*Fieldwork provides us with information that is outside the text, thus broadening the scope of study*"; "*Words are limited in bringing across the sights, sounds, feelings both physically and emotionally, it's much more interesting too and very much easier to remember lessons learnt*"; "*Fieldwork, in certain cases may help to operationalize concepts learnt in the classroom or help in crystallizing these abstract ideas. For example, when studying concepts such as 'sense of place' or legibility of a place, doing fieldwork allows us to see for ourselves the meanings behind these concepts.*" In terms of subject understanding, fieldwork is perceived to facilitate an understanding of complexity within geography, recognizing that concepts and theories do not always fit. It also provides reassurance that the subject is relevant and improves understanding of places and spaces. NUS students also placed considerable emphasis on fieldwork's development of observation skills and critical thinking. Those who had engaged in physical geography fieldwork mentioned use of equipment and techniques and project work developed confidence. In terms of transferable skills, many comment on confidence building resulting from having to engage with outside agencies, but seldom mention development of teamwork skills, although reasons for this were cited as limited fieldwork experience. No strong perceptions on the role of fieldwork for cohort identity were perceived in NUS.

New Zealand: Massey University

Summary: first-year students, observation-based, non-residential, method—questionnaire

Students were questioned at the end of a local day's fieldtrip run towards the end of a first year paper on introductory physical geography. The emphasis was on revision of material studied in class, providing local case studies of features and processes, as well as demonstration of a few techniques in the field. There was no specific technical experience and the teaching was to the group of 45 as a whole. This was the first university fieldwork experience for most.

Fieldwork was typically perceived to enhance the learning experience, summed up in one comment: "*I believe fieldtrips are far more important than lectures for metacognition, i.e. knowing and thinking about what you have learnt....*" The fieldwork was perceived to be more interesting, improved concentration and made the topics more memorable than class-based activity. Understanding of the subject was enhanced by seeing real-life examples, which reinforced the theory covered in the lecture programme: "*the fieldtrip enhanced my understanding of what I know*", "*made stuff real*". Landscape interpretation, through means of the geomorphological sketch, was considered to be the key geographical skill developed. No specific transferable skills were identified as having been developed by this fieldtrip. Students welcomed the opportunity the trip provided to get to know one another as well as their lecturer.

Section C: New Spaces of Learning

The third section of this volume highlights pioneering practices that are reshaping how, when, and where geography learning occurs in higher education. In chapter 7, Higgitt *et al.* contend that, despite the apparent seductiveness of international collaborative activities, discipline-specific evaluations of pedagogical benefit and learner outcomes require more attention than they usually receive. Some of the international collaborative projects they refer to are based on e-learning, the topic of chapter 8 by Lynch *et al.,* in which the authors explore the breadth of e-learning approaches, such as virtual communities of learners, mobile learning, and podcasting. They also argue that geographical teaching needs to be versatile to reflect the evolution of learning contexts. Increasing diversity in higher education is one of those evolving contexts, a topic considered in chapter 9 by McEwen *et al.* in the realm of taught master's courses. They discuss the meanings of "postgraduateness" and "diversity" as departments find themselves with greater numbers of postgraduates from non-traditional and international backgrounds. The final chapter in this section by Wellens *et al.* (chapter 10) argues that geographers have "a duty to teach both about and for the kinds of changes that can help to create a world which is more equal and more sustainable". Teaching for social transformation, the authors assert, can be achieved via the active learning practices of the types illustrated throughout this book.

Developing and Enhancing International Collaborative Learning

DAVID HIGGITT*, KARL DONERT**, MICK HEALEY†, PHIL KLEIN‡, MICHAEL SOLEM^ & SUSAN VAJOCZKI§

*Department of Geography, National University of Singapore, Singapore, **Deanery of Education, Liverpool Hope University, UK, †Department of Natural and Social Sciences, University of Gloucestershire, UK, ‡Department of Geography, University of Northern Colorado, USA, ^Association of American Geographers, Washington, DC, USA, §School of Geography and Earth Sciences, McMaster University, Canada

ABSTRACT *This paper is concerned with the role of international collaboration in the learning and teaching of geography in higher education. The dual aims are to provide a brief and selective review of the nature and range of international collaboration and to contextualize such observations within the internationalization project. It is argued that despite the growing interest and literature concerned with the internationalization of higher education, discipline-specific illustrations of pedagogy and practice require further attention. Several forms of collaboration in the geography arena are introduced and the factors influencing the establishment, maintenance and enhancement of international collaboration are discussed.*

Introduction: The Many Faces of Collaboration

There is no doubt that 'collaboration' has become a buzzword among senior administrators in higher education institutions throughout the world. Operating within international networks, developing strategic alliances and memoranda of understanding with other institutions is crucial to projecting an image of a well-connected university. As advances in information technology open up possibilities for enhanced communication with students within and beyond the campus, the opportunities for innovative and pedagogically informed collaboration increase, but so too do the risks.

This discussion paper has two principal aims. First, it seeks to explore the nature and range of international collaboration in geography in higher education. Though it is not possible to attempt a comprehensive review, examples of collaborative activities provide some indication of the how the discipline is delivering innovation to learning and teaching. Second, the paper attempts a critical gaze at collaboration within the context of the internationalization project.[1] Despite a burgeoning literature on the internationalization of higher education, there are many aspects of pedagogy and practice that deserve further attention and questioning. Ninnes & Hellstén (2005, p. 4) call for critique to "address the ambiguities, tensions, unevenness and contradictions in internationalization". A semantic contradiction that is immediately apparent is the double-edged meaning of the term 'collaboration'. In its positive sense, collaboration refers to cooperation with other people in a creative venture, but it also has a more sinister meaning that refers to acting traitorously with an enemy. While all manner of collaborative agreements between higher education institutions are presumably founded on the positive meaning of the term, there is an inherent conflict between pursuing goals of academic leadership and entertaining collaboration (Keohane, 2006). Competition and prestige may therefore strongly influence the nature of collaboration and access to networks. It is pertinent to ask whether the multiple agendas addressed in developing collaborative arrangements in higher education pay enough attention to enhancing the experience of the learner.

In examining the many faces of collaboration, the discussion paper raises a number of questions about the nature and usefulness of collaboration. What do we understand by the term collaboration and how is this exemplified in the context of geography in higher education? Does geography make a difference: is its subject matter particularly suited to collaboration and does the location of collaborators influence its likely success? How do the content and process of any particular collaboration interact in terms of the outcomes experienced by learners? How can collaborative ventures be initiated, championed and enhanced? Who are the stakeholders involved in collaborative activity and how do they benefit? And how do we know they benefit? To what extent is collaboration driven by pedagogic considerations?

Given that collaborative ventures are an increasing feature of the higher education landscape, what can geographers bring to the table? Does collaboration offer a key skill/competence that is central to professional development? If so, how should collaboration be incorporated into the curriculum? Should students be taught, by participation or observation, specifically how to collaborate or are collaborative alliances simply another means of enhancing student learning? In turn these questions raise issues about how the skills necessary for collaboration can be imparted and about the necessary arrangements for the assessment, evaluation and auditing of collaboration. Fundamentally identifying and measuring the benefits to the learner remains a key pedagogic and research challenge.

At the outset it is necessary to make an operational definition of the types of collaboration considered in the paper. There are, of course, multiple ways in which students and academics experience collaboration and exchange of ideas. This paper focuses on interaction with international partners at both the institutional/departmental and at the module-specific (i.e. course) scale which is centred on collaborative learning. Thus, transnational enrolment (and markets) is not a concern. Student exchanges placing individuals into a classroom setting in another country are not dealt with here because the collaboration on such exchanges is often quite peripheral. However, it is noted that many institutional exchange agreements have been formulated on alliances that offer a far broader scope for collaborative learning. Transnational projects, such as those promoted by the EU under SOCRATES, offer potential for network development that goes beyond student placements.[2] Similarly, we will not focus on local consortia arrangements that are designed to provide economies of scale because the focus of the paper is on international collaboration. National networks such as higher education groups in national geography societies or subject centres are excluded for the same reason. Nevertheless, the experience of institutions dealing with overseas students, the operation of student exchanges, development of consortia and national networks of collaboration provide a rich experience (and literature) that can inform attempts to establish and deliver international networks of collaborative learning (Reeve et al., 2000). International initiatives that hinge more centrally on collaborative learning include the establishment of networks with a focus on teaching and learning where faculty are encouraged to share ideas and best practice; programmes that develop modules jointly that are shared between multiple university partners; module logistics that enable students from more than one country to communicate with each other in pursuit for at least part of the module requirements; national organizations established to disseminate best practice (centres of excellence); joint degree programmes; and strategic alliances that seek to link a set of universities through teaching and learning initiatives.

Some examples of such forms of international collaboration are developed in the next section, followed by an identification of key issues and concerns. These are grouped around the topics of establishing, managing and sustaining collaborations.

Forms and Context of International Collaboration

Internationalization in universities has a long history. As Altbach (1998) notes, medieval universities were truly international institutions, drawing students and faculty from a wide range of countries. While increased nationalism in the nineteenth century generated a stronger national outlook, there has always been a significant migration of students and scholarly talent, not confined to the contemporary period. However, the nature of collaboration between universities has traditionally been focused around research initiatives. Collaboration is becoming more prevalent in undergraduate education and many institutions are devising (or having imposed) targets for creating international exposure for their students. Internationalization in geography in higher education has also attracted attention in the literature (Shepherd et al., 2000; Haigh, 2002).

As noted above, collaboration has many faces and serves a variety of purposes. The principal drivers for collaborative activity may be institutional networking, benchmarking (for comparison among groups of similar institutions) and the prestige of strategic alliances. The desired outcomes may be increased market share and income generation. For the faculty member seduced by the glamour of international travel and adventure, engagement in emergent collaborative networks may be a sufficient outcome in its own right. However, the purpose of the paper is to focus on the learner outcomes: the contribution of collaborative learning to cognitive, affective and inter-personal skills. It is our contention that, in establishing collaborative initiatives, the learner outcomes receive less attention than they merit. In the context of online distance education, for example, Paloff & Pratt (2001) warn that the focus on technology has often left the learner out of the equation. A central problem is the limited evidence available for evaluating the success or otherwise of collaborative learning ventures. There are a number of examples from geography that illustrate the advantages and shortcomings of attempts to collaborate between two or more departments online (e.g. Hurley et al., 1999; Warf et al., 1999; Brooks & Kent, 2001; Reed & Mitchell, 2001; Mendler et al., 2002; Chang, 2004), which provide practical guidance for others embarking on similar programmes. Yet, aspects of community building and assessing the effectiveness of the collaborative programme have not been explored as fully.

The notion that outcomes are mediated by local contexts can be represented figuratively as a lens through which the forms of collaborative activity are projected. The distortion of project aims by local contexts requires some adjustment to render the outcomes in sharp focus. Many of the points raised in the discussion are generic across higher education, but our main focus is to examine the implications of collaboration for geography in higher education. Fortunately, there are many examples of geographers engaging in international collaboration. A few selected examples are provided here before considering some of the critical issues that arise.

Networks of Practitioners

The *International Network for Learning and Teaching Geography in Higher Education* (*INLT*) was established in March 1999 with the goal of improving the quality and status of learning and teaching of geography in higher education internationally (Hay et al., 2000).[3] Its three purposes (Healey, 2006) are:

- to promote innovative, creative and collaborative research as well as critical reflection on learning and teaching of geography;
- to facilitate the exchange of materials, ideas and experiences about learning and teaching of geography and to stimulate international dialogue;
- to create an inclusive international community in higher education aimed at raising the profile and status of learning and teaching of geography.

Two previous sets of articles based on collaboration between members of INLT have been published (Healey et al., 2000; Healey, 2006).

HERODOT is a Thematic Network for geography teachers and lecturers in higher education.[4] It reports on the impacts of curriculum change and developments on geography and geographical education at national level, across Europe and beyond. It aims (Donert, 2005) to:

- promote excellence in the teaching of geography and the training of geography teachers through the development and implementation of collaborative inter-university activities;
- perform a coordinating role, disseminating information and good practice, facilitating dialogue between HE institutions in Europe and stimulating the exchange of students and teachers;
- raise awareness of the need for pedagogical considerations in the development of curricula, and in the use of specific educational products including the use of information and communications technology (ICT) and ODL in geography;
- develop a common framework for the organization of higher education professional development programmes leading to courses at Masters and PhD level as initiated by the Sorbonne and Bologna declarations.

With more than 200 participant institutions around the world, the formulation of many international collaborative projects in geography learning and teaching has resulted from this networking.

Programmes to Develop Joint Modules

The *Center for Global Geography Education* (CGGE) offers instructional materials for undergraduates, which explore contemporary geographic issues using inquiry, data-based and interactive modes (Solem *et al.*, 2003).[5] These e-learning materials aim to promote international teaching collaborations using discussion-board technology. Three prototype modules, on Nationalism, Population, and Global Economy, were written by international teams of geographers in 2003–2004 and tested in nine international trials in 2004–2005. The overall goals of the CGGE project are to:

- improve knowledge of geographic concepts and skills;
- develop understanding of both global and local aspects of contemporary issues;
- engage students in international collaborations to discuss problem-based exercises and consider international perspectives on each issue.

The CGGE experience has been instructive in respect of the issues of establishing, managing and sustaining international instructional collaborations and specific examples are provided in the sections that follow. During its pilot phase (2003–2005) the CGGE staff collected data from instructors and students participating in classroom trials of the online modules to monitor implementation and identify 'roadbumps' in the collaboration process. This paper summarizes some of these issues below and describes how the CGGE staff plans to remedy those issues as the programme expands into a second phase (2007–2010).

Module Logistics to Promote Collaboration

Most of the examples of collaborative learning in the geographic literature refer to web-based modules where staff from two or more countries arrange for students to interact online. Other areas for collaboration include fieldtrips or summer school programmes where staff and students from visiting and host institutions can be brought together. A recent example is COZIP, a coast-focused intensive programme funded by the EU SOCRATES Programme (Fletcher, 2007). Staff from partner universities participate in the teaching of the programme and all students work in international groups. Teachers are required to work collaboratively with international colleagues to devise a course of at least 10 days' duration for approximately 40 students. A central part of COZIP has been an active learning ethos, with students expected to 'learn through doing' in a format that is largely field-based. One teacher (or a small team) organizes either a day or half-day of activities for the entire group. This individual is responsible for that session and assisted by others according to need and availability.

National Initiatives for Dissemination of Best Practice

The *Centre for Active Learning (CeAL) in Geography, Environment and Related Disciplines* is based at the University of Gloucestershire, UK and is one of 74 Centres of Excellence in Teaching and Learning (CETLs) funded by the Higher Education Funding

Council for England (HEFCE).[6] CeAL aims to be an international centre of excellence reviewing, developing, promoting and embedding active learning in geography, environment and related disciplines. The approach enables students to construct theoretical understanding through reflection on inquiry in the field, studio, laboratory and classroom, using real sites, community-related and employer-linked activities. CeAL will be developed around communities of active learners where students and staff inquire together. A key innovative feature is joint student projects with related schools in the university, and initially 13 HEIs in England and 10 universities overseas. CeAL is funding an extensive programme of development and research into active learning. Each of the five postgraduate assistants is registered for a part-time pedagogic research degree. The University of Gloucestershire is committed to pursuing active learning across all undergraduate/postgraduate curricula, with CeAL as the laboratory for innovation, experimentation and evaluation.

Inter-institutional Joint Degree Programmes

The concept of a joint degree scheme between two institutions is becoming increasingly popular and many institutions are seeing competitive advantage in terms of student recruitment through the marketing of alliances with overseas universities. While the number of students enrolled in joint degrees may be small the institution gains reputation by demonstrating the potential opportunities to study in two countries and be awarded a degree recognized by both institutions. In some ways this may be regarded as the logical extension of student exchange programmes, where the student undertakes a proportion of the degree based on the campus of each partner and rules for awarding credit from both partners are formally established. Whether the joint degree is a real example of collaboration depends on the nature of the partnership. Students sit modules at each partner institution and receive credit which contributes to the final degree but individual modules at each campus do not necessarily involve engagement from each partner. The collaboration is far more likely to be at the administrative level in terms of fine-tuning the degree requirements from both partners into an acceptable compromise and establishing a framework that can be used by many subject disciplines. A question therefore follows as to whether it is possible, or desirable, to take joint degree schemes one stage further and open up collaborative opportunities for the broader learning communities, such as establishing project-based modules that involve supervision from both partners.

Another circumstance that leads to joint programmes being established is where a single institution is unable to provide sufficient expertise to run a full programme. Collaboration by necessity can be mutually beneficial in delivering a complete syllabus but will require careful articulation of the learning outcomes and expectations. Under these schemes, which are common in the USA, students may move between campuses or more likely take modules through distance learning.

Strategic Alliances

Strategic alliances are partnerships established by groups of universities with the aim of promoting some common strength or quality (Teather, 2004; Johnstone *et al.*, 2006). Alliances have long been established at national levels and have served to provide a lobbying basis. More recently international alliances have emerged. Examples include

Universitas 21, Association of Pacific Rim Universities (APRU), Worldwide University Network (WUN) and the International Alliance of Research Universities (IARU).[7] Such alliances are fundamentally driven by research aspirations but frequently have a substantial teaching and learning component. For example the first significant contribution from IARU was a symposium on graduate training in research universities. On the face of it, alliances with high kudos offer great potential for collaborative explorations but there are also considerable challenges. Alliances tend to seek multidisciplinary and multi-partner activities, whereas meaningful collaboration in teaching and learning is likely to be disciplinary focused and based on a reasonably well-established relationship between the members of faculty involved. In other words, there needs to be a strong element of self-interest and enthusiasm among the participants. A second concern about these high-profile alliances is their non-inclusiveness. Notwithstanding these concerns there is evidence that strategic alliances can deliver innovative collaboration opportunities for staff and students. Universitas 21, for example, organizes annual undergraduate conferences. Resources in economic geography have been developed by WUN (Le Heron & Lewis, 2007).

Establishing Collaboration

The examples outlined indicate that international collaboration can come in many shapes and sizes and varying degrees of formality. Incentives for establishing collaboration are likely to fall on a spectrum from a personal interest for initiating activity to co-option through an institutional programme. Despite the best efforts of practitioner networks to offer an inclusive environment, access to and power structures within partnerships are problematic. Many commentators on internationalization in higher education have problematized the process as the unrelenting spread of Western practices, culture and values framed in terms of globalization (e.g. Edwards & Usher, 2000; Mason, 2000). Who gets to participate in international collaboration and on what terms is a key issue. Most of the examples illustrated in this paper have indicated predominantly the connectivity of departments and institutions in the Anglo-American realm, although EU-funded initiatives have supported imaginative programmes across member and accession states. Mechanisms for establishing links with departments in less developed countries are more problematic, not least in terms of financing activity. There are numerous examples of collaborative activity associated with field trips (by Western universities) to the Global South, in some cases linked to development projects. For example, geography and environmental students at the University of Gloucestershire work with staff and students at Kaliro College in Uganda to train them in the use of IT as part of a field course. This raises the question of whether an overt goal of international collaboration should be to promote (sustainable) development in the less-developed world and how this can be done without avoiding criticism of paternalism. A similar concern applies to the INLT itself. Though the network is a pioneer virtual organization that has facilitated international cooperation, Hay (2008) cautions on the need to ensure that emergent networks are symmetrical and empowering and do not marginalize geography educators who operate away from a core membership in Anglo-America and Australasia.

Counterpoised with drivers of inclusiveness are the pressures of global competition to be favourably connected with prestigious institutions. Some of the strategic alliances that have been described in the previous section indicate the tendency for elite groups to emerge. Within institutions that are highly graded in global league tables, there may be considerable discouragement to pursue links with potential partners that are not regarded as equivalent rank. In effect hierarchies of partnerships emerge with institutional ties with the leading universities and faculty, departmental or ad hoc MOUs (Memoranda of Understanding) for lesser bodies. Conversely, those universities regarded favourably in global benchmarking exercises may attract many suitors. A comparative study of Australian National University and Universitas Indonesia (Marginson & Sawir, 2006) illustrates how building global capacity and facilitating international mobility and collaboration is increasingly important to both of these leading national institutions but the Australian university is more strongly placed in the global environment to react to opportunities. An analysis of the structure of links in institutional websites in Asian and European universities (Park & Thelwall, 2006) also illustrates asymmetrical relationships. Asian universities are more connected to European universities than they are to each other.

Besides the inherent unevenness of opportunity for international collaboration, there are many logistical concerns that confront the establishment of initiatives. Funding is an obvious constraint but so too is scheduling. Most online collaboration tends to be asynchronous because of the time differences between locations, but the academic calendar is a greater problem that poses difficulties for scheduling activities within modules that require collaboration.

Finally, the success of collaborative adventures is premised on the faculty involved being competent to facilitate student learning. Although there is a growing body of pedagogic research on the processes of collaboration to provide guidance there may be a need for specific training or mentoring, which in turn raises questions about pathways of professional advancement that might arise from investing time and effort in developing initiatives. For example, CGGE project staff have designed and piloted a two-day workshop to enable participants from different countries to become familiar with module contents and to devise strategies to adapt content suitable for particular international collaboration pairings (such as relevant case studies). Whether students need to be trained to learn from collaboration or 'learn by doing' is another consideration. The earlier example of COZIP implicitly assumes that learning occurs through doing, but whether such claims can be tested is a different matter. Collecting feedback and evaluation data is discussed further below.

Managing Collaboration

Key issues for the management of established collaborations concern dealing with intercultural differences, varied expectations and unevenness of engagement among students; technological constraints on communication; agreements on learning outcomes and assessment procedures; and evaluating the performance of the initiative.

Cultural differences between students of different nationalities have often been identified as a potential constraint to collaboration that needs to be handled with sensitivity, although some of the internationalization literature is at pains to point out that stereotypes of learning behaviour have often been overstated (e.g. Doherty & Singh, 2005). Nevertheless school education systems in some countries are more strongly didactic than others, such that a willingness to engage in open discussion may be more challenging for some students than others. Chang (2004) notes that Singaporean students are characterized by a 'kiasu' mentality: an anxiety about saying the wrong thing and 'losing face'. In his description of a collaborative project between students in Singapore and Hawaii, the contrast between the anxious and matter-of-fact attitudes of the former and the laid-back and relaxed attitudes of the latter raised some tensions. This scenario illustrates the significance of perceived norms in terms of behaviour. Rimal & Real (2003) distinguish between 'descriptive norms' (individuals' perceptions concerning the prevalence of a type of behaviour) and 'injunctive norms' (pressures individuals experience to conform). Thus, students engaged in group work negotiate standards based on their perceptions of expectations. Extending the group work across international borders may introduce different prevailing norms and require renegotiation of expectations. As noted above, the facilitators of collaborative learning may regard this experience of disjuncture as a useful learning experience in its own right or they may consider it necessary to give explicit training as preparation. Xu & Warschauer (2004) describe an educational reform initiative in a Chinese university that is designed specifically to prepare (English major) students for international communication and collaboration.

There is an underlying assumption that collaboration brings educational benefits through its emphasis on active learning, but examining whether the intended outcomes of collaboration have been met can be a methodological challenge. Similarly, identifying which students benefit and improving the experience of those that do not appear to take much from the experience should be considered. An example of a thorough evaluation of a collaborative activity is provided by the CGGE trials (Klein & Solem, 2006) which employed analytic induction methods to interpret qualitative responses to a pre-test/post-test item. Before using a module, students were asked if they thought people in different countries would have different perspectives on the issue they were about to study, and whether they expected international collaboration to add a useful dimension to investigating that issue. Afterwards, students were asked to identify the advantages and disadvantages of discussing that issue with an international team. On the pre-test, over 90% of respondents ($n = 285$, from seven countries) were optimistic and intrigued. They believed it would be interesting and were 'curious' as to what college students in other countries would say about these issues. Post-test responses were more varied but the clear consensus from the trial students was that collaboration's advantages outweighed its disadvantages. While few found no fault with the project, fewer still had such a distasteful experience that they saw no advantages. Where CGGE was most successful, students called it a 'great experience' and valued the opportunity to see the perspectives of people from different cultures. The problems raised by students related primarily to technical difficulties, such as scheduling differences or the time lags perceived between responses. Several mentioned challenges in getting to know their international teammates well enough to truly communicate. Student exchanges of opinions were limited by the discussion-board format and sometimes by their reticence to share thoughts on controversial issues. Differences in language, cultural referents and values, and styles of non-verbal communication could not always be bridged in a short time frame.

Data collected from instructors during the pilot phase of the CGGE project (2003–2006) identify four issues that impacted on the quality of the collaboration experience which map onto the general observations outlined above (Klein & Solem, in press). First, the geography of collaboration is important with students from similar social and economic backgrounds (e.g. UK and US students) gaining few value-added global perspectives compared with collaboration mediated between students of diverse backgrounds. Second, variability in the foundation (previous experience of geography education) appeared to have some impacts on success. Third, time management is in an issue as instructors struggle to find enough time for students to have extended and in-depth discussion with their overseas collaborators while operating within the constraints of institutional timetables. Fourth, though the online technology performed well, electronic exchanges do not capture cultural-specific and emotional contexts of communication. Related to this point, instructors report some resistance from students using online tools (such as the translation tool) and difficulties that arise when students attempt to communicate their ideas clearly in a second language.

Students' views relate to their experience with the materials, interactions with peers in other countries, own dispositions and interest in content and work ethics. Attempts to evaluate the additional benefit of collaboration by running control experiments on participating and non-participating groups led to resentment and raises ethical objections as to whether part of a cohort can be denied an opportunity in order to undertake an experiment. The evaluations of CGGE show that student engagement varied widely: some interactions were friendly and frequent, others terse and business-like. Fatigue became evident as the module lessons wore on and, unsurprisingly, some students worked harder than others. The comprehensive evaluation procedures employed here intuitively demonstrate the vitality and benefit of collaboration but the methodological challenges of measuring the 'value-added' are considerable. Furthermore, as Nairn (2005) has argued, claims for effectiveness based on students' declarations of satisfaction are not the same as testing how learning has been challenged and the degree to which objectives have been met. Where the ongoing financial support of collaboration is dependent on demonstrating the additional educational benefits this methodological dilemma requires serious attention.

Developing and Enhancing Collaboration

The establishment of collaborations is likely to be expensive in terms of time and money, in most cases supported through institutional or external grants. Once the initial funding is expended there needs to be succession planning to ensure the sustainability of the initiative, whether this involves subsequent phases of funding or the ability to run the initiative at zero net cost. Given the likelihood that the initiative has been championed by an individual, succession planning is also necessary to manage change in personnel and/or institutions.

Commitment to ongoing support of collaborative initiatives is likely to be best sustained where there is a clear perception of value of the activity. In this regard thorough evaluation of the activity is important for both guiding the practitioners in adjusting the content and structure and for 'selling' the worthiness of the initiative. The CGGE evaluation described in the previous section was undertaken as a stipulation of the grant to produce quantitative as well as qualitative indicators of performance. Publishing summaries of the collaboration in appropriate pedagogic journals is another aspect of selling the idea. Evaluation can often be the Achilles heel of pedagogic research where the evidence for learning is often predicated on student perceptions articulated in feedback. Limited attention has been given to understanding how and why collaboration enhances student learning, beyond the general recognition that active learning is encouraged. Communication strategies between student participants play a key role in the success of collaboration and an investigation of how 'ideas' are formulated, negotiated and shared would be worthwhile. Evaluation of such student projects should also examine in what ways interactions between the nationalities of the collaborators and the module content they studied influence the success of the endeavour.

Discussion: International Collaboration and Geography

The examples identified in the paper indicate that geographers are widely involved in collaborative learning initiatives in many different contexts. The 'situatedness' of collaborations as manifestations of different 'place identities' can not only be appreciated by geographers designing collaborative curricula but can also be targeted as a learning outcome. The nature of the discipline and the variability of curricula within and between countries lends itself well to benefiting from increased international interaction among staff and students. However, the majority of the issues raised in the paper are generic to higher education and important insights can be drawn from the pedagogic literature of many disciplines. It is clear that internationalization of higher education will continue to accelerate and become more complex, offering opportunities, challenges and competition for curriculum development. Innovations in communication technologies will no doubt lead the way, while institutions seek to exploit flows and exchanges to strengthen networks, increase market share and build global capacity to facilitate cross-border flows of staff, students and research projects. In pursuing these targets the benefits to the learner are often assumed and taken for granted and this paper has sought to illustrate how the pedagogic aspects of collaboration might be examined. For the faculty member plugged into networks, backed by institutional support and keen to collect frequent-flyer points, internationalization of higher education offers unprecedented and exhilarating opportunities to travel and converse. But access to collaborative opportunities is uneven both between and within universities. Issues of equity and appropriate mentoring for participants should remain key concerns.

Cultural issues arise in working practices and assessment (Keane, 2005). Difficulties of working in groups occur in some cases simply because students in one university or the other (or some minority of students) are unaccustomed to working in teams or dislike doing so (from previous distasteful experiences). Part of the issue of assessment of collaborations is recognizing varying student dispositions toward such work, often the by-product of perceived inequities in how they are graded or marked. Other dispositions are cultural in nature, requiring that we geographers recognize—and somehow account for—real cultural differences among students who are asked to work collaboratively, in terms of, for example, what kinds of communication are considered appropriate and courteous. Collaboration is also about global intercultural understanding (i.e. understanding diversity) and this is an area where a more empathetic geographical approach needs to be developed. Ideas of tolerance through understanding come to the fore with a strong spatial component. Geographers have been innovative in realizing some networking opportunities at an early stage. The subject area is often ideal for collaborations (i.e. swapping information about places) and should be the vehicle for citizenship and sustainability education.

Notes

[1] The term 'internationalization project' is shorthand to refer to the increasing importance and various trajectories of international cooperation in the higher education sector (Higgitt & Haigh, 2006). Internationalization has diverse forms that range from collaborative learning and teaching, through recruitment and marketing to infusing the curriculum with global perspectives (for further discussion see Ray & Solem, in press). Given that there are financial as well as educational objectives at stake, the phenomenon of internationalization can be critiqued as part of a neoliberal globalization agenda (e.g. Currie *et al.*, 2003).

[2] SOCRATES is the EU programme that supports the mobility of students and teachers. The programme comprises five sub-programmes: COMENIUS (schools), ERASMUS (higher education), GRUND-TVIG (adult learning), LINGUA (language instruction and learning) and MINERVA (open and distance learning, educational ICT). ERASMUS, which celebrated 20 years of activity in 2007, seeks to enhance the quality and reinforce the European dimension of higher education by encouraging transnational cooperation between universities, boosting European mobility and improving the transparency and full academic recognition of studies and qualifications throughout the Union.

[3] INLT has convened sessions and workshops in association with RGS-IBG, AAG and IGC conferences. Further information is available at: http://www.geog.canterbury.ac.nz/inlt/

[4] In 2004–2005 HERODOT organized a European survey of subject specific and generic competences in Geography. Further information may be found at: http://www.herodot.net/

[5] Further information about CGGE is available at: http://www.aag.org/Education/center/

[6] The funding from HEFCE amounts to £2.35 million capital and £2.5 million recurrent expenditure over the five-year period 2005–2010. More information about the centre is available at: http://www.glos.ac.uk/ceal

[7] Information about these strategic alliances is available at: Universitats21 (http://www.universitas21.com); Worldwide University Network (http://www.wun.ac.uk); Association of Pacific Rim Universities (http://www.apru.org); International Association of Research Universities (http://www.iaruni.org).

References

Altbach, P. G. (1998) *Comparative Education: Knowledge, the University and Development* (Westport, CT: Ablex Publishing).

Brooks, C. & Kent, A. (2001) The YoungNet Project: eLearning and the internet, in: L. Houtsonen & M. Tammilehto (Eds) *Innovative Practices in Geographical Education*. Proceedings of Helsinki Symposium. International Geographical Education, August 6–10, pp. 125–128.

Chang, T. C. (2004) Transborder tourism borderless classroom: reflections on a Hawaii–Singapore experience, *Journal of Geography in Higher Education*, 28(2), pp. 179–195.

Currie, J., de Angeles, R., de Boer, H., Huisman, J. & Lacotte, C. (2003) *Globalizing Practices and University Responses: European and Anglo American Differences* (Westport, CT: Praeger).

Doherty, C. & Singh, P. (2005) How the West is done: simulating western pedagogy in a curriculum for Asian international students, in: P. Ninnes & M. Hellstén (Eds) *Internationalizing Higher Education: Critical Explorations of Pedagogy and Policy*, pp. 53–73 (Hong Kong: Comparative Education Research Centre, University of Hong Kong and Springer).

Donert, K. (Ed.) (2005) *Aspects of Geography in European Higher Education: Geographical Information Systems* (Liverpool: HERODOT Network, Liverpool Hope University).

Donert, K. & Charzynski, P. (Eds) (2005) *Changing Horizons in Geography Education* (Torun: HERODOT Network).

Edwards, R. & Usher, R. (2000) *Globalisation and Pedagogy: Space, Place and Identity* (London: Routledge).

Fletcher, S. (2007) *The Coastal Zone Intensive Programme (COZIP): an international programme of coastal study for students from UK, Turkey, Ireland and Malta* (Cheltenham: Centre for Active Learning, University of Gloucestershire).

Haigh, M. (2002) Internationalization of the curriculum: designing inclusive education for a small world, *Journal of Geography in Higher Education*, 26(1), pp. 49–66.

Hay, I. (2008) Postcolonial practices for a global virtual group: the case of the International Network for Learning and Teaching geography in higher education (INLT), *Journal of Geography in Higher Education*, 32(1), pp. 15–32.

Hay, I., Foote, K. & Healey, M. (2000) From Cheltenham to Honolulu: the purposes and projects of the International Network for Learning and Teaching (INLT) in geography in higher education, *Journal of Geography in Higher Education*, 24(2), pp. 221–227.

Healey, M., Foote, K. & Hay, I. (Eds) (2000) International perspectives on learning and teaching geography in higher education, *Journal of Geography in Higher Education*, 24(2), pp. 217–298.

Healey, M. (Ed.) (2006) International perspectives on selected issues in the learning and teaching of geography in higher education, *Journal of Geography in Higher Education*, 30(1), pp. 63–160.

Healey, M. (2006) From Hawaii to Glasgow: the International Network for Learning and Teaching Geography in Higher Education (INLT) five years on, *Journal of Geography in Higher Education*, 30(1), pp. 65–75.

Higgitt, D. & Haigh, M. (2006) Editorial: International Advice, *Journal of Geography in Higher Education*, 30(1), pp. 1–5.
Hurley, J. M., Proctor, J. D. & Ford, R. E. (1999) Collaborative inquiry at a distance: using the Internet in geography education, *Journal of Geography*, 98(3), pp. 128–140.
Johnstone, S. M., & Conger, S. B. with Bernath, U., Husson, W. J., Maurandi, A. L. & Perez de Madrigal, M. E. (2006) Strategic alliances: collaboration for sustainability, in: A. Hope & P. Guiton (Eds) *Strategies for Sustainable Open and Distance Learning*, pp. 111–130 (Abingdon: Routledge).
Keane, M. (2005) Geography forum: intercultural learning online, in: K. Donert & P. Charzynski (Eds) *Changing Horizons in Geography Education*, pp. 236–240 (Torun: HERODOT Network).
Keohane, N. O. (2006) *Higher Ground: Ethics and Leadership in the Modern University* (Durham, NC: Duke University Press).
Klein, P. & Solem, M. (2006) Strategies for teaching geography through international collaborations, in: K. Purnell, J. Lidstone & S. Hodgson (Eds) *Changes in Geographical Education: Past, Present and Future*, pp. 259–263 (Brisbane: IGU Commission on Geographical Education).
Klein, P. & Solem, M. (in press) Evaluating the impact of international collaboration on geography learning, *Journal of Geography in Higher Education*.
Le Heron, R. & Lewis, N. (2007) Globalizing economic geographies in the context of globalizing higher education, *Journal of Geography in Higher Education*, 31(1), pp. 5–12.
Marginson, S. & Sawir, E. (2006) University leaders' strategies in the global environment: comparative study of Universitas Indonesia and the Australian National University, *Higher Education*, 52(2), pp. 343–373.
Mason, R. (2000) *Globalising Education* (London: Routledge).
Mendler, J., Simon, D. & Broome, P. (2002) Virtual development and virtual geographies: using the Internet to teach interactive distance courses in the global South, *Journal of Geography in Higher Education*, 26(3), pp. 313–325.
Nairn, K. (2005) The problem of utilizing 'direct experience' in geography education, *Journal of Geography in Higher Education*, 29(2), pp. 293–309.
Ninnes, P. & Hellstén, M. (2005) Introduction: Critical engagements with the internationalization of higher education, in: P. Ninnes & M. Hellstén (Eds) *Internationalizing Higher Education: Critical Explorations of Pedagogy and Policy*, pp. 1–8 (Hong Kong: Comparative Education Research Centre, University of Hong Kong and Springer).
Palloff, R. M. & Pratt, K. (2001) *The Virtual Student: A Profile and Guide to Working with Online Learners* (San Francisco: Jossey-Bass).
Park, H. W. & Thelwall, M. (2006) Web-science communication in the age of globalization, *New Media & Society*, 8(4), pp. 629–650.
Ray, W. & Solem, M. (in press) Gauging disciplinary support for internationalization: a survey of geographers in the United States, *Journal of Geography in Higher Education*.
Reed, M. & Mitchell, B. (2001) Using information technologies for collaborative learning in geography: a case study from Canada, *Journal of Geography in Higher Education*, 25(3), pp. 321–339.
Reeve, D., Hardwick, S., Kemp, K. & Ploszajska, T. (2000) Delivering geography courses internationally, *Journal of Geography in Higher Education*, 24(2), pp. 228–237.
Rimal, R. N. & Real, K. (2003) Understanding the influence of perceived norms on behaviours, *Communication Theory*, 13(2), pp. 184–203.
Shepherd, I., Monk, J. & Fortuijn, J. (2000) Internationalization of geography in higher education: towards a conceptual framework, *Journal of Geography in Higher Education*, 24(2), pp. 285–298.
Solem, M. N., Bell, S., Fournier, E., Gillespie, C., Lewitsky, M. & Lockton, H. (2003) Using the Internet to support international collaborations for global geography education, *Journal of Geography in Higher Education*, 27(3), pp. 239–253.
Teather, D. (Ed.) (2004) *Consortia: International Networking Alliances of Universities* (Melbourne: Melbourne University Press).
Warf, B., Vincent, P. & Purcell, D. (1999) International collaborative learning on the World Wide Web, *Journal of Geography*, 98(3), pp. 141–148.
Xu, F. & Warschauer, M. (2004) Technology and curricular reform in China: a case study, *TESOL Quarterly*, 38(2), pp. 301–323.

E-learning for Geography's Teaching and Learning Spaces

KENNETH LYNCH*, BOB BEDNARZ**, JAMES BOXALL†,
LEX CHALMERS‡, DEREK FRANCE^ & JULIE KESBY§

*Department of Natural and Social Sciences, University of Gloucestershire, UK, **Department of Geography, Texas A&M University, USA, †GIS Centre, Dalhousie University, Canada, ‡Department of Geography, Tourism and Environmental Planning, University of Waikato, NZ, ^Department of Geography and Development Studies, University of Chester, UK, §School of Physical, Environmental and Mathematical Sciences, University of New South Wales-ADFA, Australia

ABSTRACT *The authors embed their advocacy of educational technology in a consideration of contemporary pedagogy in geography. They provide examples of e-learning from a wide range of teaching and learning contexts. They promote the idea that considering best practice with reference to educational technology will increase the versatility of teaching geography in higher education. On the basis of reviewing the pedagogic options associated with e-learning using a variety of technologies, and their promotion of versatility in the use of e-learning approaches, they find and illustrate the new spaces that have become available to teachers and learners of geography.*

Introduction

The use of information and communications technology (ICT) in higher education has grown markedly. In many universities online course materials are now used to support traditional campus-based learning; in some cases courses are delivered entirely online, while others provide complementary support in the form of learning materials, learning activities or course documentation. This kind of learning is often described as 'e-learning', but 'e-learning' is used to describe a wide range of approaches to ICT-supported learning. A recent report (OECD, 2005) highlighted four main types of e-learning:

- web supplemented—where classroom-based courses are supported with online materials;
- web-dependent—where courses have required online activities, such as collaborative work, assessment or projects;

- mixed-mode—where online learning replaces significant proportions of classroom learning, but campus attendance is still required (also known as 'blended learning');
- fully online—attendance at campus is not necessary; students follow an online curriculum.

Although e-learning has the potential to improve geography learning significantly in higher education, we approach this topic critically. We are aware that many technological innovations have been introduced into teaching and learning in higher education with great fanfare, promise, and claims of efficacy. Tyack & Cuban (1995, p. 122) remind us that "Many technical inventions have in fact made their way into classrooms and are now so familiar that few people even notice them". They catalogue blackboards, cheap paper, books for individual students, globes and maps, ballpoints, calculators, film, and television. Tyack & Cuban (1995, p. 121) also point out that some of the people who made the greatest claims for the introduction of new technology "[n]ot surprisingly ... were business people who wanted to market their wares to the schools".

Some researchers argue that the medium used to deliver content is never the decisive factor. They believe that the strategies and techniques employed by the teacher and learner are the key, not the delivery technology. For example, Clark (1994, p. 26) claims that "all methods ... can be delivered by a variety of media.... It is the method which is the 'active ingredient.'" While this could be seen as a provocative view, we acknowledge that almost all of what students learn today was learned by their predecessors without the assistance of e-learning technologies. But, as e-learning develops and becomes embedded in the learning process, we think Kozma's development of Clark's view has more appeal. Kozma (1994, p. 11) says that "In a good design, media and methods are inexorably confounded.... One cannot simply replace one medium with another ... and hold everything else constant...." This argument raises the question of what improvement some technologies have provided. For example, PowerPoint, learning management systems and podcasting may not impact beneficially on the quality of learning if the underpinning philosophy of teaching and learning design fails to take full advantage of the opportunities these technologies offer. We would do well to remember the promises made on behalf of radio, television and video for education. Did these revolutionize learning? Did they revolutionize geographic education? Why will e-learning technologies be any different?

Whether one believes that it is appropriate or not, e-learning is now a mature area of interest and application in geographical education. While bibliographic searches on databases like the ISI Web of Knowledge (an online service providing subscription-based access to research journals) are problematic, the trends shown in Figure 1 support our point. As a baseline, the count of journal articles on the 'topic' *geography* in the Web of Knowledge has exceeded 300 consistently since 1993, reaching a maximum of 883. Articles on the topic *GIS* did not reach 300 until 1995 but now register more than 1000 a year. Figure 1 suggests *e-learning* matured as a field of interest around 2003, and the pattern is similar to more specific topics such as *communities of practice* and the combined *geography [and] internet* search. The search *urban [and] geography* is included as a proxy for a stable interest area.

We are also aware that e-learning does not come in one size that fits all geography courses and learning activities. In fact, one of our purposes is to encourage geography faculty to assess where any teaching–learning activity is placed in e-learning 'space', consider whether it could be re-located, and establish the most effective way to get there.

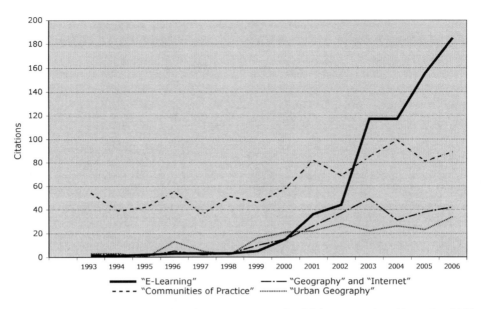

Figure 1. E-learning as a research topic. *Source.* ISI Web of Science searches, November 2005

We believe that pedagogy in geography has to be approached in this manner as there is a proliferation of technology in education at all levels. This is happening faster in some places than others, but the United Nations *One Laptop for Every Child Project* (Laptop.org, undated) is a model of producers, educators and others setting goals for the provision of educational technology, which may influence educational technology more generally. Our discussion explores questions like: Why is e-learning important? Is it an improvement on learning without the 'e'? And why is this significant for geography education?

To address these questions this paper will first provide a pedagogic rationale for the use of e-learning, and then document some representative e-learning technologies. We will then assess how reflexive practice in the teaching of geography can lead to versatile use of teaching technology and reflect on the benefits to (lifelong) e-learners. We reference our work as appropriate and list some websites that have informed our thinking in Table 1.

The Rationale for e-tools in Geography Teaching and Learning

Geography is well suited to the use of e-tools for learning. As geographers have adopted constructivist approaches to problem-based learning (e.g. Bradbeer & Livingstone, 1996; Halvorson & Westcoat, 2002) and cooperative or collaborative learning (e.g. Livingstone & Lynch, 2002), they have frequently demonstrated an appetite to adopt innovative approaches to learning and teaching and have been quick to recognize the value that technology can provide. Using information technology effectively allows students to grapple with real-world problems, access appropriate information quickly and easily, share their ideas with their fellow students (facilitating group work), and construct new knowledge and meaning for themselves in a relevant, interesting context. As Kozma (1994, p. 8) has argued, learning is "an interaction between cognitive processes and characteristics of the environment". In the constructivist learning environment, technology

Table 1. Useful websites

http://oci.open.ac.uk/ The OpenLearn site provides online free learning material taken from Open University courses. It offers good learner support, and tools for connecting learners with learners and learners with teachers. It also includes a wide range of learning media and technology comments (see also http://www.alllearn.org).

http://ocw.mit.edu/index.html This is an excellent free and open resource for educators, students and self-learners. Open Course Ware publishes MIT course materials, does not require registration, is not degree-granting and does not provide access to MIT faculty.

http://travelgeography.libsyn.com/ This is a blog site that offers travel and tourism insights, drawing upon research, theory and personal experiences from a geography and social science perspective.

http://veryspatial.com/ This is a location for the hosts and participants of 'A Very Spatial Podcast' to access sites and articles on geography. The site hosts columns, links, and downloads on relevant topics. It is a weekly source for information on geography and geospatial technologies.

http://www.alllearn.org After offering 110 online courses from Oxford, Stanford, and Yale to over 10 000 participants from 70 countries during the past five years, the AllLearn project, a consortium among Oxford, Stanford and Yale Universities to research online learning, has now closed.

http://www.createascape.org.uk/ This Futurelab website enables users to create mediascapes and to find all the resources to make them in one place. It was inspired by Futurelab research that demonstrated the enormous potential of mobile technology for learning.

http://www.dol.govt.nz/futureofwork/stocktake-summary.asp This site evaluates the impact of new technologies and ways of organizing work and suggests they will change the nature of economies and labour markets in a way similar to that of the Industrial Revolution in the nineteenth century.

http://www.exc-el.org.uk/content/index.php/main/teaching_and_learning/geography gives access to the GEOCAST site that has Geography Revision Podcasts. Podcasting is a term used to describe a group of technologies for distributing audio or video programs over the internet.

http://www.futurelab.org.uk/showcase/savannah/index.htm Futurelab supports applications like Savannah, a strategy-based game where a virtual space is mapped onto a real space. Children 'play' at being lions, navigating the augmented environments with a mobile handheld device.

http://www.itconversations.com/shows/detail978.html This is a blog site that offers a wide range of industry conversations about information technology applications. Some of the conversations relate to educational applications.

http://www.laptop.org One Laptop per Child (OLPC) is a non-profit organization (associated with MIT Media Lab) that is designing, manufacturing and distributing laptops that are sufficiently inexpensive to provide every child in the world access to knowledge and modern forms of education.

http://www.le.ac.uk/talent/elearning/why.html A University of Leicester site that provides a rationale for e-learning, and some descriptiond of Blackboard as a Virtual Learning Environment (VLE).

http://www.learninginhand.com/OurCity/index.html Our City Podcast is a podcast audio program for children and by children. Students from around the globe are invited to submit a recording all about the city they live in.

http://www.m-learning.org/ M-learning advocates the use of mobile technologies to enhance learning experiences. Mobile phones, PDAs, pocket PCs and the internet can be blended to engage and motivate learners, any time and anywhere.

can provide representations and model operations in a manner that learners cannot provide alone.

E-learning environments are particularly valuable for the display and representation of complex visual information (Hedberg, 2006). The University of Leicester (2005) e-learning website argues that e-learning provides "a very visual working environment" that "can hold the students' interest and increase motivation". E-tools which assist geographical visualization include animations to explore and explain difficult dynamic concepts or events along with cartographic and GIS technologies to assist in observing patterns and processes and virtual field trips. With reference to virtual field trips, Serafin (2005) notes these enable presentation of "(1) dynamic computer animated fly-through, (2) video footage of various sites to be visited (including animation of the use of field equipment), (3) dynamic graphing of quantitative information collected in the field, (4) annotation of images to show geographic features, (5) aims, objectives, preparatory readings, citations, and bibliographic resources, (6) logistical information and joining instructions".

Carr (n.d.) considers "the development of the virtual field course as a flagship of e-learning ... [the] completely self-paced independent virtual learning environment [is] particularly suited to geography as a discipline". Sanders (2004, p. 19) indicates that "e-based fieldwork support that allows students to be familiarized with field sites in advance of the actual field trip ... is a great way of maximizing what students can get out of the fieldwork experience". Ramasundaram et al. (2005, p. 21) stress that the virtual field laboratory that they created not only "mimicked the students' learning processes that operate during real field trips" but also provided "a simulation environment to study environmental processes in space and time". Cox & Su (2004, p. 113) note that "whether students are on another continent or in the presence of a teacher, they can have the field trip experience electronically". Virtual field e-learning materials or virtual worlds/simulations also fit well with the increasing trend in universities to explore the 'teaching–research' nexus (Parolin, 2003) and the co-learning approach re-linking research and teaching in geography as outlined by Le Heron et al. (2006).

Armastas et al. (2005, p. 27) argue that "mobile technologies cannot be ignored as part of the e-learning mix". M-learning (mobile e-learning) "is the exciting art of using mobile technologies to enhance the learning experience. Mobile phones, PDAs, Pocket PCs and the internet can be used to engage and motivate learners, any time and anywhere" (http://www.m-learning.org/). Geddes (2004) notes four main "advantages to m-learning: access, context, collaboration and appeal". Armastas et al. (2005, p. 29) and Attewell (2005, pp. 13–14) discuss identified educational benefits and various possibilities for mobile technologies in higher education. These benefits include the use of mobile technologies for delivery of multimedia materials and interactive tasks, the opportunity for independent and collaborative learning experiences, the incentive for students to actively participate in lectures and to assist learners to remain more focused for longer. Mobile technologies such as GPS, mobile phones and PDAs also enable student researchers to connect with field sites and can make field data more accessible, for example through field-related websites (McCaffrey et al., 2003).

Data repositories and libraries are important to e-learners in geography. There is an interesting variety of source materials that geography makes use of for both teaching and research. The interdisciplinary nature of the discipline often means that geographers are very high users of libraries and data repositories and other e-learning resources.

While availability and use of e-learning technologies provide an obvious rationale, critical practitioner perspectives on using technology in geography have been reported. Rich et al., (2000) reflect on their concern for "paucity of educational and pedagogic underpinnings of the developments made in the use of ICT to teach geography". This does not mean ICT is not valuable but rather that the use of the technology is not reflexive. Fletcher et al., (2007) report that in UK Geography, Earth and Environmental Science subjects "practitioners' use of C&IT is driven by technological, rather than pedagogic, developments. Nevertheless there is evidence that the educational benefits are real and being exploited."

Learning Spaces: The Final Frontiers?

In this section of the paper we review the links between evolving pedagogy and emergent technologies. The aim is to sponsor thinking about versatility in teaching and learning approaches to geography.

Communities of Learners

Tutorial software encourages 'constructivist' and learner-centred (Sherman & Kurshan, 2005) approaches to pedagogy in geography. Software (such as Blackboard, TopClass, and WebCT) constructs 'virtual communities' by managing online communication between (sometimes distant) participants in an asynchronous tutorial. Although the oldest systems claim authorship in the 1980s, the major e-learning platforms have been developed in the last five years; this e-learning approach is now mature, online and interactive. Tutors have developed skills and strategies that can make these sophisticated media for online learning (see for example Salmon, 2002).

Constructivism suggests that learning is a sense-making process where learners build new knowledge and understanding from their existing knowledge. It involves interplay between existing knowledge, and ideas and new ones embedded in material delivered via tutorial software at a time when the learner is ready to engage. Constructivist approaches to learning in geography recognize:

- the constructed nature of knowledge, and the importance of personal thoughts and reflection on them;
- the social and distributed nature of cognition;
- the situated nature of cognition; and
- sufficient time for these three elements to be worked through.

The first element involves finding new ideas, skills and materials and interpreting their meaning and significance personally; online databases are unparalleled sources, while tutorial software provides a portal and a platform for this learning. The second element emphasizes the importance of the social dimension of learning. Schlager & Fusco (2003) suggest that we learn best when working in a technology-enabled dialogue and action community. This is not the only way of engaging learning, but there are some excellent examples (some have already been discussed above) illustrating the learning power technology can bring to bear if designed appropriately, whether learning is entirely online or whether the online resources are supplementing classroom-based learning and teaching. The third element recognizes that learning in geography needs to be closely tied to the situation of the learners. Learners need to be able to apply, experiment and reflect on new ideas and approaches in real situations. With reference to the fourth, it takes time to develop a vibrant social community where reasons for change and underlying philosophies and concepts can be fully and openly explored.

Oliver & Bane (1971, p. 268) note that the tutorial group must be important enough to the individuals involved that (they) take seriously the ideas of others; communities of learners should be open and egalitarian. Power & Power (1992, p. 196) suggest that such groups feature cooperation, informality and spontaneity. Tutorial software, facilitated by the internet, can empower discussion and debate in conditions where face-to-face meetings are problematic: reflection is encouraged by asynchronous communication. Tutorial groups have the opportunity to share their knowledge, the chance to learn with each other and from each other and to develop common approaches to their learning (McDermott, 2001).

Mobile learning

What will mobile technologies (m-technologies) produce with regard to e-learning (m-learning) strategies? Peter Cochrane (former Chief Technical Officer of British Telecom) argues that computing power is accelerating so fast that very soon a 'super-iPod' will be available that will hold all the music that has ever been produced. Storage, speed of processing and connection will not be the main constraints in computing. This will free computers from the desktop and change the nature of teaching and learning with computers.

Developments in mobile technology suggest that resources can be delivered to learners anywhere and at anytime (Anderson & Blackwood, 2004). As a result, there are already changes to the design principles for new learning spaces. For example, Alexander (2006) has argued that educators previously concerned about designing libraries as spaces for learning will, in the future, have to design learning for any space. These approaches are not contradictory, but require a different starting point. Alexander has suggested that providing learning resources in the palm of learners' hands through mobile technology is going to result in a revolution for all learners.

FutureLab (2006) has developed two interesting packages that use mobile technologies to encourage learning in place. Savannah equips students with location-aware PDAs connected to a virtual savannah environment. Each PDA takes the student through a scenario of a different animal and they navigate around a virtual space in a real space (such as a playground) in an effort to find the food and/or watering holes. Students learn how the ecosystem of the savannah operates through locational simulation. In Mudlarking (a second package from FutureLab) students take a PDA to a location and use it to record images, video, audio and text data relating to the location. They can then edit and link these data and make them available to other students to illustrate the particular features of the place. Descriptions range from sense of place to scientific data collected from samples in the field. In each case the students are interacting with resources that are designed for learning, or what is becoming known as 'learning objects' (Beck, 2007). The students' interactions may involve entering and receiving information and learning about the theme while moving around a particular place, whether real or virtual.

If Alexander (2006) is correct, then academics' versatility may have to increase to provide more portable learning resources. We may need to work with m-technology providers, learning resource providers, libraries and learning technologists. We need to create futures that take advantage of opportunities to *locate* learning in space and place and make geography education accessible, attractive and exciting for all.

Podcasting

Podcasting is an excellent example of an emergent technology that can increase our pedagogic versatility. Podcasting is a term used to describe a group of technologies for distributing audio or video content over the internet. You do not need an iPod or any Mp3 player to download from sources such as Geocast. Geocast (2006) provides audio and video learning objects that are short and to the point on the Scottish Standard Grade Geography curriculum, mainly focusing on explaining physical geography processes.

One of the most listened to geography podcasts is one put together by a group of PhD students, A Very Spatial Podcast (VSP). It started with GIS and remote sensing, but has broadened its focus to discussing a range of geography-related themes, providing software comments, conference reports and topical discussions. This is an informal and informative podcast that is accessible and enjoyable.

These two examples are very much learner centred. Geocast was started by a teacher to give his students revision audio and video learning resources and the VSP was launched by students for students as a bit of fun, but has turned into an extremely useful resource for students. The podcasters provide email and blog facilities for any listeners to get in touch and they respond to questions. Much has been written on the *potential* of podcasting, but as yet not very much on how learners engage with them and how they influence learning. An early example is Chan & Lee (2005) in which they provide evidence that five-minute student-centred audio programmes can address students' preconceptions and anxieties about subjects and learning activities. This isolated example is set to be joined with the completion in 2007 of IMPALA (Informal Mobile Podcasting And Learning Adaptation), a major cross-institution study on podcasting in higher education led by the University of Leicester and funded by the Higher Education Academy. This study is shortly to be followed up by IMPALA 2 to focus on geography, earth and environmental sciences (GEES) disciplines, jointly led by the University of Leicester and the UK GEES Subject Centre (details are available from www.impala.ac.uk).

Distance/Blended/Flexible Learning

More and more educational content will be made available online. There are experiments with how this will complement traditional modes of learning. Robertson & Fluck (2004) for example made learning objects available to high school students in Australia and reviewed the experiences of both teachers and students. The main responses were that the learning was enjoyable. However, one of the interesting findings related to the importance placed on being able to find friends in the chat areas. The students took responsibility for keeping in contact because of the institutional challenges of arranging chat sessions during school times in different schools and different states.

The popularity of sites such as myspace.com and bebo.com demonstrates the fascination of sites that allow for the posting of information and the capability to make connections between people and content. These sites provide the opportunity to post video, images and text, to link this content and create social networks with people of similar interests. One development that may provide models for the future is initiatives making learning available more widely. These include the open content initiatives of the USA's MIT (2006) and the UK's Open University (2006). In contrast, the Alliance for Lifelong Learning (2006) provided through Oxford, Stanford and Yale collapsed in 2006. It is therefore important to understand more about how and why this blended classroom–internet learning approach works and avoid the pitfalls.

We argue that technology will change the future of work and life, and that higher education teaching needs to be versatile to reflect the evolution of learning contexts.

Blended learning approaches may support lifelong learning skills where graduates change careers up to eight times, there is more self-employment and project work, and fewer hierarchies (Hewitt Associates, 2004). Malone (2005) provides a podcast that explores what is happening in organizations and how this impacts on education and the Department of Labour (2006) in New Zealand provides comparable arguments.

Versatility in Teaching Practice: Discovering Ways to Implement e-learning

There is some research to guide evaluation and implementation methods. Baldwin-Evans (2006, pp. 157–163) identifies various steps in the implementation of new learning strategies. The steps include: ensuring learner readiness (including student orientation); gaining attention of learners (including an overview of learning objectives and stimulation of prior learning); providing students with opportunities for experiential learning; instructors considering appropriate sectioning of information; providing students with opportunities to try out and support learning (case studies, role playing, simulations, self-evaluation); ensuring assessment mechanisms provide good feedback to students, providing ongoing support and assistance to expand learning (by FAQ or mentor or peer in coaching role); and enabling opportunities for collaboration with others.

The model presented in Figure 2 encourages versatility in teaching approaches by focusing on learner-centred activities. E-learning contributes through contemporary engagement and widening the potential participant set through effective distance education. This model should not be seen to be definitive but a starting position for practitioners, since e-learning practice is constantly evolving to incorporate new learning and teaching methods.

Research in other disciplines also provides useful insights into the implementation of e-learning for both students and teachers (Ruiz *et al.*, 2006). Gotthard *et al.* (2006, p. 379) acknowledge that "it is not easy to develop electronic learning (e-learning) strategies that

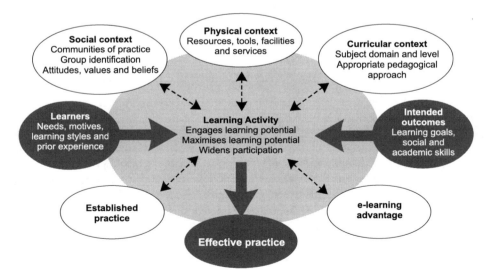

Figure 2. A model of effective practice with e-learning. *Source.* Joint Information Systems Committee (2004)

are widely accepted by teachers and students". Conacannon *et al.* (2005, p. 511) indicate that "students saw e-learning as an expected and integral part of the learning process within higher education". The major finding in a study of students' perceptions of e-learning in university education was "that the strategy of implementing e-learning may play a crucial role for students' perception of the new technology" (Keller & Cernerud, 2002, p. 66). Westbrook (2006, p. 480) concludes that in order "for online courses to be effective there needs to be appropriate training and support for both teachers and learners as they develop new strategies in response to new technologies for learning". Such training and support should focus on issues of availability, access and affordability for example as illustrated in the issues affecting practice with e-learning in Figure 2.

Student and Employer Interest

Teachers of geography in higher education need to address the issue of e-learning because of the pressure from students and their potential employers. It is important for tutors to acknowledge that students are more technologically capable than ever before. The Trust for the Study of Adolescence (2005) suggests that mobile phone ownership in the UK is at its highest level ever and the same is true of teenagers using social software sites such as Facebook, Bebo and MySpace and Microsoft's Instant Messenger. The corollary of this is that businesses are now also using such technology and that they are expecting it of their potential employees. White & Wyn (cited in Knight *et al.*, 2006, p. 28) argue that:

> The arrival of the post-industrial society has brought a realization that the new economy will be increasingly focused on the trade in knowledge through the medium of communication technology, which brings the educational systems into the debate about how to best adapt to an information society to provide the best educational opportunities for young people.

It is no surprise to find information literacy is a key requirement of the UK undergraduate Geography Benchmark, a consultative document written by practitioners that indicates what one might expect to be in the undergraduate curriculum of all universities (Quality Assurance Agency, 2000).

One of the challenges for those managing geography education has been the fact that the discipline requires use of laboratories like sciences, tutorial classes and lectures like the humanities, libraries and map rooms like social sciences, architecture and planning and computing laboratories like computing sciences and information systems. Far from being a challenge, adopting versatile e-learning strategies can mean geography students develop an ability to work with cartographers, librarians and technicians with common technology practices. A recent survey (ASTD, 2006) of US business executives found that 37 per cent of respondents searched for information for more than four hours per week. Nine out of 10 of them routinely use the internet rather than sources such as paper-based trade journals, books and traditional media. Half reported that the main challenges of using the internet are unproductive searches and having to sift through too much information. If this is a problem for contemporary executives we need to consider how we prepare current students for their future careers.

In this context, Knight *et al.* (2006) argue that the old model of one-time teacher training provided by a university and a discipline curriculum handed down by academics will have to be replaced by new forms of development and support. The model they propose is based on communities of learning that include the university, college and school, as well the communities they serve. This view resonates strongly with the collaboration of the UK Department for Education and Skills, the Geographical Association and the Royal Geographical Society in the Action Plan for Geography launched in 2006. A key strategy of this plan is for subject associations to provide a framework for networks of subject leadership to support and enhance geographical education. In the United States the Association of American Geographers (AAG, 2006) is taking a similar tack with the project entitled *My Community, Our Earth Project: Geographic Learning for Sustainable Development*.

A key challenge is to ensure that e-learning initiatives provide graduates with information literacy skills that include making sense of data and information, connecting and learning from relevant information and applying what they have learned. The emergence of Web 2.0 developments (frequently led by teenagers and students) indicates a level of sophistication with the technology, if not with the critical abilities to turn content into learning. These developments are beginning to provide content that competes with more formal content in existing curricula.

We can resist the growth of such developments, encouraging students to use institutional learning management systems, log onto ScienceDirect, Ingenta and other electronic versions of print media, or we can equip them to analyse, make sense of and interpret a wide range of sources. One way we can prepare them for this is to model versatility and build on the discipline's existing strengths to make their geography education experience more connected. Educational technology provides a wide range of flexible e-learning opportunities that develop communication, information literacy, project management, team and independent working skills.

Conclusion

This paper has discussed a range of aspects of e-learning to illustrate that the term describes a broad and complex range of approaches, many of which have been in existence for some time and have matured in educational use. One of the first challenges faced in the interpretation of the broad issue of e-learning in geography is that it is just that: a broad concept. We have identified a number of continua in this complexity:

- face-to-face (f2f) teaching and learning, through a blended approach to entirely online teaching and learning;
- passive learning to interactive, as in a traditional didactic lecture compared with an enquiry-based learning activity;
- low technology use to high technology use, ranging from 'chalk and talk' through to some of the examples discussed (such as a PDA with a global positioning system, video-conferencing or social software).

One of the main challenges appears to have been the complex and often difficult to interpret evidence of the efficacy of many of these technological applications to teaching and learning. A second is the assessment of the range of e-learning activities in relation to the external forces on a course. We have therefore proposed a graph that illustrates these continua and suggests that users of e-learning approaches can map geography's ever-expanding e-learning space. Most learning activities can be placed on this graph.

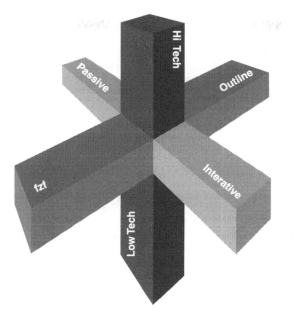

Figure 3. Versatility and geography's learning spaces

We therefore conceptualize the e-learning 'landscape' in geography to be a continuum. As Figure 3 illustrates, this landscape is multi-dimensional. If we understand the e-space we describe and configure, and recognize the context of teaching and learning experiences, we can facilitate the use of versatile and pedagogically appropriate e-learning technologies. This diagram can also illustrate where potential barriers may be. The intention of the diagram is that all e-learning approaches can be located and this will give an indication of each approach in the broader context of e-learning.

This paper has provided a broader context for the integration of e-learning into the curriculum in a way that maximizes its potential and ensures the student learning experience is enhanced by the adoption of technology, rather than that the technology is an additional bolt-on to the existing model of learning and teaching. This is intended to aid in the identification of the barriers and pathways to progress from the current approach to the desired space on the model in Figure 3.

Acknowledgements

The authors thank Eric Pawson for coordinating the INLT workshop where this paper was conceived, the anonymous reviewers who assisted in the birth (well over nine months later!) and Eric again for overseeing whole process. They would also like to thank Trudi James and Max Oulton for the illustrations.

References

Alexander, B. (2006) Web 2.0: a new wave of innovation for teaching and learning?, *Educause Review*, 41(2), pp. 32–44.

Alliance for Lifelong Learning (2006) Oxford, Stanford and Yale Universities. Available at http://www.alllearn.org (accessed November 2006).

Anderson, P. & Blackwood, A. (2004) *Mobile and PDA Technologies and their Future Use in Education* (Bristol: Joint Information Systems Committee Technology and Standards Watch). Available at http://www.jisc.ac.uk/uploaded_documents/ACF11B0.pdf (accessed October 2006).

Armastas, C., Holt, D. & Rice, M. (2006) Balancing the possibilities for mobile technologies in higher education. Available at http://www.ascilite.org.au/conferences/brisbane05/blogs/proceedings/04_Armatas.pdf (accessed October 2006).

Association of American Geographers (2006) *My Community, Our Earth Project: Geographic Learning for Sustainable Development*. Available at http://www.aag.org/sustainable/ (accessed October 2006).

ASTD (American Society for Training and Development) (2006) Learning circuits. http://www.learningcircuits.org/ (accessed November 2006).

Attewell, J. (2005) *Mobile Technologies and Learning: A technology Update and m-learning Project Summary* (London: Learning and Skills Development Agency). Available at http://www.m-learning.org/docs/The_m-learning_project_-_technology_update_and_project_summary.pdf. (accessed November 2006).

Baldwin-Evans, K. (2006) Key steps to implementing a successful blended learning strategy, *Industrial and Commercial Training*, 38(3), pp. 156–163.

Bradbeer, J. & Livingstone, I. (1996) Problem-based learning and fieldwork: a better method of preparation?, *Journal of Geography in Higher Education*, 20(1), pp. 11–18.

Carr, S. (n. d.), Embedding e-learning: A cautionary tale with a happy ending? Available at http://ssl.brookes.ac.uk/teachingLearningWeek/downloads/teachingSeminarE-learning.ppt (accessed May 2007).

Beck, R. (2007) Learning objects (Milwaukee: Center for International Education, University of Wisconsin Milwaukee). Available at http://www.uwm.edu/Dept/CIE/AOP/learningobjects.html (accessed May 2007).

Chan, S. & Lee, M. (2005) An Mp3 a day keeps the worries away: exploring the use of podcasting to address preconceptions and alleviate pre-class anxiety amongst undergraduate information technology students. Charles Sturt Student Experience Conference. Available at http://www.csu.edu.au/division/studserv/sec/papers/chan.pdf (accessed May 2007).

Clark, R. E. (1994) Media will never influence learning, *Educational Technology Research and Development*, 42(2), pp. 21–29.

Conacannon, F., Flynn, A. & Campbell, M. (2005) What campus-based students think about the quality and benefits of e-learning, *British Journal of Educational Technology*, 36(3), pp. 501–512.

Cox, E. S. & Su, T.-Y. (2004) Integrating student learning with practitioner experiences via virtual field trips, *Journal of Educational Media*, 29(2), pp. 113–123.

Department of Labour (2006) The Future of work. http://www.dol.govt.nz/futureofwork/stocktake–summary.asp (accessed November 2006).

Fletcher, S., France, D., Moore, K. & Robinson, G. (2007) Practitioners' perspectives on the use of technology in fieldwork, *Journal of Geography in Higher Education*, 31(2), pp. 319–330.

FutureLab (2006) Available at http://www.futurelab.org.uk/showcase/savannah/index.htm (accessed October 2006).

Geddes, S. (2004) *M-learning in the C21st: Benefits for Learners*. Available at http://knowledgetree.flexiblelearning.net.au/edition06/html/pra_simon_geddes.html (accessed November 2006).

Geocast (2006) Geocast revision area. Available at http://www.exc-el.org.uk/content/index.php/main/teaching_and_learning/geography/geocast_revision_area (accessed November 2006).

Gotthardt, M., Siegert, M., Schlieck, A., Schneider, S., Kohnert, A., Gro, M., Schäfer, C., Wagner, R., Hörmann, S., Behr, T., Engenhart-Cabillic, R., Klose, K., Jungclas, H. & Glowalla, U. (2006) How to successfully implement E-learning for both students and teachers, *Academic Radiology*, 13(3), pp. 379–390.

Halvorson, S. & Westcoat, J. (2002) Problem-based inquiry on world water problems in large undergraduate classes, *Journal of Geography*, 101(3), pp. 91–102.

Hedberg, J. G. (2006) E-learning futures? Speculations for a time yet to come, *Studies in Continuing Education*, 28(2), pp. 171–183.

Hewitt Associates (2004) *Building the Management and Organizational Disciplines to Grow* (Houston, TX: Hewitt Associates).

Joint Information Systems Committee (2004) *Effective Practice with e-learning*. Higher Education Funding Council for England. Available at http://www.jisc.ac.uk/whatwedo/programmes/elearning_pedagogy/elp_practice.aspx (accessed November 2006).

Jonassen, D. H., Dyer, D., Peters, K., Robinson, T., Harvey, D., King, M. & Loughner, P. (1997) Cognitive flexibility hypertexts on the web: rngaging learners in meaning making, in: B. Khan (Ed.) *Web-based Instruction*, pp. 119–134 (Englewood Cliffs, NJ: Educational Technology Publications).

Keller, C. & Cernerud, L. (2002) Students' perceptions of E-learning in university education, *Journal of Educational Media*, 27(1–2), pp. 55–67.

Knight, C., Knight, B. & Teghe, D. (2006) Releasing the pedagogical power of information and communication technology for learners: a case study, *International Journal of Education and Development using ICT*, 2(2), pp. 27–34.

Kozma, R. B. (1994) Will media influence learning? Reframing the debate, *Educational Technology Research and Development*, 42(2), pp. 7–20.

Le Heron, R., Baker, R. & McEwen, L. (2006) Co-learning: re-linking research and teaching in geography, *Journal of Geography in Higher Education*, 30(1), pp. 77–87.

Livingstone, D. & Lynch, K. (2002) Group project work and student-centered active learning: two different experiences, *Journal of Geography in Higher Education*, 26(2), pp. 217–237.

Malone, T. (2005) The future of work. Available at http://www.itconversations.com/shows/detail731.html (accessed November 2006).

McCaffrey, K., Holdsworth, R., Clegg, P., Jones, R. & Wilson, R. (2003) Using digital mapping tools and 3-D visualization to improve undergraduate fieldwork, *Planet*, (5), pp. 34–37.

McDermott, R. (2001) The public and private space of community, *Knowledge Management Review*, 4(5), p. 5.

MIT (2006) MITOPENCOURSEWARE. Massachusetts Institute of Technology. Available at http://ocw.mit.edu/index.html (accessed November 2006).

OECD (2005) *E-learning in Tertiary Education: Where Do We Stand?* (Paris: Organization for Economic Cooperation and Development).

Open University (2006) Openlearn. Available at http://oci.open.ac.uk/ (accessed November 2006).

Oliver, D. & Bane, M. (1971) Is reasoning enough?, in: C. Beck, B. Crittenden & E. Sullivan (Eds) *Moral Education: Interdisciplinary Approaches*, pp. 252–270 (Toronto: University of Toronto Press).

Parolin, B. P. (2003) The geography research–teaching nexus, in: R. Freestone, A. Bagnara, M. Scoufis & C. Pratt (Eds) *The Learning Community First Explorations of the Research–Teaching Nexus at UNSW*, pp. 56–58. Available at www.ltu.unsw.edu.au/content/userDocs/Parolincasestudy.pdf (accessed June 2007).

Power, F. & Power, A. (1992) A craft of hope: democratic education and the challenge of pluralism, *Journal of Moral Education*, 21(3), pp. 193–205.

Quality Assurance Agency (2000) *Geography: Benchmarking Statement* (Gloucester: Quality Assurance Agency for Higher Education). Available at http://www.qaa.ac.uk/academicinfrastructure/benchmark/honours/geography.pdf (accessed November 2006).

Ramasundaram, V., Srunwald, S., Mangeot, A., Comerford, N. & Bliss, C. (2005) Development of an environmental virtual field laboratory, *Computers and Education*, 45, pp. 21–34.

Rich, D., Robinson, G. & Bednarz, R. (2000) Collaboration and the successful use of information and communications technologies in teaching and learning geography in higher education, *Journal of Geography in Higher Education*, 24(2), pp. 263–270.

Robertson, M. & Fluck, A. (2004) Capacity building in geographical education: strategic use of online technologies, *Geography*, 89(3), pp. 269–273.

Ruiz, J., Mintzer, M. & Leipzig, R. (2006) The impact of e-learning in medical education, *Academic Medicine*, 81(3), pp. 207–212.

Salmon, G. (2002) *E-tivities: The Key to Active Online Learning* (London: Kogan Page).

Sanders, M. (2004) Engaging with e-learning in geography, earth and environmental sciences. Available at http://www.exchange.ac.uk/files/eissue6.pdf (accessed October 2006).

Schlager, M. & Fusco, J. (2003) Teacher professional development, technology, and communities of practice: are we putting the cart before the horse?, *The Information Society*, 19, pp. 203–220.

Serafin, E. (2005) *E-Learning for fieldwork—description of demo*, e-Learning @ Edinburgh Conference March 2005. Available at http://www.elearn.malts.ed.ac.uk/issues/news/elearn@ed/#fieldwork (accessed November 2006).

Sherman, T. & Kurshan, B. (2005) Constructing learning: using technology to support teaching for understanding, *Learning and Leading with Technology*, 3(5), pp. 10–39.

Stokes, S. (2000) Preparing students to take online interactive courses, *The Internet and Higher Education*, 2(2–3), pp. 161–169.

Trust for the Study of Adolescence (2005) Key data on adolescence. Available at http://www.tsa.uk.com/ (accessed November 2006).

Tyack, D. & Cuban, L. (1995) *Tinkering Toward Utopia* (Cambridge, MA: Harvard University Press).

University of Leicester (2005) Why use learning technology?. Available at http://www.le.ac.uk/talent/elearning/why.html (accessed November 2006).

UNSW Educational Development & Technology Centre (undated) *Guidelines on Application of Educational Technology* Available at http://www.edtec.unsw.edu.au/inter/dload/flex_ed/application/index.htm (accessed November 2006) (Sydney: University of New South Wales).

Westbrook, V. (2006) The virtual learning future, *Teaching in Higher Education*, 11(4), pp. 471–482.

Strength in Diversity: Enhancing Learning in Vocationally-Orientated, Master's Level Courses

LINDSEY MCEWEN*, JANICE MONK**, IAIN HAY†, PAULINE KNEALE‡ & HELEN KING^

*Pedagogic Research and Scholarship Research Institute (PRSI), University of Gloucestershire, UK, **School of Geography and Development, University of Arizona, USA, †School of Geography, Population and Environmental Management, Flinders University, Australia, ‡Geography, Earth & Environmental Sciences Subject Centre, Plymouth University, Plymouth, UK, ^Higher Education Consultant, Virginia, USA

ABSTRACT *Postgraduate education in geography, especially at the Master's level, is undergoing significant changes in the developed world. There is an expansion of vocationally oriented degree programmes, increasing recruitment of international students, integration of workplace skills, and the engagement of non-traditional postgraduate students as departments respond to policies for a more 'inclusive' higher education. This paper sets the context by outlining some programmatic changes in selected countries (Australia, the UK, and the USA). The authors briefly reflect on how postgraduate 'bars' or 'levels' are defined and explore in detail what 'diversity' or 'heterogeneity' means in these new postgraduate settings. They then explore some practice examples drawn from their own experiences, recognizing that relevance will vary in other contexts. Finally they consider how diversity can be harnessed as a strength that has potential to enhance taught elements of contemporary postgraduate education in and beyond the discipline.*

Changing Directions in Postgraduate Education

Postgraduate education in geography, especially at Master's level, is undergoing significant changes in the developed world. Among these are the expansion of vocationally orientated degree programmes that go beyond the traditional research-orientated focus, increasing recruitment of international students, and the need to respond to policies for widening access in a more 'inclusive' higher education. The more academic 'research training' Master's course is equally expected to step up to these pedagogic challenges. Few studies provide reflective guidance on Master's teaching (Knight, 1997; Keller & Kros, 2000; Fejes *et al.*, 2005) are valuable exceptions), although geography colleagues have been striving to develop curricula that explicitly integrate more workplace skills and deal with non-traditional postgraduates. Two contributions with an explicit focus on postgraduate diversity include Scheyvens *et al.* (2003) who evaluated impediments to learning (e.g. language problems) for international postgraduate students in geography in New Zealand and Ridley (2004) who explored the experiences of international students on Masters' courses in business, finance and management at a UK university. However, much of the existing diversity literature focuses on undergraduates (e.g. Hall *et al.*, 2002; Sanders, 2006).

This paper aims to chip away at these lacunae, outlining some dimensions of change in Australia, the UK and the USA, evaluating and offering examples of guidance drawn from our experiences on ways to draw constructively on the diversity of students enrolled in such programmes. These see heterogeneity as 'strength', not an 'obstacle', benefiting the co-learning of peers and staff. We focus primarily on 'taught' postgraduate programmes (including nested Postgraduate Certificate, Postgraduate Diploma and full Master's awards with a research thesis), although our discussion is also relevant to research-focused postgraduate courses with more limited taught elements, but from which students progress to careers outside academe.

Internationally postgraduate education follows different models, levels and learning outcomes with varying proportions of taught and research elements. In the USA, course work has traditionally been included in both Master's and PhD curricula, with independent research having compulsory or optional status in Masters' awards. Recently taught postgraduate programmes, such as the Master's in Geographic Information Sciences (M.GIS/M.GInfS) and Certificates in GIS (Geographical Information Systems) have been introduced. Similarly in the UK, academic research-dominated Master's awards (Thorne, 1997), have been complemented by vocationally orientated 'taught' courses (Eastwood, 2005; McEwen, 2005). In Australia, Master's level education has shifted substantially from research-based degrees to programmes involving coursework that are often vocationally oriented. Postgraduate certificates—non-existent in 1984—have grown rapidly, reaching 11 703 enrolments in 2000 (DETYA, 2000).

Several currents are fostering these changes, among them increasing demands for vocational preparation from employers, professional and funding agencies, and students. Student demand comes from the traditional post-Bachelors' or undergraduate pool but increasingly postgraduate students are also recruited from new constituencies. For instance, in the UK, 'money rich, time poor' workplace learners are a key target group, seeking to change or enhance their career prospects through taught postgraduate study, linking personal development planning to continuing professional development. To meet their needs, various models of integrated postgraduate-workplace study are being promoted (e.g. Learndirect, 2007; National Centre for Work Based Learning Partnerships, 2007). The ends of both social justice and economic competitiveness are being pursued by widening access in ways that attract and support more diverse student groups. The Higher Education Funding Council in England (HEFCE, 2006) has widening access and participation as a key priority in its five-year strategic plan (2006–2011). New efforts and patterns of recruitment of international students add to the complexity. The UK Government's *Initiative for International Education* (launched in April 2006) aims to attract an additional 100 000 overseas students, with numbers set to reach 870 000 by 2020 (BBC News, 2004). In Australia, the number of overseas postgraduate students soared from 54 928 in 2001 to 90 231 in 2005 (DEST, 2006). In the USA, the issue of international student enrolments is a subject of continuing discussion, with more than half a million foreign students enrolled in 2004–2005. The greatest numbers come from South Korea, Japan, India, China, and Taiwan (Batalova, 2006).

The Postgraduate 'Bar' and Diversity

As the recruitment imperatives and target markets evolve, debates are focusing on various areas:

- What does 'postgraduate' mean in terms of knowledge and skills levels and how does it differ from undergraduate education?
- What are the implications for research dominated Master's (Thorne, 1997)?
- What impact does the changing character of postgraduate education have on educational and academic standards (HEFCE/CVCP/SCOP, 1996; Thorne, 1997)?
- What are effective models of graduate education (Tobias et al., 1995; Colker & Day, 2003; Golde & Dore, 2004)?
- How can the transition to Master's level be managed and supported so students make the most of their vocational, and cultural experiences?
- How can co-learning groups be created to capitalize on diversity and ensure engagement, while avoiding pitfalls such as learning ghettos and negative stereotyping of culturally and visibly different groups (Collins, 2006), negative aspects of 'disciplinary tribes' in interdisciplinary postgraduate courses (Lattuca, 2001), and issues such as how poor academic practice and plagiarism can be avoided (Leask, 2006)?

To explore these questions, we first reflect on what 'postgraduateness' means then discuss ways to define 'diversity'.

Defining 'Postgraduateness'

> Even within one university, taught Master's programmes serve many different clients, embody a diversity of purposes and reflect different notions of the 'masterness' of postgraduate study. (Thorne, 1997, p. 16)

Defining 'postgraduateness' involves establishing a shared understanding of the nature of such study, the associated level of the 'bar(s)' and how high these are raised vis-à-vis undergraduate study. These 'bars' may be established generically in university terms and then applied to geography. 'Postgraduateness' can be construed in terms of Master's level ('M-level'): knowledge and skills, distinctive approach to learning activities, and socialization. Several attempts have been made in the UK and Europe to formalize and standardize the demands of postgraduate study through generic 'level descriptors' for Master's level (independent of the proportions of taught and research elements). These typically seek to determine what knowledge and skills a student will have upon completion of the award. Regional, national and international agencies have set a proliferation of learning level descriptors focused on staged learning outcomes to which Higher Education Institutions (HEIs) are being asked to adhere (e.g. in the UK, QAA, 2007 and SEEC 2003, and the shared European 'Dublin' descriptors, JQI, 2004). These outline the nature of 'postgraduateness' in relation to 'undergraduate' knowledge and skills. As an example, Table 1 illustrates the distinctions made between final-year undergraduate and Master's level, with excerpts from the full set of SEEC-level indicators.[1] These encompass knowledge and understanding, cognitive and intellectual skills (e.g. analysis and synthesis), key/transferable skills (e.g. communication) and practical skills (e.g. technical expertise). At the same time, the Bologna Process with its focus on lifelong learning, employability, and graduate skills in the curriculum has generated debates across Europe about the comparability of demands and duration of Master's programmes (or the 'second cycle'; Europe Unit, 2007). Table 2 shows JQI's (2004) draft differentiation from undergraduate to PhD level or 'cycles', which are broadly comparable to SEEC and QAA.

Calls for outcome-based assessments of degree programmes in the USA are creating similar pressures to generate level descriptors, although the approaches lack the central models described above as individual departments respond to their own university's policies. From our perspective, in relation to diversity, these 'level descriptor' models have a number of limitations. While they may recognize a diversity of qualifications, the overlap and differentiation is often confusing. Furthermore, their language is too restricted to traditional knowledge and skill domains, largely failing to elaborate on the affective/attitudinal domains and personal skills (Fink, 2003)[2] which are important in all levels of higher education but especially so as the nature and aspirations of the student body become more diverse.

Several pedagogic characteristics are generally accepted as distinguishing postgraduate from undergraduate learning (e.g. McEwen *et al.*, 2005). These include: the development of more self-reliance and autonomy; more critical evaluation and self-reflection; more opportunity for originality in developing or applying ideas; and acknowledgement of students as producers of research on a scale not normally seen in undergraduate courses. Vocational postgraduate courses frequently have a more explicit skills focus. Employers recruiting such postgraduates over undergraduates normally expect not only specialist knowledge and skills but also 'creative professionalism' (Kennedy, 2002), the ability to self-direct learning and acquire new skills quickly, undertake advanced problem-solving, work flexibly and lead teams. Professional organizations, departments, and students themselves are recognizing the importance of more collaborative activities, more autonomy and negotiated study, more experiential learning, and more engagement with cutting edge literature in Master's level programmes.

The current research and resource development efforts of the Association of American Geographers (AAG), 'Enhancing Departments and Graduate Education' (EDGE, 2007), for example, incorporate attention to an array of issues in the culture and 'climate' of postgraduate education, in particular how students are being socialized and prepared for professional tasks (e.g. team work, networking, and communication with various audiences). At Flinders University in Australia, the School of Geography, Population and Environment has several approaches to integrating postgraduate students into professional activities in departmental research and practice, identified as 'pastoral care' (Flinders, 2007). In the USA, postgraduate students may organize themselves to foster professional advancement and lobby for their own interests (e.g. MSU, 2007) and to address concerns about diversity, such as efforts to increase and support gender diversity in the profession through Supporting Women in Geography (e.g. SWIG, 2007) groups.

Table 1. Example learning descriptors (based on SEEC, 2003) that differentiate between HE Level 3 (final-year undergraduate) and HE Level 4 (Master's level)

Learning Descriptor category	Learning Descriptor sub-heading	Undergraduate final year (HE Level 3) The learner:	Master's level (HE Level 4) The learner:
Development of Knowledge and Under-standing (subject specific)	Knowledge base	has a comprehensive/ detailed knowledge of a major discipline(s) with areas of specialization in depth and an awareness of the provisional nature of knowledge	has depth and systematic understanding of knowledge in specialized/applied areas and/across areas and can work with theoretical/ research-based knowledge at the fore front of their academic discipline
	Ethical issues	is aware of personal responsibility and professional codes of conduct and can incorporate a critical ethical dimension into a major piece of work	has the awareness and ability to manage the implications of ethical dilemmas and work proactively with others to formulate solutions
Cognitive/ Intellectual skills (generic)	Analysis	can analyse new and/or abstract data and situations without guidance, using a range of techniques appropriate to the subject	with critical awareness can undertake analysis of complex, incomplete or contradictory areas of knowledge communicating the outcome effectively
Key/transferable skills (generic)	Group Working	can interact effectively within a team/learning/ professional group, recognize, support or be proactive in leadership, negotiate in a professional context and manage conflict	can work effectively with a group as leader or member. Can clarify task and make appropriate use of the capacities of group members. Is able to negotiate and handle conflict with confidence
	Communications	can engage effectively in debate in a professional manner and produce detailed and coherent project reports	can engage confidently in academic and professional communication with others, reporting on action clearly, autonomously and competently
Practical skills (subject specific)	Autonomy in skill use	is able to act autonomously, with minimal supervision or direction, within agreed guidelines	is able to exercise initiative and personal responsibility in professional practice

Table 2. The 'Dublin' learning level descriptors: differentiating between cycles across Europe

Cycle	
	Knowledge and understanding:
1 (Bachelor)	[Is] supported by advanced textbooks [with] some aspects informed by knowledge at the forefront of their field of study ...
2 (Master)	provides a basis or opportunity for originality in developing or applying ideas often in a research context ...
3 (Doctorate)	[includes] a systematic understanding of their field of study and mastery of the methods of research associated with that field ...
	Applying knowledge and understanding:
1 (Bachelor)	[through] devising and sustaining arguments
2 (Master)	[through] problem-solving abilities [applied] in new or unfamiliar environments within broader (or multidisciplinary) contexts ...
3 (Doctorate)	[is demonstrated by the] ability to conceive, design, implement and adapt a substantial process of research with scholarly integrity ... [is in the context of] a contribution that extends the frontier of knowledge by developing a substantial body of work some of which merits national or international refereed publication ...
	Making judgements:
1 (Bachelor)	[involves] gathering and interpreting relevant data ...
2 (Master)	[demonstrates] the ability to integrate knowledge and handle complexity, and formulate judgements with incomplete data ...
3 (Doctorate)	[requires being] capable of critical analysis, evaluation and synthesis of new and complex ideas ...
	Communication:
1 (Bachelor)	[of] information, ideas, problems and solutions ...
2 (Master)	[of] their conclusions and the underpinning knowledge and rationale (restricted scope) to specialist and non-specialist audiences (monologue) ...
3 (Doctorate)	with their peers, the larger scholarly community and with society in general (dialogue) about their areas of expertise (broad scope) ...
	Learning skills:.
1 (Bachelor)	have developed those skills needed to study further with a high level of autonomy ...
2 (Master)	study in a manner that may be largely self-directed or autonomous ...
3 (Doctorate)	expected to be able to promote, within academic and professional contexts, technological, social or cultural advancement...

Defining 'Diversity'

Issues of diversity, especially in relation to undergraduate teaching and to the concerns of women geographers, have received sustained attention in *JGHE* (see Monk, 2000 for a review). Perhaps most relevant for postgraduate education are the papers by Hansen *et al.* (1995), and Moss *et al.* (1999) which consider strategies that women students and staff might use to 'survive and thrive' and to mentor students at all levels and one another. Our focus, however, is on Master's level courses, especially those attracting vocationally orientated students, including mature and international students. In so doing, we recognize that ideas from the earlier literature are salient: for example, paying attention to communication issues, power relations, networking, and drawing on students' lived experiences.

Our definition of 'diversity' goes beyond considerations of cultural and bodily diversity to embrace diversity of:

- students' background, prior knowledge and experience, course expectations and future goals;
- prior experience of different teaching models;
- teaching methods/approaches/learning environments experienced;
- programme styles experienced;
- the scale and imperatives of the institution of previous study; and
- the extent, character and demands of previous work experience (Table 3).

Some dimensions are enduring while others can be transient or changeable, developing either through the learning experience or independent of it. Some have possible commonality with undergraduate education, but other factors (e.g. students' prior learning experiences in higher education, personal skill development) will normally differentiate postgraduate learners. An agenda for supporting postgraduate diversity needs to involve attention to access and success of all groups, to inter-group relations and campus climate, to education and to scholarship, and to institutional viability and vitality (Smith *et al.*, 2000).

Diversity and the Learning Environment

Student diversity brings opportunities and challenges as quotations from students and staff (Table 4) attest. In the quotations students tend to focus on cultural diversity; the staff extend this to consider prior work experience and discipline background. International perspectives, student aspirations for careers within and beyond academe and variety in background are recurrent themes. It is important to focus on capitalizing proactively on, *not just coping with*, diversity and to recognize not only what teachers bring but also the potential of peer support in facilitating learning. Graduate student participants in focus groups for the AAG's EDGE project, for example, have discussed how they share skills and experiences, including those gained from internships (placements) beyond campus. They recognize and draw on these as opportunities for networking and subsequent employment. Advanced graduate students and early career faculty attending the US Geography Faculty Development Alliance workshops repeatedly report that they learn from, and are supported by, the diversity of the group which brings together a mix of genders, ages, foreign- and US-born, and teachers from diverse types of institutions. The heterogeneity of the learning community is further extended by the disciplinary, vocational, research, cultural and personal experiences of staff. All can affect students' learning environments.

The location of institutions influences the mix of staff and students, which then affects important peer learning opportunities and practices. Contrasting cultures were very evident in the department visits conducted for the EDGE project. Those in metropolitan regions, for example, tend to attract mature-age students who commute and may study part time while holding down jobs. They spend less time in the department and so are less engaged with shared informal learning than students in departments in the 'campus town' environments of large universities in relatively small communities who often study and socialize together. The differences among institutions in the international student presence is also evident, partly a function of recruiting policies.

Table 3. Dimensions of diversity within postgraduate education

Form of diversity	Characteristics
Student body	Personal characteristics (e.g. age, gender, race, culture, linguistic skills); personal commitments (part-time/full-time; with dependants), vocational experience (career stage, workplace and professional development aspirations); discipline-base and nature and extent of prior academic experience of geography; natural learning style; expectations and aspirations
Teaching models	Teachers encountered (diversity in background and experience, roles and status, gender, ethnic, class, national backgrounds) Class sizes (a small number of students writing a thesis on a self-selected topic to large classes on a vocational programme with limited curriculum options) Varying roles and conceptions of research (e.g. research-led, research-informed, scholarship-based teaching, memorization of prescribed knowledge); level of research activity Higher education framework; international variants
Teaching methods	Range of approaches from independent research and peer-supported group learning, or from emphasis on critical thinking to memorization and application of prescribed knowledge and approaches (predominance of deep or surface learning); learning environments (staff-led versus student-led); class size Experience of different models of workplace learning including internships/placements Development of student designed methodologies in research beyond methodologies prescribed by staff Experience of formative individual constructive feedback and critique of scholarship
Programme styles	Differences in qualification titles, course length and potential duration; flexibility in time for completion; mode of delivery (part time/full time; face to face, open, blended and distance learning); balance of research to teaching, vocational or theoretical emphases. Differences within the discipline (e.g. practice-based programmes such as Geographical Information Science (GIS), theoretically focused research-based Master's courses)
Institutional context	Differences in type/scale of institution and associated character of the student body (e.g. PhD or Master's as highest degree offered). Status research and knowledge exchange at institutional level: research-led, research informed or teaching college? Large institutions with benefits from a graduate school across campus Significant presence of cultural diversity in institution, staff, study body, and surrounding community Effects of geographic location on curriculum (e.g. focus on urban studies in large metropolitan institutions, on GIS in those located near concentrations of information technology industries)
Work experience	Presence or absence of work experience Subject relevance of work experience Nature, duration and demands of previous work experience Work experience during course (including work-based learning, WBL)

Table 4. Perspectives on diversity and postgraduate learning environments

Student quotes:
"The topic encouraged me to consider the world—not just Australia—due to its multicultural outlook and students." (Australian postgraduate student 2003)
"On the whole our university is located in an area that is very open, very diverse, and very progressive. That is the strength of the department. The student body and the faculty are diverse as well. As a result, it's an open atmosphere." (USA EDGE project preliminary focus group participant, 2006)
"Much more personal with smaller classes. High proportion of international students give [study] a different, positive emphasis with other views." (UK postgraduate student)

Problems:
In classes with people of diverse language experience and national backgrounds:
"There was a tendency for [a small group] of people to dominate class discussion and make it hard for other people to speak." (Australian postgraduate student 2006)
"GIS students tend to be international students and they tend to socialize and collaborate on their own, separate from the rest of the graduate students." (USA EDGE project preliminary focus group participant, 2006)
Students express disappointment when teachers provide significant support only for those considering academic careers:
"My degree program is not providing many professional opportunities outside of academia. Within the school in which the department is situated there are more opportunities for those considering careers outside academia. The department doesn't seem to be open to offering possibilities for students who aren't considering academia." (USA EDGE project preliminary focus group participant, 2006)

Staff quotes:
"The students who join our classes bring many new challenges. Often they do not have academic backgrounds in the areas in which they undertake postgraduate study (e.g. mechanical engineers and lawyers studying environmental management); some do not have well-developed English-language skills; and huge diversity within a class adds great value to conversation and discussion but also presents interesting teaching-and-learning challenges. For example, one postgraduate class of 18 I had two years ago included 15 students all from different countries including Norway, Mongolia, Papua New Guinea, Hong Kong, Sudan." (Faculty/staff member, Australia)
"I am teaching a comparative planning course where I am trying to compare and contrast US approaches to planning with selective other countries... I would normally be hamstrung if the class makeup was only US students. I was talking one day about economic development and there was a South Korean student who used to be a city planner. He was saying 'in my country we are losing all our factories along the coast to China.' ... And I said, 'See, American students, it not just here.' So it's a good two-way learning experience for me." (County Planner/Part-time faculty/staff interviewed for EDGE project, USA)
"One of the greatest challenges that I face is to engage new postgraduate students direct from undergraduate study, work-based learners and international students in the same learning environment. When this diversity actually works for co-learning, the knowledge and skill development goes far beyond the traditional postgraduate norms into the realms of attitude and advanced personal skill development." (Faculty/staff member, UK)

Drawing Strength from Diversity

We suggest that it is critical to bring diversity positively and explicitly into learning design to enable students to engage with and learn from each other through discussions, group work and peer support. If staff/faculty members are to succeed in supporting diverse students to achieve ultimate postgraduate success, they must take up the challenge of anticipating and planning to capitalize on that diversity as strength. In addition, there may be potential for staff themselves to learn from, encourage and adapt to student diversity.

In the 10 practice examples below, drawing on our knowledge and experiences in geography and related discipline areas, we illustrate a variety of ways to improve students' and staff experiences of taught postgraduate learning by capitalizing on diversity. We go beyond the traditional knowledge/skills domains that define 'postgraduateness' (see Tables 1/2) to include the affective domain and to draw on prior learning experiences. The examples are aspirational, raising the 'bar' or 'level of achievement' and pitching learning at the postgraduate level. We have not attempted to offer a comprehensive set of practices but aim to suggest ways in which the effectiveness of practice in postgraduate teaching can be increased. We have not explicitly linked the examples to level descriptors because their integrated learning objectives go beyond these to embrace, for example, the development of values and personal skills of judgement. There is no attempt to evaluate each example's effectiveness; rather we offer them to stimulate thinking about ways in which a diversified student body might be brought productively into co-learning communities. We have grouped the examples into 'setting-up' for postgraduate learning; communication skills; and specialist skills and knowledge for the workplace. Further details of individual practice examples are provided elsewhere (see http://gees.ac.uk/events/2006/inlt/pgtsd/) along with a table breaking down each example by the dimensions of diversity on which it explicitly capitalizes.

Setting up Skills for Effective Postgraduate Learning

Practice Example 1: Being 'Postgraduate'

New postgraduate students bring different experiences from their undergraduate programmes and backgrounds, and their expectations of postgraduate study vary widely. Good practice involves making the demands of postgraduate study explicit. Ideally this should start in the recruitment and induction processes with recognition of diverse students' 'transitions' and support needs (see Garner & Wallace, 1997; Kneale, 2005). While some universities make explicit their expectations of postgraduate students and teachers (e.g. Flinders University, 2006), students also bring their own expectations to these relationships and to their relationships with peers. Encouraging small groups of students to engage with postgraduate learning outcomes from the outset, discuss their various hopes and beliefs and present their consolidated view to academic staff can encourage early responsibility for learning and help to ensure a match between expectations and possibilities. In setting the agenda within individual modules, space can usefully be left for the student body to negotiate inputs into the curriculum—though willingness to participate in such negotiations will also be influenced by aspects of diversity within the student group. Creating opportunities in the programme for personal reflection and action planning through journal or log records allows the individual to take ownership of his/her studies (Davis, 1997). In this way, there is the prospect that students will co-learn and the consolidated view will offer an opportunity for conversation about differences and misconceptions that might be addressed in curriculum design.

Practice Example 2: Developing Effective Co-learning Communities

In fostering respect for multiple forms of diversity among students it is important to recognize and capitalize on strengths within the group. Ice-breaker activities can perform this function and foster peer support and respect.

Sample activities include:

- asking students to write a personal introduction to their peers in their 'second best language'. This task has been shown to sensitize US native speakers of English to their own limitations while demonstrating the diverse skills of international students (Daniels, 2002);
- getting students to write a piece in the language and style of their disciplinary home, then unpick the differences in the examples and writing collaboratively on an interdisciplinary theme (e.g. sustainable development principles and practice);
- asking students in the first weeks to share an audit of their individual skills in a supportive way with a student partner, and then with a broader group of peers, helps people to identify strengths that can be capitalized on within co-learning environments as well as areas of challenge that may benefit from peer support:
- encouraging students to reflect on and share reasons for embarking on postgraduate study, why now, and how this venture fits into their personal development planning. Articulating individual formal and informal pathways for learning, paying attention to their goals and the means and resources they will need to attain them, can foster a shared understanding of opportunities and constraints on study (e.g. returning to study after a period of absence);
- introducing the sharing of note-taking early in the course brings students with diverse academic, vocational, and cultural backgrounds more effectively into class discussions. Posting notes on shared web space or bulletin boards allows students of different backgrounds to become more confident and prepared for class discussions, seeing and learning from others' practices. It is especially useful for students for whom the classroom language is not their first, offering access to materials and nuances they might otherwise have missed. Importantly, it offers an additional opportunity to develop an awareness of the diverse positionalities and perspectives of fellow students;
- early in the course, having staff and students present their previous experiences of research and research-informed teaching and, if appropriate, articulate their research aspirations. This encourages a shared understanding of the potential for enquiry-based learning and also establishes potential synergies in research interests in preparation for a Master's thesis.

Practice Example 3: Engaging Diverse Postgraduates in Career Planning

Moving beyond the specifics of study for a module to students' futures in workplaces where colleagues have different strengths and limitations, students can be asked to initiate a longer term professional development plan beyond the degree programme. A personal values, skills and resources audit can prepare students for the reality of the workplace. The concept of a road map as a metaphor for career planning can alert students to think about changing opportunities and obstacles and reflect on how to handle new situations. Some of the routes may be within the degree programme, others outside it. In developing such a plan, students can be asked to articulate their personal and professional values and goals for sample time periods (e.g. the semester, the year, two years); to reflect on what they do well and what they need to improve;

and to identify resources they need to accomplish specified goals for a selected time span. As one student wrote:

> I realized that if I was to do research on refugees in the future I would need to learn Spanish, so I was prompted to take a local authority evening class while I was doing the Master's. It was hard work but when I applied for the research place, it made a difference because I could get into the field so much faster. (UK postgraduate student)

Practice Example 4: Enhancing Personal Practice—Effective Time Management

For mature-aged students in particular, balancing the competing demands of study, paid work, and personal commitments may vary widely (see Hansen *et al.*, 1995 for issues associated with female postgraduates). Interviews with postgraduates conducted in 2006/2007 for the AAG's EDGE (2007) project indicated that time management is one of the most challenging aspects of completing their studies. Keeping and analysing a time log for 3–5 days, noting specific tasks, and discrepancies between actual and 'ideal' time can provide a useful, 'experience-based' backdrop to peer discussions. Sharing successful time management strategies within the group offers a supportive exercise.[3] Reflection on the experiences of those students who already have workplace experience where time 'is money' and is recorded can be an instructive experience for those developing time-management skills for first-time employment. Used each week in a UK Master's module, most students admitted to totally changing their reading, thinking time and writing processes:

> ... it never occurred to me that thinking needed planning, but when you wrote it on the sheet I could see I needed to read on Monday and then have time to think through and do the PowerPoint on Wednesday. [And:] This seemed so stupid at first but having to hand it in each week [the time sheet] made me look at what I do properly. And I started planning my other modules. What I do in the library has totally changed. (UK postgraduate student)

Capitalizing on Diversity to Develop Communication Skills

Practice Example 5: Capitalizing on Diverse Communication Skills through Professional Posters

Some postgraduate students (e.g. in environment or GIS) may wish to present posters rather than papers at professional meetings as part of their training. Peers who may be strong in oral presentation may value peer learning with those whose past academic and vocational experience and aptitudes are strong in visual representation. Introducing reviews of posters by diverse audiences (other students, staff, outside consultants) can enhance awareness of the importance of tailoring the style and message to audiences. Displaying high-quality student and staff posters with different academic, vocational and cultural experiences in departmental hallways also models and rewards those whose work is featured (for example, Howenstine *et al.*, 1988).

Practice Example 6: Communication Skills Fitted to Purpose: Drawing on Prior Experiences of Writing for Different Audiences

As the goals of postgraduate programmes diversify, assignments need to match writing formats and style for professional and commercial clients, and community audiences. Students with vocational experience may have valuable insights to share about report writing and producing executive summaries. Through role play, students can be asked to convey the same advanced scientific knowledge to different audiences or for different purposes. For example, they may be asked to play a government employee writing both environmental reports and a one-page summary briefing statement, or an environmental consultant writing for the local press and a trade paper in order to get the environmental message across to the local community and fellow professionals. Some of this writing might be taken beyond role play to the public domain. Students might be encouraged to write short 'Opinion-Editorial' commentaries for local newspapers or to write letters to politicians about contentious issues. Professional practitioners, journalists and alumni can be invited to discuss with students the ways in which they write and assure the quality of their writing.

Capitalizing on Diversity to Prepare Specialist Skills for the Workplace

Practice Example 7: Capitalizing on Diversity in Dealing with Ethical Issues in an Advanced Professional Context

Dealing with difficult value judgements and exploring complex ethical issues is a postgraduate-level skill. Students may be presented with—or have to uncover—ethical dilemmas associated with their professional/research practice (see, for example, Israel & Hay, 2006; Stuart *et al.*, 2006). Small-group discussion of these dilemmas can involve participants from diverse backgrounds in uncovering assumptions and values. Groups can be challenged to generate a group-consensus response to each dilemma and to reflect on the significance of, and complexities generated by, diversity in the learning community in that process. For example, students can be asked to comment on the 'dual-use' dilemma by reflecting on instances of the decimation of rare and endangered plant and animal species by commercial 'collectors' following publication of site locations in scientific journals (Stuart *et al.*, 2006). Should scholars withhold key location and other information in their publications? What does this imply for science as a free exchange of information?

Practice Example 8: Working in an Interdisciplinary Context—Designing Innovative Methodologies

Developing innovative approaches to research problems can be significantly helped through group work with students and staff with contrasting skills, subject expertise and learning styles from different disciplines. Interdisciplinary settings require a range of approaches, flexible and holistic thinking, and the exploration of contrasting methodologies to investigate new and complex problems with the potential for "enhanced creativity, original insights or unconventional thinking" (Ivanitskaya *et al.*, 2002, p. 100; see also Field *et al.*, 1994). Bringing together staff/faculty members from the natural and social sciences to integrate teaching of quantitative and qualitative methods can add interest to postgraduate research methods modules. Research simulations that draw together students and staff/faculty members with contrasting disciplinary perspectives stimulate reflection on the value of different research approaches in interdisciplinary learning. Tasks might include groups designing methodologies to evaluate: the impact of large-scale dam building in a physical and cultural context; barriers to geohazard management or sustainable tourism in a developing world context; and climate change impacts in a specific economic sector or domain. The groups peer review and critique each other's methodologies with special attention to innovation and thinking 'outside the box'. Reflections by a group of postgraduate students in an urban ecology programme (Graybill *et al.*, 2006) offer an indication of the value of interdisciplinary endeavours.

Practice Example 9: Capitalizing on Diversity in the Wider Learning Community—Learning through Professional Service

Promoting and encouraging informal learning and reflection through 'service', in, for example, student and community organizations, departmental and professional committees and community outreach activities can contribute to students' personal and professional development while drawing on diverse strengths and aspirations. Such activities can be particularly valuable, for example, in assessing the challenges of team leadership or the benefits of networking beyond peers in the programme. They can reveal the need to practise diplomacy and also assertiveness, and to engage in transdisciplinary learning beyond academe (Monk, 1999).

Practice Example 10: Capitalizing on Distilled Experience—Integrating Alumni in the Learning Community

Arguably, academics whose careers have been entirely within academe offer students limited insights into the opportunities and nature of work in private and public national and international arenas. Students benefit from contacts with professionals who validate the specific and generic skills and knowledge that have longer term currency in the workplace (McEwen *et al.*, 2003). To meet the needs of a diverse group of students, departments can draw on their alumni taking care to mirror the employment patterns and diversity of their graduates. Effective practices include: inviting alumni, as individuals or groups, to give guest presentations (Baker, 2007); establishing alumni advice and mentoring networks; and offering annual workshops or conferences integrating students and alumni. Contacts can also be made by including information on departmental and professional websites (e.g. 'my graduates' websites, Baker, 2007; the alumni 'business card' map model, Akron, 2007; and the interviews with geographers in the careers section of the AAG's website). Course assignments can involve students researching alumni contacts and reflecting on ways to prepare further to help capitalize personally on similar vocational opportunities.

Capitalizing on Diversity in Geography and Related Disciplines?

It is worth questioning the extent to which postgraduate teaching in geography is distinctive in its own right in the opportunities it provides to capitalize on diversity? Geographical training has traditionally valued a wide-ranging skills portfolio and a diversity of assessment patterns. Geographers engage in interdisciplinary and multidisciplinary debates and there is a major applied research focus foci around 'environment–society relations' within the sustainable development realm. They continue to bring something distinctive to the intellectual table with the ability to engage and develop insights at different spatial and temporal scales. Geography is well placed in terms of both traditions in teaching and learning methods and in developing subject foci of global concern and engagement to capitalize on diverse postgraduate cohorts. This can help ensure broad and inclusive perspectives, where identifying sustainable solutions requires holistic thinking, interdisciplinary expertise and cultural insights and sensitivity.

The potential to draw strength from diversity in geography and related disciplines is, however, also determined by whether independent or group work forms the sub-disciplinary norms. Debates occur regarding the degree of independence in project creation and implementation at postgraduate level. For example, should postgraduate students be expected to develop an entirely independent piece of work comparable to a thesis or should they be involved in supervisor-'dictated' or -'directed' research? The question takes particular salience in contexts where research clusters and team-based research are being encouraged. Moreover, physical and human geography traditionally differ in their cultures. The science model is built on the notion that group research offers better training for the practice of collaboration in real research. Geographers taking a 'humanities' approach tend to work alone, practising and developing a different range of skills. For these groups, the shift to capitalize on diversity may be greater. In addition, in some Master's programmes in geography and environment, students may have a first degree in another field. Thus these students bring the perspectives of those fields, but also have to work to develop their geography background.

Summary and Conclusions

This paper highlights the potential of diversity to enhance learning and teaching in taught postgraduate programmes. This international, albeit Anglophone discussion has recognized student variations within countries. We have identified six categories of diversity in terms of student background and experiences of different teaching models and methods, programme styles and institutional contexts and prior or concurrent workplace experience (see Table 3). Drawing from our practice examples, we argue that diversity of student peers and staff, beyond the more obvious discipline and cultural types and particularly in the affective and prior learning areas, can be capitalized in raising the 'bar' from undergraduate to postgraduate level in a variety of ways. These include:

- by developing high-level affective learning skills and personal skills valued in leaders in the workplace;
- by developing the potential for advanced co-learning within groups; and
- by active learning in problem situations that require holistic thinking, taking in a range of perspectives and involving sophisticated and informed personal selection from different higher-level knowledge and skills.

Our practice examples show how diversity can be leveraged to support and induct students into professional practice and develop 'creative professionalism' in a variety of ways. Alumni, staff and the wider learning community of employers can also contribute a broad range of potential resources. Workplaces, employees and employment are characterized by diversity; learning how to capitalize on this diversity is an important generic skill worth developing.

There is no 'standard' workplace for geography postgraduates but developing flexible and considerate approaches through study can be important in securing employment.

Principles for capitalizing on diversity involve:

- Enabling individuals to recognize their own skills, expectations and aspirations, and to acknowledge responsibility for their own learning from day one. This 'self-efficacy' can also be supported through understanding others' perspectives and identifying similarities and differences from one's own.
- Integrating students from the workplace as role models for their student peers through face-to-face or virtual networking opportunities. Students with prior experiences of conference attendance in industry or higher education should be encouraged to cascade that experience within the group (Hay *et al.*, 2005).
- Fostering learning on how to capitalize on diversity by engaging with alumni, simulating work-type environments (e.g. mock conferences, writing for different audiences) and offering students opportunities for workplace learning through internship placements.
- Encouraging teachers to learn with students and adapt flexibly to diversity in learning communities, for example by researching and learning together in collaborative, enquiry-based projects that allow different skills and insights to be brought to particular problems (e.g. Le Heron *et al.*, 2006).

Rather than taking a 'one size fits all' approach to learning and teaching, we advocate bringing diversity positively and explicitly into learning design to enable students to engage with and learn from each other in ways that benefit both students and staff/faculty members. We identify three key areas for further research and awareness raising:

(1) The vocationally orientated Master's degree should be distinctive, but the paucity of generic and discipline-specific literature leaves staff/faculty members relatively unsupported. Sharing examples of good practice on how to capitalize on student and staff diversity to enhance the richness of the postgraduate student learning experience, through conference discussion and an appropriate online repository, would be a useful staff-development initiative. Moreover, we believe research must be undertaken into the changing character of the postgraduate student learning experience and the environments within which learning occurs.
(2) The paucity of literature about learning and teaching at Master's level provides an opportunity for geography as a discipline to lead the way forward in this pedagogic research area.
(3) Although debate on the currency of the postgraduate degree is heating up in Europe through the Bologna process (Europe Unit, 2007), perhaps we should also be seeking more commonality between continents and including developing countries in the discussion of qualifications, titles, level descriptors and comparability between postgraduate programmes.

Master's level education needs to retain its traditional academic strengths—development of curiosity, independent learning, and critical thinking—while accepting responsibilities for contributing to society and enhancing students' opportunities to pursue careers beyond academe.

Acknowledgements

This paper originated from discussions at the International Teaching and Learning Network in Geography in Higher Education (INLT) meeting in Brisbane, July 2006. The authors acknowledge the contributions of individuals working on other projects in the postgraduate area: EDGE project director Dr Michael Solem and principal researcher Dr Beth Schlemper and the LTSN-GEES funded 'postgraduateness' project team (Professor Martin Haigh, Oxford Brookes University; Dr Steve Smith, Coventry University; Professor Rob Duck, Dundee University and Dr Liz Wolfenden, Farnborough College of Technology, all UK).

Notes

[1] The full set of SEEC level descriptors involves 17 categories under these four overarching headings.
[2] Fink (2003) offers a complementary taxonomy which includes cognitive and other important domains of learning (e.g. social significance, caring, new feelings, values, making connections) and illustrates how these are interconnected in creating significant learning experience.
[3] Ken Foote has introduced such an activity into Geography Faculty Development Alliance sessions.

References

Akron (2007) Nationally employed department alumni. Available at http://www3.uakron.edu/geography/alumni_memb/Alumni_Files/alumnimapworking.htm (accessed June 2007).

Baker, R. (2007) My graduate students. Available at http://srespeople.anu.edu.au/richard_baker/mygrad.html (accessed June 2007).

Batalova, J. (2007) Spotlight on foreign students and exchange visitors. *Migration Information Source*, 1 November. Available at http://www.migrationinformation.org (accessed June 2007).

BBC News (2004) Overseas students 'set to triple'. Available at http://newsvote.bbc.co.uk/mpapps/pagetools/print/news.bbc.co.uk/2/hi/uk_news/education/3640141.stm (accessed June 2007).

Colker, R. & Day, R. (2003) Educational institution responsibilities and new skill sets, *Renewable Resources Journal*, 21(4), pp. 20–23.

Collins, F. L. (2006) Making Asian students, making students Asian: the racialisation of export education in Auckland, New Zealand, *Asia Pacific Viewpoint*, 47(2), pp. 217–234.

Daniels, J. K. (2002) Writing across borders: an exercise for internationalizing the women's studies classroom, in: M. M. Lay, J. Monk & D. Rosenfelt (Eds) *Encompassing Gender: Integrating International Studies and Women's Studies*, pp. 404–412 (New York: Feminist Press).

Davis, M. (1997) Adult learning: the place of experience, in: P. Knight (Ed.) *Masterclass: Learning, Teaching and Curriculum in Taught Master's Degrees*, pp. 28–38 (London: Cassell).

DEST (Department of Education, Science and Training—Australia) (2006) *Students 2005 [full year]: selected higher education statistics*. Available at http://www.dest.gov.au/NR/rdonlyres/F1331710-F793-4E81-8867-B5FAF1AEC4DE/13781/2005_student_full_year_data.pdf (accessed June 2007).

DETYA (Department of Education, Training and Youth Affairs, Australia) (2000) *Higher Education Students Time Series tables*. Available at http://www.dest.gov.au/NR/rdonlyres/AE11F01D-E517-4BF7-8ECA-8553C31EF206/2481/timeseries00.pdf (accessed June 2007).

Eastwood, D. (2005) A growth market: the increase in taught postgraduate numbers in the environmental sciences, *Planet*, 14, p. 7.

EDGE (2007) Enhancing Departments and Graduate Education. Available at http://www.aag.org/EDGE/edge_research.cfm (accessed June 2007).

Europe Unit (2007) Bologna process. Available at http://www.europeunit.ac.uk/bologna_process/uk_position_on_qualification_length.cfm (accessed June 2007).

Fejes, A., Johansson, K. & Dahlgren, M. A. (2005) Learning to play the seminar game: students' initial encounters with a basic working form in higher education, *Teaching in Higher Education*, 10(1), pp. 29–41.

Field, M., Lee, R. & Field, M. L. (1994) Assessing interdisciplinary learning, *New Directions for Teaching and Learning*, 58, pp. 69–84.

Fink, L. D. (2003) *Creating Significant Learning Experiences: An Integrated Approach to Designing College Courses* (San Francisco: Jossey Bass Higher and Adult Education Series). Available at http:www.ou.edu/idp/significant/WHAT%20IS.pdf (accessed June 2007).

Flinders University (2006) *Student Related Policies and Procedures Manual*. Available at: http://www.flinders.edu.au/ppmanual/student.html (accessed June 2007).

Flinders University (2007) *Pastoral Care Activities for Postgraduate Students*. Available at http://www.ssn.flinders.edu.au/geog/postgrad/pastoralcarepostgrads.php (accessed June 2007).

Garner, M. & Wallace, C. (1997) Supporting Master's degree students, in: P. Knight (Ed.) *Masterclass: Learning, Teaching and Curriculum in Taught Master's Degrees*, pp. 53–62 (London: Cassell).

Golde, C. & Dore, T. (2004) The survey of doctoral education and career preparation: the importance of disciplinary contexts, in: D. Wulff & A. Austin (Eds) *Paths to the Professoriate: Strategies for Enriching the Preparation of Future Faculty*, pp. 19–45 (San Francisco: Jossey Bass).

Graybill, J., Dooling, S., Shandas, V., Withey, J., Dreve, A. & Simon, G. I. (2006) A rough guide to interdisciplinarity: graduate student perspectives, *BioScience*, 56(9), pp. 757–763.

Hall, T., Healey, M. & Harrison, M. (2002) Disabled students and fieldwork: from exclusion to inclusion, *Transactions of the Institute of British Geographers*, 27, pp. 213–231.

Hansen, E., Kennedy, S., Mattingly, D., Mitchneck, B., Monzel, K. & Nairne, C. (1995) Surviving and thriving in graduate school and beyond, *Journal of Geography in Higher Education*, 19(3), pp. 307–315.

Hay, I., Dunn, K. & Street, A. (2005) Making the most of your conference journey, *Journal of Geography in Higher Education*, 29(1), pp. 159–171.

HEFCE/CVCP/SCOP (Higher Education Funding Council For England, Committee of Vice-Chancellors and Principals Standing Conference of Principals) (1996) *Review of Postgraduate Education: Evidence Volume* (Bristol: HEFCE).

HEFCE (Higher Education Funding Council) (2006) *Strategic Plan 2006–2011* (Bristol: HEFCE).

Howenstine, E., Hay, I., Delaney, E., Bell, J., Ross, A., Whelan, A. & Pirani, M. (1988) Using a poster exercise in an introductory geography course, *Journal of Geography in Higher Education*, 12(2), pp. 139–147.

Israel, M. & Hay, I. (2006) *Research Ethics for Social Scientists: Between Ethical Conduct and Regulatory Compliance* (London: Sage Publications).

Ivanitskaya, L., Clark, D., Montgomery, G. & Primeau, R. (2002) Interdisciplinary learning: process and outcomes, *Innovative Higher Education*, 27, pp. 95–111.

JQI (Joint Quality Initiative) (2004) *Shared 'Dublin' descriptors for short cycle, first cycle, second cycle and third cycle awards*. Available at http://www.jointquality.com (accessed May 2007).

Keller, C. & Kros, J. (2000) Teaching communication in an MBA operations research/management science course, *Journal of the Operational Research Society*, 5(12), p. 1433.

Kennedy, H. (2002) *Postgraduate Multimedia Education: Practices, Themes and Issues*. Report from International Institute of Infonomics, School of Cultural and Innovation Studies, University of East London. Available at http://ecdc.info/publications/reports/cmd_benchmark.pdf (accessed April 2007).

Kneale, P. E. (2005) Enthusing staff delivering taught Masters programmes, *Planet*, 14, pp. 13–15.

Knight, P. T. (1997) *Masterclass: Learning, Teaching and Curriculum in Taught Master's Degrees* (London: Cassell).

Lattuca, L. R. (2001) *Creating Interdisciplinarity: Interdisciplinary Research and Teaching among College and University Faculty* (Nashville, TN: Vanderbilt University Press).

Learndirect (2007) *Learning through Work*. Available at http://www.learndirect.co.uk/ (accessed June 2007).

Leask, B. (2006) Plagiarism, cultural diversity and metaphor—implications for academic staff development, *Assessment and Evaluation in Higher Education*, 31(2), pp. 183–199.

Le Heron, R., Baker, R. & McEwen, L. J. (2006) Co-learning: re-linking research and teaching in geography, *Journal of Geography in Higher Education*, 30(1), pp. 77–87.

MSU (2007) The Geography Graduate Group at Michigan State University. Available at http://www.tripleg.geo.msu.edu (accessed June 2007).

McEwen, L. J. (2005) Postgraduate taught course developments in geography, earth sciences and environment in the UK: an initial assessment of drivers, *Planet*, 14, p. 6.

McEwen, L. J., Duck, R., Haigh, M., Smith, S., Wolfenden, L. & Kelly, K. (2005) Evaluating the 'postgraduateness' of vocational taught Masters environmental courses: student perspectives, *Planet*, 14, pp. 8–12.

McEwen, L. J., Haigh, M., Smith, S., Steele, S. & Miller, A. (2003) 'Real world' experiences? Reflections of current and past students on practitioner inputs to environmental taught masters' courses, *Planet*, 10, pp. 18–22.

Monk, J. (1999) Valuing service, *Journal of Geography in Higher Education*, 23(3), pp. 285–289.

Monk, J. (2000) Looking out, looking in: the 'Other' in the Journal of Geography in Higher Education, *Journal of Geography in Higher Education*, 24(2), pp. 163–177.

Moss, P., De Bres, K. J., Cravey, A., Hyndman, J., Hirschboeck, K. K. & Masucci, M. (1999) Toward mentoring as feminist practice: strategies for ourselves and others, *Journal of Geography in Higher Education*, 23(3), pp. 413–427.

National Centre for Work Based Learning Partnerships (2007). Available at http://www.mdx.ac.uk/www/ncwblp/ (accessed June 2007).

Planet (2003) Special Issue: Special Educational Needs and Disabilities—Learning and Teaching Guidance for Geography, Earth and Environmental Sciences, *Planet*, 3(6), GEES Subject Centre, Plymouth. Available at http://www.gees.ac.uk/planet/#PSE3 (accessed June 2007).

QAA (2007) Quality Assurance Agency. Available at: http://www.qaa.ac.uk/ (accessed June 2007).

Ridley, D. (2004) Puzzling experiences in higher education: critical moments for conversation, *Studies in Higher Education*, 29, pp. 91–107.

Sanders, R. (2006) Social justice and women of color in geography: philosophical musings, trying again, *Gender, Place and Culture*, 13, pp. 49–55.

Scheyvens, R., Wild, K. & Overton, J. (2003) International students pursuing postgraduate study in geography: impediments to their learning, *Journal of Geography in Higher Education*, 27(3), pp. 309–323.

Smith, D. G., García, M., Hudgins, C. A., Musil, C. M., Nettles, M. T. & Sedlacek, W. E. (2000) *A Diversity Research Agenda* (Washington, DC: Association of American Colleges and Universities).

SEEC (Southern England Consortium for Credit Accumulation and Transfer) (2003) *Credit Level Descriptors for Further and Higher Education*, Available at http://www.seec-office.org.uk/SEEC%20FE-HECLDs-mar03def-1.doc (accessed June 2007).

Stuart, B. L., Rhodin, A. G. J., Grismer, L. L. & Hansel, T. (2006) Scientific description can imperil species, *Science*, 312, pp. 1137.

SWIG (2007) Supporting Women in Geography. Available at http://www.geog.psu.edu/swig (accessed June 2007).

Thorne, P. (1997) Standards and quality in taught Master's courses, in: P. Knight (Ed.) *Masterclass: Learning, Teaching and Curriculum in Taught Master's Degrees*, pp. 16–27 (London: Cassell).

Tobias, S., Chibin, D. & Aylesworth, K. (1995) *Rethinking Science as a Career: Perception and Realities in the Physical Sciences* (Tucson, AZ: Research Corporation).

Triple, G. (2007) The Geography Graduate Group at Michigan State University. Available at http://www.tripleg.geo.msu.edu/forum/ (accessed June 2007).

Teaching Geography for Social Transformation

JANE WELLENS*, ANDREA BERARDI**, BRIAN CHALKLEY[†],
BILL CHAMBERS[‡], RUTH HEALEY[§], JANICE MONK[^] & JODI VENDER[#]
*Graduate School, University of Nottingham, UK, **Open Systems Research Group, Open University, UK, [†]Teaching and Learning Department, University of Plymouth, UK, [‡]External Relations and Widening Participation, Liverpool Hope University, UK, [§]Department of Geography and Development Studies, University of Chester, UK, [^]School of Geography and Development, University of Arizona, USA, [#]Department of Geography, Pennsylvania State University, USA

ABSTRACT *This paper considers how higher education geography is a discipline that can make a significant contribution to addressing inequality and engaging with the agenda for social change. It adopts the view that the teaching of geography can promote social transformation through the development of knowledge, skills and values in students that encourage social justice and equity. The paper explores how teaching about social transformation is closely interlinked with teaching for social transformation and considers some of the pedagogical approaches that might be used to achieve these. It considers how the lack of diversity of higher education geography teachers impacts on these issues before moving on to consider how the nature of different higher education systems supports or constrains geographers' abilities to teach for social transformation. Finally, the paper ends by asking individuals and geography departments to consider their commitment to teaching for social transformation.*

Introduction

This paper focuses on higher education geography as a discipline that can make a significant contribution towards teaching for social transformation. In arguing for a stronger commitment to the agenda for social change, the paper acknowledges that this is by no means new territory for academic geography. Geographers, have, for example, long been interested in issues of equity and social justice. However, for reasons referred to below, the time is now right for us to re-examine and strengthen our commitment to teaching for change. In so doing, this paper engages with questions such as 'What do we mean by social transformation?', 'What contextual constraints and opportunities do we face?' and 'What pedagogic approaches are most appropriate in teaching for transformation?'

It is recognized, of course, that the answers to these questions will depend, in broad terms, on what kind of social transformation is envisaged. There is inevitably a wide array of societal models and envisaged futures that could be considered as representing strategic, long-term ambitions. However, at the risk of considerable over-simplification, we suggest that the concept of teaching for social transformation can be interpreted in two principal ways:

1. teaching that aims to promote knowledge, skills and values amongst all students that, through critical thinking, encourages social justice and equity;
2. teaching that fosters conservative and neo-liberal goals such as the re-production of the labour force through vocationally oriented education.

The authors wish to make clear at the outset that this paper adopts the first position and is focused around issues of social justice and inclusivity. This reading of teaching for social transformation encompasses the multi-faceted nature of social justice, as described by Gewirtz & Cribb (2002), compared with the second and more utilitarian reading. It reflects a desire for curricula not only to address issues related to the distribution of economic, cultural and social resources, but also to recognize and draw from the plurality of cultural perspectives and knowledge, particularly of students and faculty. However, as Thrupp & Tomlinson (2005, p. 549) point out, "although social justice is a central concept in many academic discussions of education policy it tends to suffer from the charge of utopianism or idealism, as well as accusations of vagueness and oversimplification". They also highlight that this vagueness and oversimplification "often just reflect the complexity and contestedness of achieving social justice in education" which "require more than liberal 'problem-solving' approaches, with their technicist and reductionist assumptions" (p. 549).

For many, the achievement of neo-liberal goals is negatively bound up with the 'new managerial' agendas in higher education (Riddell *et al.*, 2005), which are associated with teaching audits and target setting, for example, requirements to include the development of transferable skills within the curricula to enhance students' employability. These issues are addressed elsewhere and readers are pointed in particular to Brown *et al.* (2004), Maguire & Guyer (2004), the (2001) special collection of *Planet* on Embedding Careers Education in the Curricula of Geography, Earth and Environmental Sciences (http://www.gees.ac.uk/pubs/planet/index.htm) and others, which focus, for example, on promoting geographers' employability (see Rooney *et al.*, 2006).

Why Social Transformation?

Our paper opens by highlighting the need for change in geographical education. In part, this is because of major developments in the world we study: in particular, the growing and increasingly complex forms of economic and social inequality at all scales of analysis (Kanbur & Venables, 2005). At the global level, 80% of the world's Gross Domestic Product is held by 1 billion people largely in the developed world and the remaining 20% is shared by 5 billion people living in developing countries (UN, 2005). At local and regional scales too there is a growing gap between the rich and the poor and an increasing differentiation between their economic situations, access to health and education and representation in legislation and judicial processes (UN, 2005). For example, whilst the proportion of the global population living in extreme poverty declined between 1981 and 2001, in sub-Saharan Africa the situation has worsened, exacerbated by the HIV/AIDS epidemic (UN, 2005). For geographers, exploration of these intense spatial and social contrasts provides both new opportunities for academic enquiry and important issues to be addressed within geographical curricula. They also give a renewed moral imperative to teaching for change in an increasingly divided world. Moreover, these issues of equity and justice are inter-generational as well as contemporary. The launch in January 2005 of the United Nations Decade for Sustainable Development raises major questions about resource use, climate change and species extinction, which require us all to think critically about long-term equity issues and meeting the needs of future generations.

Of course many geographical curricula already address issues of economic and social inequality within modules or courses. These provide students with an understanding of the issues resulting in inequality; however, teaching about social transformation develops the relationship between activism and the academy (Hay 2001a; Cloke, 2002). Previously the argument has been that solutions to societal problems lie in hands outside the classroom, such as government bodies. However, classrooms can be "a microcosm of the emancipatory societies we seek to encourage" (Hay 2001a, p. 170). bell hooks (1994, p. 12) argues that "the classroom remains the most radical space of possibility in the academy". Hay (2001b), while recognizing the danger of naïve idealism, believes that through changing classrooms we may change the world. Geography offers an opportunity "to include the voices of marginalised people in academic representations of their lives" (Cook, 2000, p. 13). It can provide a critical approach to addressing inequalities in power relations (Curran & Roberts, 2001). Bondi (2004) and Heyman (2000) argue that the geography classroom should be a site of political engagement and highlight the importance of students' examining the meaning of social justice and equity in their own lives. However, as Valentine (2005, p. 486) stresses, "this does not mean telling students what to think or value but rather giving them the skills to think through problems for themselves and to value argument". In addition, Merritt (2004, p. 95) argues that "geographers are particularly well suited to study and teach concepts related to social justice because social injustice is caused by and expressed in such intrinsically geographical ways as ghettos, borders, margins, peripheries and regions at different scales".

The importance of re-focusing geography teaching in the directions outlined above is further reinforced by a number of trends and pressures affecting the health and status of our discipline and by its ability to recruit students. Arguably, we need to change not only to keep abreast of major global developments and problems but also to protect and enhance the welfare of our subject. Many recent surveys in a variety of different countries point to a decline in the subject's popularity at both school and university levels. The international evidence is generally not encouraging. Gerber (2001) surveyed the situation in 31 countries and found the position of geography a cause for concern. A recent European survey by Donert (2004) indicated that the subject is under serious threat in 38 per cent of school and 45 per cent of higher education systems. Similarly, in a survey of 14 countries, Rawling (2004, p. 168) identified the "uncertain place" of geography in both the primary and secondary school curriculum. In the UK, Gardner & Craig (2001) highlighted the declining popularity of school geography and the threat this poses to the discipline at higher education level. In the United States, Bednarz & Bednarz (2004, p. 210) have expressed the view that, faced with increasing competition from other disciplines, geography runs the risk of being left behind.

In the schools sector the position and role of disciplines within the curriculum is normally centrally controlled by governments. It seems that geographers have not been sufficiently active or successful in persuading politicians and education bureaucrats of the value of our subject (Rawlinson *et al.*, 2004). Moreover, the difficulties facing geography in schools inevitably impact on the discipline's status and success at higher education level, although here the curriculum is generally less centrally controlled and more responsive to factors such as student demand. However, if fewer students take geography in schools this of itself is likely to reduce recruitment for degree courses. As a result in the UK, for example, some smaller and less well known geography departments have been forced to close (Gardner & Craig, 2001).

Although geography's position is by no means entirely negative, the current problems do provide a prompt for the discipline to review its relationship with government, with education policy-makers, with the public and with our students. There are, of course, many different ways of improving the discipline's position, particularly with regard to its impact on public policy (Martin, 2001; Massey, 2001; Lee, 2002; Dorling & Shaw, 2002; Murphy *et al.*, 2005; Wong, 2005), but certainly one of these is to strengthen our engagement with the agenda for social change. Ruth Wilson Gilmore, writing in Murphy *et al.* (2005, p. 181) specifically addresses the role of scholar-activists and the production of geography and concludes that: "Geography is ... so wide open for good use. Certainly the key words of the contemporary moment—globalization, racism, migration, war, new imperialism, environmental degradation, fundamentalism, human rights—bespeak and connect all kinds of complexities."

Geography must enable its students to play a part in engaging with these major questions and of contributing intelligently and knowledgeably to debates about social transformation and how to achieve it. However, it is acknowledged that for some geographers such a reorientation may be extremely difficult due to governmental and/or institutional opposition. Quinn & Stuart (2004) provide examples of the real threats faced by academics working in nations with oppressive regimes whose activities move beyond officially sanctioned limits. These can include arrest on false charges, trial and imprisonment, torture disappearance and death. Even within democracies, where academic freedom is highly valued, criticizing government policy and challenging public preconceptions can have negative impacts. Derek Gregory writing in Murphy *et al.* (2005) draws on examples from the 'war on terror' to urge geographers to counter the 'imaginative geographies' that reside in the public arena, but identifies that such approaches face obstacles which are more than intellectual. He highlights how, in the United States, scholars of area studies and, in particular, Middle Eastern Studies have been adversely affected because their views do not conform to those of the Bush government.

Teaching about and for Social Transformation

Teaching social transformation has three aspects. These are: teaching *about* social transformation; teaching *for* social transformation and, finally, *how* to teach for social transformation. These three topics are closely interlinked. Teaching *about* social transformation can lead to teaching *for* social transformation as the students' views are affected through a wider understanding of society, both locally and globally. Likewise, teaching *for* social transformation inevitably leads to teaching *about* social transformation. In addition, both are influenced by the forms of pedagogy that are employed (as discussed later in the paper).

The aim of social transformation within the lens of higher education is, as we see it, to challenge students' preconceived perceptions of the economy, society, environment and politics constructed through social structures. By engaging with higher education, students develop the skills and knowledge to analyse critically their perceptions of the world around them, and its various national and cultural groups.

Geography can play an important role in extending beyond national and international stereotypes and in promoting cultural empathy. In some countries, students of geography are predominantly white and middle class. Through geographers teaching *about* social transformation, the distinction between 'us' and 'them' can be challenged (Cook, 2000). Teaching about social transformation challenges categories of the 'other', which in turn creates awareness of 'self' (Jackson, 2000). Raju (2004) discusses how she came to teach geographies of gender in India. She explains how teaching about the 'other', in contrast to traditional geography courses, was initially discouraged by her colleagues. However, she argues that her "teaching of gender, both pedagogically and conceptually, remains interlinked with the legacy of the discipline of geography in India that [she has] inherited" (p. 64). Teaching about the 'other' is important to achieve social transformation. Further examples of othering can be seen in the categories of gender (Oberhauser, 2002; Smith, 2004), race (Wall, 2001; Goudge, 2003), sexuality (Valentine, 1994), class (Ulrich, 2000), disability (Hall *et al.*, 2002) and nationality (Scheyvens *et al.*, 2002).

Geographers teaching *about* social transformation can also lead to teaching *for* social transformation. As Robinson (1988) illustrates, teaching about social transformation can deconstruct students' initial hostility, sympathy or paternalism towards the 'other' and move towards achieving what he terms "realistic empathy", that is "a willingness to accept another person as equal; an understanding of the context within which the other person lives (social, environmental, economic and political); and an acceptance that the other person's value system and 'way of looking at things' is a valid alternative to one's own" (pp. 154–155). Geography as a subject can develop this view. Students are taught to build respect for the 'other'. Once students have learnt the value of the perspective of the 'other' within the discipline of geography, they can also transfer it to non-academic situations.

The increasing social diversity of students in higher education can assist and enrich the teaching of social transformation. In many countries the expansion of higher education is associated with the inclusion of a wider range of students in terms of factors such as class, age and ethnicity. This greater social mix will open up new opportunities for learning alongside and at first hand from people with very different social backgrounds. This kind of experience can sometimes produce deeper learning than that acquired simply through lectures and textbooks. A variety of students in the classroom enables teachers to build upon and utilize the range of perspectives that are present (Cook, 2000).

Pedagogy for Social Transformation

In exploring the issue of how to teach for social transformation, our discussion begins with the concept of positionality. This is the notion that where an individual is located in the social structure as a whole and which institutions he/she is in affect how she/he understands the world. In higher education the positionality of both the teacher and the researcher needs to be acknowledged. First, the positionality of the teacher influences his/her knowledge and approach to social transformation. Second, teaching that acknowledges the positionality of the researcher is important in enabling students' full understanding of the research findings. For example, Besio (2003), in her work in Pakistan, explicitly discusses how her positionality as a researcher impacted on the data she collected, and hence the information she could teach to students. Due to her whiteness she was treated as a 'sahib'—a masculine, colonial subject position—by the villagers. Although in a privileged position, Besio was uncomfortable with this image as she could not participate in the 'goings-on' of the village. However, through this position she was given power over the villagers to talk to people that she would not have been able to if she was a woman of their ethnicity.

The positionality of the students impacts on the output of social transformation in higher education. Students need to "learn to trust their own, rather than solely the teacher's, interpretations of things" (Cook, 2000, p. 15). Through approaches such as active learning, the student's positionality is integral to the learning process. The views that students have are impacted through the structural position from which they have experienced the world. Angus *et al.* (2001) argue that students who take personally the issues they study draw these ideas into their everyday lives. The students' positionality is a part of their opinions, yet their studies enable them to analyse critically their views of the world at large.

The key question that we need to ask is whether our teaching reinforces the established order or helps to transform society. There is a danger that the role of teachers as 'professionals' places students in a situation of relative incompetence, where teaching could be seen as the exclusive domain of the teachers, in that the active participation of students is a challenge to teachers' professional practice. This approach limits feedback mechanisms that would challenge the students' and teachers' positionality. This absence of a 'co-evolution of teaching and learning' maintains the status quo, within both education and society.

Several attempts to establish dialogue between teachers and students have emerged, most notably Paulo Freire's critical pedagogy, where teachers engage students in a process of 'conscientization' that reveals social reality with all its often oppressive manifestations. Although proven to be effective in social transformation, this approach raises problematic issues in that it is questionable whether students are able to develop their own understanding of social reality or are yet again provided with pre-formulated dogmas by the teaching profession. One can envisage how Freire's critical pedagogy could transform society from one oppressive established order to another. In this paper we steer away from prescribing in detail a particular pedagogical approach for social transformation, in that a prescribed approach can become "a blind spot when it evolves into practice lacking any manner of critical reflection being connected to it" (Ison, 2000).

If we want to establish a method of social transformation through critical reflective practice, we need to introduce a process of self-questioning that challenges our positionality as defined by our own value system and lays it open to the critique of all those who may be concerned. (The term 'we' is used in the generic sense, and should include the teachers, the students and the studied context/participants.) But challenging an individual's perspective is not enough. Most of our teaching is based on a flawed assumption that learning is an individual process. Teaching for social transformation is aimed at changing society, and thus should be underpinned by a new paradigm based on learning as a social phenomenon. As Etienne Wenger writes: "learning is an issue of engaging in and contributing to the practices of [an individual's] communities" (Wenger, 1998, p. 7). He goes on to say that "what looks promising are inventive ways of engaging students in meaningful practices, of providing access to resources that enhance their participation, of opening their horizons so that they can put themselves on learning trajectories they can identify with, and involving them in actions, discussions and reflections that make a difference to the communities that they value" (1998, p. 10). At the core of a social process of learning is that learning should be underpinned by social interaction, collaboration and students working together (Brown et al., 1998). Co-learning, with students and staff engaging in inquiry-based learning (Le Heron et al., 2006) provides another potential opportunity to engage with social transformation.

Another form of learning that aligns particularly well with social transformation is learning linked to public scholarship and service to the community. In many universities students, in effect, withdraw from participating in society for the duration of their course rather than connecting to their communities. *Public scholarship* refers to the conceptualization and practice of knowledge that applies scholarship—the "discovery and creative performance generated by faculty and students in their teaching and learning, research and service—to the civic, cultural, artistic, social, economic, and educational well-being of the community" (Cohen & Yapa, 2003, pp. 5–6). *Service learning* is a pedagogy that integrates community service into an academic context. Essential elements of *service learning* that distinguish it from *service projects* include academic learning and reflection that occur before, during and after the actual experience. Service learning becomes public scholarship when issues of civic and social consequence are engaged in ways that both learn from and give back to the communities involved, and engagement with the community "becomes an integral part of how new knowledge is generated" (ibid., p. 6).

Geographers have incorporated community-based service learning into coursework covering introductory geography (Orf, 1998; Zeigler, 1999); urban geography (Bouman et al., 1998; Yapa, 2000; Downey, 2001; Veness, 2001); poverty/hunger issues (Jarosz et al., 1996; Yapa, 2000); community development (Kotval, 1998; Waddington, 2001; Dennis, 2003) land-use planning (Dorsey 2001); gender geography (Oberhauser, 2002); regional geography (Bein, 2002; Vender et al., 2002, Vender, 2004); field/research methods (Buckingham-Hatfield, 1995; Crump, 2002); geomorphology (McEwen, 1996); water resources (Fearn, 2001), GIS (Benhart, 1998; Dennis, 2003); and pre-service teacher education (Rice, 2003). Service learning may be incorporated as part of a single-semester/term course, or as a multi-course sequence covering several semesters/terms; the service component may be optional (e.g. as an alternative to a library-based research project) or a mandatory, integral part of the course.

Who will do the Teaching?

In developing appropriate forms of pedagogy and in teaching for and about social transformation within geography, a major consideration has to be who the current and future teachers of geography in higher education are. Numerous surveys have shown that there is a lack of diversity within the higher education teaching faculty in general (see, for example, Sax et al., 1999 cited in Becher & Trowler, 2001, and HESA, 2003). Moreover, it is generally considered that diversity within geography faculty is less than for many other disciplines. This is illustrated by the fact that the INLT itself is so UK/USA dominated and

Anglophone (Shepherd *et al.*, 2000), as highlighted by the nationalities of the authors of this paper.

This has implications for the discipline in terms of the ability of faculty to teach for and about social transformation. Indeed, it might be questioned whether social transformation can be taught effectively by faculty comprising mainly white, male, upper-middle-class academics. There are also questions about the extent to which the discipline can attract and recruit students from more diverse backgrounds. Haigh (2002, p. 53) highlights that many faculty have limited personal knowledge of the cultural backgrounds of many of their international students, and this is also true of those home students from cultural and ethnic groups different from their own. Oberhauser (2002) and Lee (1997) discuss how many geography faculty have lived only briefly, or not at all, as 'foreigners' or as 'social minorities' in other, usually non-European, regions. Lee (1997, p. 265) stresses the important point that "While the faculty remains relatively homogeneous, higher education has a limited capacity to offer majority students opportunities to learn about their culture from the perspectives of other cultures and groups" because as Johnson-Bailey & Cervero (1997) point out: "When learners and teachers enter classrooms they bring their positions in the hierarchies that order the worlds, including those based on race, gender, class, sexual orientation and disability."

Furthermore, the divergent nature of the sub-disciplines within geography, and particularly the human–physical schism, mean that faculty vary in their willingness to embrace, or even engage with, research and hence teach topics that are of social relevance. For physical geographers in particular, the drivers of the research funding bodies mean that they have to be pragmatic in ensuring that grant proposals meet the needs of funding bodies, and including elements that address issues of social transformation may be problematic. Even in human geography, there has been an insufficient focus on research and teaching for and about issues of social transformation. Cloke (2002, p. 591) reflects that "the self serving nature of contemporary research conditions is conspiring against the development of a sustained sense for the other". McDowell (1992) highlighted how the paucity of women in the discipline contributed to the lack of attention to gender issues in the curriculum and pedagogy in general. However, to some extent this situation has slowly started to be addressed and Monk (2000) explores some of these issues, highlighting how, in articles in the *Journal of Geography in Higher Education*, the most visible 'others' have been women, with a paucity of articles on development issues. The 2004 multi-country Symposium section of the *Journal of Geography in Higher Education* on gendered patterns of staff and student participation lends credence to this idea, though it highlights how the effects are dynamic and relate to specificities of context (Droogleever Fortuijn, 2004; Garcia-Ramon & Pujol, 2004; Monk *et al.*, 2004; Timar & Jelenszkyne, 2004; Yeoh *et al.*, 2004). In the same issume Mahtani (2004) highlights issues for women of colour in Britain, the US and Canada.

It is clear that as well as teaching for and about social transformation, geography faculty have to question how they can ensure that the discipline is attractive and relevant to people from all sectors of society in order that over time the diversity of both staff and students increases (Monk, 2000). If the social transformation agenda is to be addressed effectively, geography will need both a more diverse staffing mix and also professional support and development for those colleagues who wish to contribute to the agenda but who do not yet feel equipped to do so.

Higher Education Contexts

The nature of systems of higher education also has a substantial bearing on how we are constrained or supported in efforts to teach for social transformation. Some systems are nationally centralized, others decentralized, influencing the extent to which institutions and individuals within them have freedom to innovate. Furthermore, higher education has changed considerably over the past two decades and factors such as increased student numbers and changes in their demographic profile, changes in the nature of funding, greater demands for accountability, emphasis on the economic benefits of higher education, and increased variety in teaching and learning methods all are important issues that limit or provide opportunities for teaching for social transformation. Altbach and Davis (1999) provide a more detailed overview of the challenges and changes to higher education and compare the international situation. The relative significance of these different issues is highly system specific and we illustrate this through a comparative look at three different cases.

Indiresan (2000) has identified the difficulties of instigating change in Indian higher education. In a society that has been highly diverse yet stratified in terms of caste, gender, religion, region and language, desires for social change have seen rapidly increasing demands for higher education over the last several decades. Progress is potentially facilitated but also constrained by the highly centralized system and the nature of decision-making. Government policies have promoted diversity and advancement for those who have been excluded, especially members of scheduled castes and scheduled tribes. But there have been an array of legal challenges to national policies that attempt to set aside enrolment quotas for those who have been disadvantaged (Sharma, 2000). An emphasis on teaching for external examinations, coupled with the continuation of the colonial system whereby the curriculum and examinations of a high proportion of colleges are controlled by the universities of which they are 'affiliates', creates another set of obstacles. The prestige of English-language medium institutions and the inadequate preparation of disadvantaged students, including secondary education in local languages, present additional problems. Motivating change in institutions and populations that have been privileged by existing conditions, and also among teachers who have limited resources and who may not be inclined to take risks, remains a major challenge.

Social transformation through reshaping of the higher education system is also on the agenda in South Africa, presenting some of the same challenges that have been noted in the Indian case, such as dealing with language differences. Most obvious are the goals of redressing the disadvantages to African, Coloured and Indian students that were brought about by separation of educational institutions during the apartheid era (Badsha & Harper, 2000). Among key issues are the widening of participation without provision of the finance to support it; dealing with the legacy of failing to prepare non-white students in the schools; attracting students and staff to the historically Black institutions that are frequently in remote locations; and the historical divisions in curricular orientations that channelled Black students into arts, humanities and educational fields while they remained under-represented in scientific and technical areas.

Initially, it would seem as if the substantial decentralization and plurality of institutional types in American higher education (public/private; undergraduate/graduate; teaching oriented/research oriented) offer a significantly different model, with greater freedom for curricular innovation than in systems more subject to central public control. Cultural values support competing models of education: commitment to transmission of a core culture and reliance on 'classic' texts in some institutions; marked experimentation and more radical commitments in others; technical and vocational orientations in yet others. Cutting across institutional types is a distinctive national expectation that the bachelor's degree will include a substantial component of 'general education' in the humanities, social sciences and natural sciences, as well as preparation in written expression and quantitative skills. This expectation would suggest that openings exist for curricular innovations that promote teaching for social transformation. Funding for curriculum projects, not only from governmental agencies but from private sources, also adds to a climate of pluralism. In this setting, and in response to larger social pressures and local interest and leadership, over the last three or more decades innovations have been made in introducing ethnic studies (such as African-American, Chicano/a Mexican-American, Asian-American, and American Indian Studies) and women's, gender, and gay, lesbian, bisexual and transgender studies, as well as initiatives to 'mainstream' multicultural or 'diversity' initiatives into other courses. Still, these initiatives are not immune from national governmental directions. More liberal governments have offered targeted funds for changes of particular kinds (such as projects to create materials in women's studies or 'mainstreaming' ethnic studies). More conservative governments have made it very difficult to secure support for such undertakings.

We could expand the examples of systemic issues, but instead will conclude these comments by noting some international trends that are inhibiting teaching for 'progressive' social transformation in a number of contexts: declining budgets for higher education; increased external scrutiny of 'quality'; tuition fee increases; increasing casualization of the teaching staff; pressures on students to pursue technical education rather than undertake studies that promote critical thinking and exposure to alternative world-views (Arriaga Lemus, 2002). As we strive to pursue teaching for social transformation, it is important that we understand and develop strategies to work with and against the contexts as necessary.

Conclusions

As we move further into the twenty-first century, it is becoming increasingly clear that many of the world's major problems are strongly geographical in nature. The misuse of the earth's resources, environmental degradation, climate change, global inequality and intercultural relations are all central parts of geography's territory. While retaining its academic rigour and scholarship, geographical education has, we would argue, a duty to teach both about and for the kinds of changes that can help to create a world which is more equal and more sustainable. A more explicit focus on social transformation would enrich our students' education and also help to raise the discipline's status and profile. It would help to release us from the present paradoxical situation where our discipline appears in many countries to be faltering at the very moment when its knowledge, insights and skills have never been more needed.

In describing a vision of teaching for social justice, Bigelow *et al.* (1994) called for curriculum and classroom practice to have the following characteristics:

- grounded in the lives of students;
- critical and linked to real-world problems;

- multicultural, anti-racist and pro-justice;
- participatory and experiential;
- hopeful, joyful, kind and visionary;
- activist;
- academically rigorous;
- culturally sensitive;
- concerned with issues beyond the classroom walls.

In the years since Bigelow's paper the effects of globalization, climate change, increased geo-cultural tensions and rising inequality have made stronger still the case for geographical education to adopt these qualities. Given the variety of institutional, cultural and national contexts within which geography is taught, there are, of course, many different ways in which these principles can be turned into practice. However, they do provide a broad template against which both geography departments and individual academics can review and assess their own curriculum and their teaching methods. So, this paper ends with two challenging questions for both departments and individuals to consider. To what extent are you committed to teaching about/for social transformation? And in so far as social transformation is part of your vision and values, how far do your curriculum and teaching match up?

Acknowledgements

The authors would like gratefully to acknowledge the valued contribution of Hans de Jong to the discussion that provided the initial basis for the article.

References

Altbach, P. G. & Davis, T. M. (1999) Global challenge and national response: notes for an international dialogue on Higher Education, *International Higher Education*, 14, pp. 2–5.

Angus, T., Cook, I. & Evans, J. (2001) A manifesto for cyborg pedagogy?, *International Research in Geographical and Environmental Education*, 10(2), pp. 195–201.

Arriaga Lemus, M. de la Luz (2002) Pubic education is not for sale: constructing continental social alliances, in: International Committee of the Professional Staff Congress (Eds.) *Globalization, Privatization, War: In Defence of Public Education in the Americas*, Summary of Proceedings of a Conference held 26 October 2002, pp. 9–11 (New York: City University of New York).

Badsha, N. & Harper, A. (2000) South African higher education: diversity overview, in: E. F. Beckham (Ed.) *Diversity, Democracy and Higher Education: A View from Three Nations*, pp. 11–31 (Washington, DC: Association of American Colleges and Universities).

Becher, T. & Trowler, P. R. (2001) *Academic Tribes and Territories*, 2nd edn (Buckingham: Society for Research into Higher Education & Open University Press).

Bednarz, S. W. & Bednarz, R. S. (2004) School geography in the United States, in: W. A. Kent, E. Rawling & A. Robinson (Eds) *Geographical Education: Expanding Horizons in a Shrinking World*, pp. 209–212 (Glasgow: Scottish Association of Geography Teachers and Geographical Education Commission of the International Geographical Union).

Bein, R. (2002) Service learning for a Latin American geography course, Paper presented at the 87th Annual Meeting of the National Council for Geographic Education, October 2002, Philadelphia, PA.

Benhart, J. (1998) Teaching Geographical Information Systems through applied project work for local organizations Paper presented at the 94th Annual meeting of the Association of American Geographers, March 1998, Boston, MA.

Besio, K. (2003) Steppin' in it: post-coloniality in northern Pakistan, *Area*, 35(1), pp. 24–33.

Bigelow, B., Christensen, L., Karp, S., Miner, B. & Peterson, B. (1994) *Creating Classrooms for Equity and Social Justice, Rethinking Our Classrooms: Teaching for Equity and Justice* (Milwaukee: Rethinking Schools).

Bondi, L. (2004) Power dynamics in feminist classrooms: making the most of inequalities?, in: J. Sharp, D. Thein & K. Browne (Eds) *Gender and Geography: 20 Years On*, pp. 175–182 (Glasgow: Women in Geography Study Group).

Bouman, M., Peterman, W. & Martin, W. (1998) Communiversity: a model for faculty, student and community collaboration, Paper presented at the Annual Meeting of the West Lakes Division of the Association of American Geographers, Madison, WI.

Brown, J. S., Collins, A. & Duguid, S. (1998) Situated cognition and the culture of learning, *Educational Research*, 18(1), pp. 32–42.

Brown, S., Butcher, V., Drew, L., Elton, L., Harvey, L., Kneale, P., Knight, P., Little, B., Moreland, N. & Yorke, M. (2004) *Pedagogy for Employability*, Learning and Employability Series, No 8 (York: Higher Education Academy).

Buckingham-Hatfield, S. (1995) Student–community partnership: advocating community enterprise projects in geography, *Journal of Geography in Higher Education*, 19(2), pp. 143–150.

Cloke, P. (2002) Deliver us from evil? Prospects for living ethically and acting politically in human geography, *Progress in Human Geography*, 26(5), pp. 587–604.

Cohen, J. & Yapa, L. (2003) Introduction: what is public scholarship?, in: J. Cohen & L. Yapa (Eds) *A Blueprint for Public Scholarship at Penn State*, pp. 5–8 (University Park: Pennsylvania State University Office of Undergraduate Education).

Cook, I. (2000) Nothing can ever be the case of 'us' and 'them' again: exploring the politics of difference through border pedagogy and student journal writing, *Journal of Geography in Higher Education*, 24(1), pp. 13–27.

Crump, J. R. (2002) Learning by doing: implementing community service-based learning, *Journal of Geography*, 101(4), pp. 144–152.

Curran, M. & Roberts, S. M. (2001) Dilemmas of difference: teaching the 'Non-West' critically, *International Research in Geographical and Environmental Education*, 10(2), pp. 179–183.

Dennis, S. F. (2003) Action research at the intersection of youth development, urban planning, and qualitative GIS: the South Allison Hill youth mapping project, Paper presented at the 99th Annual meeting of the Association of American Geographers March 2003, New Orleans, LA

Donert, K. (2004) HERODOT: a thematic network for geography departments in higher education, in: W. A. Kent & A. Powell (Eds) *Geography and Citizenship Education Research Perspectives*, pp. 102–113 (London: University of London, Institute of Education, International Geographical Union Commission of Geographical Education).

Dorling, D. & Shaw, M. (2002) Geographies of the agenda: public policy, the discipline and its (re)'turns, *Progress in Human Geography*, 26(5), pp. 629–646.

Dorsey, B. (2001) Linking theories of service-learning and undergraduate geography education, *Journal of Geography*, 100(3), pp. 124–132.

Downey, G. (2001) Teaching urban geography with community-based service learning, Paper presented at the 97th Annual Meeting of the Association of American Geographers, March 2001, New York.

Droogleever Fortuijn, J. D. (2004) Gender representation and participation in Dutch human geography departments, *Journal of Geography in Higher Education*, 28(1), pp. 133–141.

Fearn, M. L. (2001) Service learning in geography, *Journal of College Science Teaching*, 30(7), pp. 470–473.

Garcia-Ramon, M. D. & Pujol, H. (2004) Gender representation in academic geography in Catalonia (Spain): towards a masculinization of discipline?, *Journal of Geography in Higher Education*, 28(1), pp. 111–119.

Gardner, R. & Craig, L. (2001) Is geography history?, *Journal of Geography in Higher Education*, 25(1), pp. 5–10.

Gerber, R. (2001) The state of geographical education around the world, *International Journal of Geographical Education*, 10(4), pp. 349–362.

Gewirtz, S. & Cribb, A. (2002) Plural conceptions of social justice: implications for policy sociology, *Journal of Education Policy*, 17(5), pp. 499–509.

Goudge, P. (2003) *The Whiteness of Power: Racism in Third World Development and Aid* (London: Lawrence & Wishart).

Haigh, M. J. (2002) Internationalisation of the curriculum: designing inclusive education for a small world, *Journal of Geography in Higher Education*, 26(1), pp. 49–66.

Hall, T., Healey, M. & Harrison, M. (2002) Fieldwork and disabled students: discourses of exclusion and inclusion, *Transactions of the Institute of British Geographers*, 27(2), pp. 213–231.

Hay, I. (2001a) Engaging lessons: classrooms as sites of engagement in activist critical geography, *International Research in Geographical and Environmental Education*, 10(2), pp. 168–173.

Hay, I. (2001b) Editorial: Critical geography and activism in higher education, *Journal of Geography in Higher Education*, 25(2), pp. 141–146.
HESA (2003) Full time academic staff in UK institutions by location of institution, gender, principal source of salary and clinical status 2002/03 Available at http:www.hesa.ac.uk/holisdocs/pubinfo/staff/staff0203.htm (accessed September 2005).
Heyman, R. (2000) Research, pedagogy and instrumental geography, *Antipode*, 32(3), pp. 292–307.
hooks, b. (1994) *Teaching to Transgress: Education as the Practice of Freedom* (New York: Routledge).
Indiresan, J. (2000) The dynamics of diversity and higher education: initiatives and challenges in the Indian Context, in: E. F. Beckham (Ed.) *Diversity, Democracy and Higher Education: A View from Three Nations*, pp. 51–72 (Washington, DC: Association of American Colleges and Universities).
Ison, R. L. (2000) Supported open learning and emergence of learning communities: the case of the Open University UK, in: R. Miller (Ed.) *Creating Learning Communities: Models, Resources and New Ways of Thinking about Teaching and Learning*, pp. 90–96 (Brandon, VT: Solomon Press).
Jackson, P. (2000) Other/otherness, in: Johnston, R. J., Gregory, D., Pratt, G. & Watts, M. (Eds) *The Dictionary of Human Geography*, 4th edn, p. 568, (Oxford: Blackwell).
Jarosz, L. & Johnson-Bogart, K. (1996) New concepts of the relationship between college and the community: the potential of service learning, *College Teaching*, 44(Summer), pp. 83–88.
Johnson-Bailey, J. & Cerveo, R. M. (2005) Beyond facilitation in adult education: power dynamics in teaching and learning practices Paper delivered at the 27th Annual Standing Conference on University Teaching and Research in the Education of Adults Conference "Crossing Borders, Breaking Boundaries: Research in the Education of Adults", 1–3 July 1997, University of London. Available at http://www.leeds.ac.uk/educol/documents/000000248.htm (accessed September 2005).
Kanbur, R. & Venables, A. J. (Eds) (2005) *Spatial Inequality and Development* (Oxford: Oxford University Press).
Kotval, Z. (1998) Opportunities and constrains to community outreach in the planning curriculum Paper presented at the 94th Annual Meeting of the Association of American Geographers, March 1998, Boston, MA.
Le Heron, R., Baker, R. & McEwen, L. (2006) Co-learning: re-linking research and teaching in geography, *Journal of Geography in Higher Education*, 30(1), pp. 77–87.
Lee, D. O. (1997) Arena Symposium: multicultural education in geography in the USA, *Journal of Geography in Higher Education*, 21(2), pp. 261–268.
Lee, R. (2002) Geography, policy and geographical agendas—a short intervention in a continuing debate, *Progress in Human Geography*, 26(5), pp. 627–628.
Maguire, S. & Guyer, C. (2004) Preparing geography, earth and environmental science (GEES) students for employment in the enterprise culture, *Journal of Geography in Higher Education*, 28(3), pp. 369–379.
Mahtani, M. (2004) Mapping race and gender in the academy: the experiences of women of colour faculty and graduate students in Britain, the US, and Canada, *Journal of Geography in Higher Education*, 28(1), pp. 91–99.
Martin, R. (2001) Geography and public policy: the case of the missing agenda, *Progress in Human Geography*, 25(2), pp. 189–210.
Massey, D. (2001) Geography on the agenda, *Progress in Human Geography*, 25(1), pp. 5–17.
McDowell, L. (1992) Engendering change: curriculum transformation in human geography, *Journal of Geography in Higher Education*, 16(2), pp. 185–197.
McEwen, L. (1996) Student involvement with the Regionally Important Geomorphological Site (RIGS) Scheme: An opportunity to learn geomorphology and gain transferable skills, *Journal of Geography in Higher Education*, 20(3), pp. 367–378.
Merritt, C. D. (2004) Social justice: what is it? why teach it? *Journal of Geography*, 103(3), pp. 93–101.
Monk, J. (2000) Looking out, looking in: the 'other' in the Journal of Geography in Higher Education, *Journal of Geography in Higher Education*, 24(2), pp. 83–90.
Monk, J., Droogleever, J. D. & Raleigh, C. (2004) The representation of women in academic geography: contexts, climate and curricular, *Journal of Geography in Higher Education*, 28(1), pp. 83–90.
Murphy, A. B., de Blij, H. J., Turner, B. L., Wilson Gilmore, R. & Gregory, D. (2005) The role of geography in public debate, *Progress in Human Geography*, 29(2), pp. 165–193.
Oberhauser, A. M. (2002) Examine gender and community through critical pedagogy, *Journal of Geography in Higher Education*, 26(1), pp. 19–31.

Orf, T. M. (1998) Utilizing service learning in a collegiate geography curriculum, Paper presented at the 94th Annual Meeting of the Association of American Geographers March 1998, Boston, MA.

Quinn, R. & Stuart, C. (2004) Academic freedom and the promise of international higher education, *International Higher Education*, 37, pp. 2–3.

Raju, S. (2004) Teaching and researching the geography of gender: a journey of negotiations and contestation, in: J. Sharp, D. Thein & K. Browne (Eds) *Gender and Geography: 20 Years On*, pp. 64–67 (Glasgow: Women in Geography Study Group).

Rawling, E. (2004) School geography around the world, in: W. A. Kent, E. Rawling & A. Robinson (Eds) *Geographical Education: Expanding Horizons in a Shrinking World*, pp. 177–180 (Glasgow: Scottish Association of Geography Teachers and Geographical Education Commission of the International Geographical Union).

Rawlinson, S., Essex-Carter, L., Bolden, D. & Constable, H. (2004) Have geographers lost their way? Issues relating to the recruitment of geographers into school teaching, *Journal of Geography in Higher Education*, 27(1), pp. 39–56.

Rice, G. (2003) Pre-service geographical education through service learning, Paper presented at the 99th Annual Meeting of the Association of American Geographers, March 2003, New Orleans, LA.

Riddell, S., Tinklin, T. & Wilson, B. (2005) New Labour, social justice and disabled students in higher education, *British Educational Research Journal*, 31(5), pp. 623–643.

Robinson, R. (1988) Development issues: sympathy and paternalism, empathy and realism, in: R. Gerber & J. Lidstone (Eds) *Developing Skills in Geographical Education*, pp. 152–155 (Brisbane: International Geographical Union Commission on Geographical Education with The Jacaranda Press).

Rooney, P., Kneale, P., Gambini, B., Keiffer, A., Vandrasek, B. & Gedye, S. (2006) Variations in international understandings of employability for geography, *Journal of Geography in Higher Education*, 30(1), pp. 133–145.

Sax, L., Astin, A., Korn, W. & Gilmartin, S. (1999) *The American College Teacher: National Norms for the 1998–1999 HERI Survey* (Los Angeles: HERI at UCLA).

Scheyvens, R., Wild, K. & Overton, J. (2002) International students pursuing postgraduate study in geography—impediments to their learning experience, *Journal of Geography in Higher Education*, 27(3), pp. 309–323.

Sharma, M. C. (2000) Affirmative action policies in higher education: the Indian experience, in: E. F. Beckham (Ed.) *Diversity, Democracy and Higher Education: A View from Three Nations*, pp. 117–135 (Washington, DC: Association of American Colleges and Universities).

Shepherd, I. D. H., Monk, J. J. & Fortuijn, J. D. (2000) Internationalising geography in higher education: towards a conceptual framework, *Journal of Geography in Higher Education*, 24(2), pp. 285–298.

Smith, F. (2004) 'It's not all about grades': accounting for gendered degree results in geography at Brunel University, *Journal of Geography in Higher Education*, 28(2), pp. 167–178.

Thrupp, S. & Tomlinson, S. (2005) Introduction: Education policy, social justice and 'complex hope', *British Educational Research Journal*, 31(5), pp. 549–556.

Timar, J. & Jelenszkyne, I. (2004) Female representation in the higher education of geography in Hungary, *Journal of Geography in Higher Education*, 28(1), pp. 101–110.

Ulrich, W. (2000) Reflective practice in the civil society: the contribution of critically systemic thinking, *Reflective Practice*, 1, pp. 247–268.

United Nations (2005) *Report on the World Social Situation 2005: The Inequality Predicament* (New York: UN Department of Economic and Social Affairs).

Valentine, G. (1994) Ode to a geography teacher: sexuality and the classroom, *Journal of Geography in Higher Education*, 21(3), pp. 417–424.

Valentine, G. (2005) Geography and ethics: moral geographies? Ethical commitment in research and teaching, *Progress in Human Geography*, 29(4), pp. 483–487.

Vender, J. C. (2004) Community action research: a three-part service-learning course model, in: J. M. Carubia & R. S. Engel (Eds) *Innovations in Undergraduate Research and Honours Education: Proceedings of the Second Schreyer National Conference*, pp. 90–98 (Ames, IA: National Collegiate Honours Council).

Vender, J. C., Yapa, L. & Kelley, M. (2002) Service learning through geography: an illustrated panel discussion, Paper presented at the 87th Annual Meeting of the National Council for Geographic Education, October 2002, Philadelphia, PA.

Veness, A. (2001) Whose space is this? Negotiating place and promoting citizenship in Newark, Delaware, Paper presented at the 97th Annual Meeting of the Association of American Geographers, March 2001, New York.

Waddington, S. B. (2001) Working with the community: improving the learning experience for large classes, *Journal of Geography in Higher Education*, 25(1), pp. 67–82.

Wall, M. (2001) Normalcy, freakishness and critical pedagogy: struggling 'in here' with lessons in whiteness, *International Research in Geographical and Environmental Education*, 10(2), pp. 184–188.

Wenger, E. (1998) *Communities of Practice: Learning, Meaning and Identity* (Cambridge: Cambridge University Press).

Wong, P. P. (2005) A wave of geographical research?, *Singapore Journal of Tropical Geography*, 26(2), pp. 257–261.

Yapa, L. (2000) Integrating teaching, research and service: a Philadelphia field project, *Bulletin of Science, Technology and Society*, 20(3), pp. 175–176.

Yeoh, B., Huang, S. & Wong, T. (2004) Gender representation in geography: Singapore, *Journal of Geography in Higher Education*, 28(1), pp. 121–131.

Zeigler, D. J. (1999) The value of voluntary public service in the introductory geography course, Paper presented at the 95th Annual Meeting of the Association of American Geographers March 1999, Honolulu, Hawaii.

Section D: Beyond the Classroom

This final set of chapters examines issues beyond campus that nonetheless carry important implications for learning in higher education. The topic of engaging students in community-based learning is taken on by Bednarz *et al.* in chapter 11. This approach involves widely ranging practices for embedding learning in the work of communities, a strategy that the authors note carries some degree of risk. Nevertheless, the authors note the potential of community engagement for broadening the horizons of learning and maintaining student commitment. In chapter 12, Rooney *et al.* deconstruct the concept of "employability" in a range of national contexts. Although recognizing the dangers of following short-run and politically inspired agendas, the authors argue that it is essential that geography graduates acquire "the skills to sustain success in a globalized labor market". The theme of professional development is further investigated by Solem *et al.* in chapter 13, particularly with regard to the continued education of adult professionals in the workforce via distance education. These three chapters, then, complete the cycle of learning that begins with formal instruction and results in the application of geographic knowledge and skills in professional work settings. Yet the need for lifelong learning is a common theme that emerges from this section, one that is built on principles of active learning and student engagement.

Community Engagement for Student Learning in Geography

SARAH WITHAM BEDNARZ*, BRIAN CHALKLEY**,
STEPHEN FLETCHER†, IAIN HAY‡, ERENA LE HERON^,
AUDREY MOHAN§ & JULIE TRAFFORD¶

*College of Geosciences, Texas A&M University, USA, **Teaching and Learning Development, University of Plymouth, UK, †School of Conservation Studies, Bournemouth University, UK, ‡School of Geography, Population and Environmental Management, Flinders University, Australia, ^School of Environment, University of Auckland, New Zealand, §Department of Geography, Texas State University A San Marco, USA, ¶Student Learning Centre, University of Auckland, New Zealand

ABSTRACT *This article examines the role and purpose of community engagement as a learning and teaching strategy within higher education geography. It explores different interpretations of the concept of community engagement and illustrates different examples of this kind of learning through six case studies drawn from Australia, New Zealand, the UK, and the USA. Key factors which can lead to success in community engagement and also some of the risks and challenges are discussed. Geographers are encouraged to become involved in this kind of experiential learning and to share practice across a wide range of institutions and countries.*

Introduction

Community engagement is often discussed in geography without much recognition that it is interpreted in a range of ways and takes a wide variety of forms. The notion of formal community engagement appears to be most prevalent in the United States where it is often referred to as service learning (see for example Colby *et al.*, 2003; Cantor & Lavine, 2006) and in the United Kingdom and Ireland (see for example Buckingham-Hadfield, 1995; Waddington, 2001; Connor, 2005). It predominantly pertains to notions of service and learning, where these activities form elements in undergraduate or postgraduate degree programmes (Waddington, 2001). The essence of community engagement is that students combine academic study with some form of direct, practical involvement, usually with a community close to the university (Mohan, 1995). Students undertake work, extended field experiences, or conduct investigations in community settings which are incorporated into their education.

Most research on community engagement in both geography and education (see for example Astin *et al.*, 2000; Cohen, 2002; Billig & Waterman, 2003) provides persuasive arguments for its value, presents in-depth examples and case studies, enumerates the associated benefits and challenges to diverse stakeholders (faculty, students, the community, society) involved (see for example, Buckingham-Hadfield, 1995; Waddington, 2001), and suggests how community engagement might be integrated into formal curricula and assessed. This research also indicates that community engagement has multiple interpretations and contested meanings (Pain, 2003). These appear to depend significantly and understandably on university, community, regional, and national contexts and are related to varying economic, social and political agendas. From a review of this literature it seems that little or no attention has been given to comparisons of community engagement activities across institutions or nations. Nor does it appear that community engagement has been investigated specifically as a tool to directly and explicitly enhance teaching, learning and/or research activities within higher education geography curricula.[1]

The purpose of this paper is, therefore, to present a transnational vision of community engagement, from a faculty (staff) perspective, and to extend conventional perceptions of community engagement. We begin by critically highlighting existing research and previous results on community engagement as a teaching and learning tool and providing a detailed rationale and set of purposes to make our case for its inclusion in higher education geography. In the third section, we share the practical knowledges derived from our experiences by presenting a series of studies as designed and delivered in our various national settings. These studies are a mechanism to explore three broadly identifiable forms of community engagement: service-based community engagement; research-based community engagement; and work-based community engagement. Drawing from these experiences, in the last portion of the paper we set out for geographers a summary of the reasons to engage with the community, and provide a discussion of strategies to ensure successful community engagement, together with potential benefits to be gained and associated challenges for faculty.

This is a faculty-driven paper. While we acknowledge the importance of students and the community in community engagement projects, this point of view is well expressed in other research. We are particularly concerned here with the promotion of student learning, where the effectiveness of community engagement activities in enhancing students' acquisition of skills and knowledge can be assessed against specific learning outcomes, from a faculty perspective. Accordingly, we limit our discussion to community engagement's direct and explicit relevance to formal geography curriculum goals. Although they can undeniably be significant to students' wider learning, we exclude placements of students in paid employment or voluntary service where the engagement is not integrated into the academic curricula. This paper similarly excludes, therefore, students' part-time and vacation jobs.

Community Engagement as a Learning and Teaching Tool

As we reviewed existing definitions of community engagement in the light of our experiences, we found they seemed narrow and somewhat restrictive. We seek to promote a broader understanding of community engagement to meet the diverse needs of geography practitioners in a range of academic, community, and national contexts. Thus, we take community engagement to refer to any ethical, reciprocal, and interactive relationship of shared learning fostered between the geography academic discipline (both faculty[2] and students) and the external community or communities, however defined. Community engagement, we maintain, can be achieved through a variety of activities and practices, including, for example, service-based community projects, volunteer work, work-based learning, and fieldwork and research collaborations (Figure 1). We recognize that community engagement is a complex, multi-faceted process that involves activity in, for, with, and/or through communities, with potential benefits and challenges for all the parties involved.

We also recognize that the term 'community' is a contested notion with varying definitions, uses, scales of inclusions, and significance to different constituencies and stakeholders (Smith, 2001; Panelli & Welch, 2005). We also acknowledge that individuals belong to multiple and often overlapping communities. We therefore encourage the view that a community (or communities) of interest should be defined in whichever ways are deemed most appropriate given the particular circumstances involved and the derived learning outcomes of the engagement exercise. A 'community' might, for example, be as tightly defined as the membership of a particular town planning committee, or less prescriptively, members of the general public interested in, shall we say, nature conservation or winter sports.

Nonetheless, we believe it is crucial for community engagement to be seen by both faculty and students as an integral and important component of the curriculum, linked seamlessly with other learning and teaching activities and providing an important form of experiential learning (Kolb, 1984). To achieve its objectives, community engagement needs to be a three-stage, active learning process involving (i) preparation, thinking and

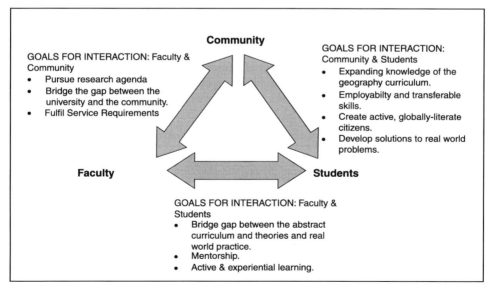

Figure 1. Community engagement goals and learning outcomes

discussion in the classroom prior to engagement; (ii) active and effective engagement with the community to meet specific pre-determined, yet evolving, objectives; and (iii) reflection on the experiences and learning upon returning to the classroom (see Spronken-Smith *et al.*, 2008). As one of numerous learning and teaching tools used within geography curricula, community engagement can enhance and complement other academic activities rather than replace, conflict, contradict or compete with them.

Most forms of community engagement are with physically proximate groups and agencies, partly because of convenience, but also because of local knowledge and the fact that many universities have mission statements that direct attention to their local and regional context. However, community engagement may be undertaken at a range of geographical scales—from the immediate or local community to inter-, cross-, multi- or transnational communities—and with communities founded on other diverse delimiting characteristics such as education, occupation, ethnicity or social, sporting, political and environmental affiliations. Engagement may also involve multiple, spatially dispersed communities simultaneously. It can be conducted in person or virtually and can be undertaken by students as individuals or collaboratively. Incorporating collaboration within at least some aspects of the process is deemed likely to enhance the students' learning experience.

Community engagement can also have varying temporal dimensions. The length of engagement or degree of student involvement may vary from a few hours to several months. From our collective experiences we feel that it is very important that the time and energy invested equates to the *quality* of learning outcomes achieved, whether measured over the short or long term. Engagement can also be a one-off or more frequent event. In cases of episodic re-engagement involving a single group of students, community engagement can be viewed as a cyclical process in which students repeatedly journey through a process of academy-based learning, community application, and personal reflection on how their community engagement has enhanced their geographical knowledges.

In addition, research and experience tells us that community engagement can take place at varying stages in students' academic experiences—from part of a discipline induction to a capstone learning experience—with each intended to achieve different learning outcomes. Students may also be engaged in multiple community engagements, both simultaneously and consecutively, to fulfil the desired learning outcomes of different geography courses. In these circumstances it is important to students' learning that geography faculty attempt to communicate clearly with one another, for instance helping to make more relevant and useful those overlaps, synergies and cross-references that may occur. Where students are involved in more than one community engagement, the total learning experience can be more than the sum of its parts.

Finally, we assert that our discipline, geography, lends itself naturally to community engagement for enhanced teaching and learning. Expanding vocational opportunities for geographers in geographic information systems, remote sensing, biogeography, geotechnology, and urban/regional planning bring new imperatives and opportunities for geography students to engage with the communities in which they may be living or employed (Buckingham-Hadfield, 1995). Community engagement offers students opportunities to contribute classroom-acquired knowledge to public activity and decisions: for example, balancing the needs of communities, economies and natural environs. Simultaneously, community engagement provides geography students with opportunities to demonstrate both specific knowledges and transferable skills of interest to potential employers (Chalkley & Harwood, 1998). The next section of this paper further explores various rationales for and purposes of community engagement in geography.

Rationale and Purposes of Community Engagement

Community engagement is undertaken for various reasons contingent upon the mission of a university and the ambition or goals of university faculty and students. Specifically, the purpose of community engagement is dependent on several factors: (1) university context, (2) student group involved, (3) community group involved, and (4) desired learning outcomes. Community engagement projects may take various forms (e.g. service-based or work-based learning projects), but their primary goal is to create a working relationship where the academic and intellectual ideas of the institution of higher education can be used to help meet the needs of the community. In some cases, community engagement may be initiated for academic or cognitive reasons, while in other cases citizenship issues or student employability are the main focus. In many instances, the goals of community engagement projects overlap; for example, a service-based learning project may enhance a student's academic learning in geography as well as aim to promote responsible citizenry. Figure 1 illustrates some of the goals and outcomes of community engagement with reference to the three main 'actors' involved, namely the community, the faculty and the students. Ultimately, whatever the form of community engagement being undertaken, the two principal goals can generally be summarized as enhancing student learning in geography and meeting community needs.

Community engagement enhances geographic knowledge and skills by encouraging students to apply curricular materials to 'real-world' situations and to reflect on that experience. Whether it is incorporating GIS to solve a community problem or learning about urban watersheds, community engagement projects allow students to apply geography first hand. The literature is replete with articles that discuss the academic outcomes of community engagement projects from land-use planning and watershed initiatives to learning about community gender roles and issues (Buckingham-Hatfield, 1995; Dorsey, 2001; Oberhauser, 2002; Yarwood, 2005; Eflin & Sheaffer, 2006). Placing the academic curriculum into a 'real world' context helps students realize geography's applications: "After having found an appropriate community-based organization whose work relates thematically to course objectives, these students have not only benefited from class activities, they also have a built-in site and context for testing and applying classroom knowledge" (Krumme, 2006, p. 2).

In addition to enhancing academic content, community engagement also brings cognitive benefits. Active, experiential education that provides time for student reflection is becoming increasingly common in university programmes (Dorsey, 2001). In particular, for geography, "experiential learning ... may expand upon the reflection process to include questions asking where problems exist or where solutions might be best applied" (Dorsey, 2001, p. 1). Community engagement also allows students more autonomy over their learning, allowing them to become active learners on a deeper level (Waddington, 2001). Students involved in community engagement must, however, find the projects interesting and relevant to their course of study in order to find real value in the learning experience (Buckingham-Hatfield, 1995; Dorsey, 2001; Waddington, 2001).

Development of interpersonal communication skills in combination with academic learning and increased student motivation is a frequently observed result of community engagement (Eflin & Sheaffer, 2006).

Community engagement offers students opportunities to work with communities to understand and help resolve the problems they face. This is a hallmark feature of applied geography: addressing societal problems within the spatial perspective of geography (Kenzer, 1989). Although geographers have always conducted fieldwork, service-based learning and other forms of community engagement can be used to encourage students to participate in communities while also offering service to them (Buckingham-Hatfield, 1995).

Following from this, community engagement may encourage heightened levels of moral and civic responsibility. Students are often disengaged from communities, politics and the environment, despite intensifying global interdependence and the growing complexity of environmental, social, political, and economic problems (Colby et al., 2003). Overcoming this disengagement is a responsibility of higher education institutions (Colby et al., 2003). It is an obligation that fits well within the geography curriculum (Yarwood, 2005) and can be achieved through community engagement. A number of studies show such positive effects of community engagement, including students' intention to participate in volunteer work in the future (Yarwood, 2005), enhanced understanding of culture and racial diversity, development of attitudes that value democracy, and heightened awareness of the importance of political participation (Colby et al., 2003).

Students can become stakeholders in the community as a result of community engagement projects. This offers multiple benefits for communities and students, "the most notable of which was fostering a culture of interaction between and a mutual respect among community leaders and students as consultants" (Eflin & Sheaffer, 2006, p. 41). Other geography community engagement programmes have tackled cultural issues such as gender power relations, in which the goals of the project were to "break down traditional power relationships and raise awareness of unequal gender relations in the classroom and society at large" (Oberhauser, 2002, p. 23).

Increased awareness of community needs and moral responsibility are important for student learning, but many students are also concerned with future career choices and employability (Dorsey, 2001).[3] In this field too, community engagement can bring benefits. While learning professional and workplace skills is important to students and faculty, employers are sometimes dissatisfied with the lack of relevant skills amongst higher education graduates (Chalkley & Harwood, 1998). Key employment-related skills are more likely to be developed by an active learner in a contextual situation than by a passive learner in a traditional classroom lecture (Waddington, 2001). Higher-level skills are linked with an increase in economic performance, and "In order to continue to compete internationally ... requires a continually better skilled and educated workforce, which is self-motivated, flexible and adaptive to change" (Connor, 2005, p. 1). These characteristics are also more likely to be developed through active, community engagement opportunities than through some more 'traditional' and passive teaching techniques.

For the purposes of this paper, we wish to emphasize that faculty benefits are also important considerations. Unfortunately, there is relatively little reward for faculty involvement in the community in most academic tenure and promotions systems. A recent article in the US publication, *Chronicle of Higher Education*, specifically addresses these constraints:

> Today's system of tenure and promotion extracts a high price. It is costly to communities, as it deprives them of relationships with education partners. It is costly to faculty ... who find it difficult to make their public and community-based intellectual and artistic work count at tenure time. And it is costly to students looking to the curriculum for opportunities for significant public work. (Cantor & Lavine, 2006, p. 20)

Community engagement can, however, provide a useful outlet for course content, and even fulfil service requirements that are part of a faculty member's academic duties. Community organizations, both public and private, can also provide future research opportunities.

In addition to faculty benefits, the community benefits arise when engagement addresses community needs, not only the needs of the university students and faculty. Helping to find solutions to a community problem or developing ideas to promote a community organization are common objectives for engagement projects (Dorsey, 2001; Yarwood, 2005; Eflin & Sheaffer, 2006), with students providing much needed support and human resources for community organizations (Buckingham-Hatfield, 1995; Yarwood, 2005).

Case Studies of Community Engagement

In most situations, as indicated above, community engagement projects have in practice multiple and overlapping purposes. In the next part of the paper we set out six studies of community engagement by geographers working in different parts of the world, the USA, Australia, New Zealand and the UK, organized under three distinct but overlapping categories: service-based community engagement; research-based community engagement; and work-based community engagement. These cases illustrate the diversity of current practice and are also used later in the conclusions as the basis for highlighting some particularly successful strategies and also some pitfalls and challenges. Each provides a brief summary of the main elements of the community engagement process and, where appropriate, a brief comment by way of evaluation.

Service-Based Community Engagement

Advancing Geospatial Skills in Science and Social Science, USA (AGSSS) is a community engagement project funded by the United States' National Science Foundation GK–12 Programme and housed at Texas A&M University. AGSSS connects geospatially skilled Master's and PhD students (called Fellows) with local science and social studies teachers, grades 6–12 (years 11 to 18), in a collaborative partnership. The project seeks to enhance teachers', students', and Fellows' knowledge and skills in spatial thinking (defined as the knowledge, skills, and habits of mind to use concepts of space, tools of representation, and processes of reasoning) to structure and then solve problems. Since its inception in August 2005, Fellows have worked in classrooms, directly with teachers and students on a daily basis, to develop and implement spatially rich curricula supported by geospatial technologies such as GIS, remote sensing and GPS. Fellows and teachers are engaged in a 'respectful dialogue' to conduct action research, to co-learn about spatial thinking, and to help teachers acquire ways to use geospatial technologies in their classrooms. Frequent email, monthly meetings with teachers, and biweekly journals from Fellows provide data to assess alignment to project goals and to monitor progress.

Fellows benefit from the programme by developing their geotechnical and spatial thinking expertise and by gaining confidence and skills in communicating their own understandings of spatial thinking and technology. They are also learning about the teaching/learning process and ways to communicate with the general public in clear terms. Fellows are engaged with and connected to the local community in a mutually beneficial way. Their daily encounters with students and teachers cause Fellows to participate fully in the place they live, and to attain both intellectual and technical skill. Although such initiatives can be costly in that they require careful coordination and planning, plus the briefing and preparation of all the 'actors' involved, there can be real benefits to the school pupils and their teachers. Meanwhile the university students develop new competencies, interpersonal skills and the habits of mind required of citizens in a democracy.

Community Engagement for Experiencing Indigenous Values, New Zealand. A very different form of community engagement is illustrated by those courses in New Zealand, as at the University of Auckland, where learning with a Maori community is an integral component of residential fieldtrips. Understanding Maori cultural frameworks is critical for many of the career paths that New Zealand geographers follow, in such areas as resource management and community planning. The relevant legislation requires that the principles of the Treaty of Waitangi, which *inter alia* protects indigenous rights, be taken into account.

To many New Zealand students, who may have had little if no direct experience of Maori world-views, such engagement involves travelling outside their own worlds. Initial classroom preparation focuses on the protocol and behaviours appropriate to the marae (meeting house and grounds) at which the class will be hosted; this sets the scene for a constructive visit, usually involving an overnight stay, and focusing on local Maori histories, environmental meanings and community stories. It is then vital to reflect on the experience upon return to the classroom, with students considering how their experience of indigenous perspectives might enhance their understanding of how people interact with the environment as well as their geographical knowledge.

Not all marae are willing to work in these ways, but many tribes do provide educational opportunities of this sort. The motivation is the opportunity to add voice to the formal education of students who are showing themselves open to gaining some practical experience that might be part of a much longer series of steps to working in Treaty-related areas. More immediately both the students and their Maori hosts benefit from developing shared understandings and from an enhanced appreciation of each other's world-views and values.

Research-Based Community Engagement

The Hamble Estuary Partnership, UK. This case study serves to illustrate how activities such as a faculty's research (especially small-scale action research), voluntary work or consultancy can open up opportunities for student engagement in some aspects of the local community. The Hamble Estuary Partnership (HEP) is a group of statutory and voluntary organizations with a stake in the management of the River Hamble, a small but intensively used estuary that discharges into the Solent on the central south coast of England. The HEP is currently chaired on a voluntary basis by an academic geographer from Bournemouth University. The academic involvement supports directly the community-based management of the estuary and contributes to the university's mission to engage with the local community. Staff involvement has also had spin-off benefits for students through curriculum connections and research opportunities. Curricular connections have arisen in the following ways: (1) use of the HEP as a case study of coastal management practice in undergraduate and postgraduate teaching, (2) student involvement in HEP meetings and events in order to provide an insight into the process of community-based management, and (3) enhanced guest speaker involvement in the teaching schedule through the network derived from the HEP.

Research opportunities arise in two main ways. First, as a result of involvement in the HEP, awareness of issues that matter to stakeholders is enhanced and research opportunities are more readily identified. Second, the HEP has formed a Student Research Fund that offers financial support to students undertaking small personal research projects that directly support the delivery of the Hamble Estuary Management Plan. Students who receive funding are required to present their findings to an HEP meeting and provide a written summary of their research. Student involvement in the HEP requires little management and is assessed formally only where it coincides with curricular activities. However, it is important to emphasize that not all areas of the HEP's activities provide a basis for academic work. Success depends on the development of clear links between community engagement and the curriculum and providing opportunities in the curriculum to take advantage of community involvement opportunities that link directly to the professional practice of academics.

Supporting Emergency Planning using GIS, USA. In response to a stated need, a faculty member of Texas State University met with the local fire chief and city officials to discuss the development of a GIS program to be used by the city in the event of a major disaster. From this initial consultation came a service learning project that would allow advanced GIS students to design prototype software programs for the city to aid in more efficient emergency response. The fire chief met with the students to: (1) discuss the needs of the fire department, and (2) allow students to ask questions about the duties and decisions involved in emergency response situations. This discussion or 'knowledge solicitation' period allowed students to establish the needs of the emergency response officials and helped them to develop an extensive concept map of the decisions involved in emergency response. From this concept map, students were able to develop prototype software that would fit the needs of the emergency response officials while allowing students to practise their geographic skills. The prototype software programs mapped building structures, fire hydrants, and quickest driving routes for emergency response officials. These prototypes were presented to the city officials at the end of the course. A particular difficulty facing this project was the lack of time (15 weeks) to fully develop and implement the software program. However, the city officials were adequately trained in the use of GIS and city data sets were readily available, both of which contributed to the success of the project. Student benefits included using GIS software in 'real-world' application, conversing with community officials about their needs, and creating a network for future employability.

Community Consultancy Projects, Australia. In 1997, students studying a third-year undergraduate 'Research Methods in Geography' class (about 12 students at the time) at Flinders University, South Australia, were commissioned to conduct a study for a community association on recreational services needs in its neighbourhood. The community association sought the information for an ongoing struggle it was having with the local city council over the location of a proposed skateboard park. As a group, students negotiated the terms of the 'consultancy' with the President of the Association, designed the study, pre-tested it, completed a large-scale questionnaire survey of over 300 residents selected randomly, wrote a formal group report based on the results of that survey, and presented their work at a special public meeting of the Association. In a letter of thanks to students, the Association's President wrote that the work was a "magnificent effort in establishing the social and recreational needs of local residents". Not only had the students provided a useful and high-quality service to a community near the university and gained valuable practical research skills, but it was clear they had gained insights to the 'politics' of social research. Following the success of that initiative, subsequent, and larger, groups of students studying the same 'Research Methods' topic have participated in other similar research projects that provide a service to the community; for example, providing expert advice to a consultant preparing a very large questionnaire survey of volunteers in the South Australian Country Fire Service. Prerequisites of this approach include the availability of suitable projects and faculty members with local community networks. Another possible challenge is that of helping students to ensure that the work they undertake is of an appropriate, professional standard.

Work-based Community Engagement

UK, Australia and USA. One means of promoting community engagement is through curriculum-related placements, or 'internships' (Foster *et al.*, 1979; Ballinger & Lalwani, 2000). Placements involve the student in learning through working in an appropriate organization, usually external to the university, but within a reasonably accessible distance. Placements vary in their character, but all require the student to practise and develop his/her geographical skills in a work-based setting (Shepherd, 1995). Placements can vary from a whole year of full-time activity to perhaps simply a day a week for a term or semester. In the UK and Australia, an increasing number of geography degree programmes (perhaps up to a quarter in the UK) now offer work-based learning as an accredited and assessed unit of study. The extent to which placements can legitimately be considered as community engagement activities depends on the nature of the host organization and the student's particular programme of work. Where the host is a commercial enterprise, there may be little or no engagement with broad social, environmental or citizenship issues. However, in practice students are often placed with governmental or voluntary sector agencies in fields such as conservation, housing, health or environmental enhancement. In these cases, the student's work may well involve some contact with local people and some investigation of their views, of problems or of local community-based policies or initiatives (Yarwood, 2005).

It must be recognized that in work-based learning the quality of the student experience is variable and in part dependent on the attitude of the host and on the nature of the work students are asked to undertake. There needs to be a clear focus on applying geography in the workplace and on encouraging students to develop their technical and inter-personal skills. While work-based learning can bring real benefits to geography departments (not least in terms of raising their local profile) it can also be an expensive form of learning in terms of faculty supervision and time (Chalkley, 2000)—although some departments have overcome these difficulties by contracting out to commercial employment firms the task of finding appropriate placements. The issue of how to assess work-based learning has sometimes been another impediment to its wider adoption. However, there is now increased experience and expertise in using a wide range of methods including project reports, student logs, reflective diaries/essays, student presentations and interviews (vivas).

In the past the prime motive for providing work-based learning has often been to enhance students' employability. There has been a tendency, therefore, to overlook the merits of arranging placements that will both achieve career benefits and give students the advantage of working with local communities. Placing work-based learning more explicitly within the context of community engagement and citizenship could therefore open up interesting new opportunities and further enrich the student's placement learning.

In summary, in looking across the range of case studies outlined above, we observe a service-based engagement model with volunteerism at its core practised in the US and a variant in New Zealand with a premium on gaining different cultural perspectives; a work-based engagement model with a work skills emphasis in the UK; and a research-based approach in Australia and the US, in which it seems that all of these strands come together in a general commitment to making in-class learning experiences more 'relevant'. However, it is important to stress that the above characterizations are no more than broad generalizations. It is also important to emphasize that each model/approach has much to offer and that no one model/approach should necessarily be held up as the preferred option. Learning through community engagement has to be a response to particular circumstances, needs, and opportunities.

Conclusion

We began our discussions on community engagement unaware of the significant differences in the basic community engagement model that we each were carrying to the discussion. We all agreed that community engagement is a valuable strategy and used it in our teaching for somewhat similar reasons but were unaware that we were taking very different routes towards the same general goals.

Community engagement offers many benefits but also presents significant challenges. It is undertaken in many formats, with varying degrees of success. This article has explored the ways in which we believe community engagement can be beneficial for student learning in geography. The benefits include:

- challenging students' preconceived notions;
- developing interpersonal skills including the ability to network and build social capital;
- demonstrating the value and relevance of the academy;
- offering useful resources/knowledge and more direct ways to access the community;
- understanding and experiencing other cultural frameworks;
- learning how organizations work;

Table 1. Strategies that contribute to success and challenges to community engagement

Success in community engagement relies on a mixture of the following strategies:	Some of the challenges of community engagement are:
• start small • work with someone experienced • derive opportunities from the organizers' personal knowledge of suitable case studies • develop good community networks • run a pilot • maintain the goodwill of the community concerned • train and prepare students for their part in community engagement; discuss expectations • make the rationale/purposes explicit to students (and yourself) • ensure strong connections to the academic curriculum • see community engagement as another teaching strategy • have clear learning outcomes • follow ethical protocols • review, evaluate, reflect (especially in the case of a pilot). • liaise with the community and students about what has been learnt • be aware that benefits (to students and/or community) might have a time lag • highlight employability gains to students • base assessment (and particularly formative assessment) in part on community feedback • remember that the length or extent of community engagement does not have to be huge in order to affect student learning—focus on the quality rather than the quantity of engagement	• it can be risky • lack of time; workload issues • lack of networks • institutions may be perceived as elite and not part of their local community • lack of suitable opportunities in the community for this kind of work • is media involvement beneficial or detrimental to the community? Will these activities generate good or bad PR? • student resistance/fear • the possibility that students do not engage, leading to a failure of outcomes • problems in maintaining a balance between practice and theory • staff resistance (sometimes this is considered time away from the 'proper' curriculum) • variable levels of engagement within the student group • ethical issues, e.g. confidentiality • sustainability—how do you keep the community involved? • benefits might have excessive time lags • turnover of students—lack of longitudinal commitment • undervalued by institutions; tenure and promotion implications • possibility of negative impacts on the community • how far do you go to find your 'community'? Will it be your local community or elsewhere?

• enhancing students' preparedness for the world of work and citizenship;
• providing services to the community that they would not otherwise have.

Of course, we acknowledge the difficulties involved in 'doing successful community engagement'. To this end, we identify strategies that have contributed to success. These are shown in Table 1.

Table 1 also lists the challenges to community engagement. Although we believe in the value of community engagement to student learning in geography, it is worth listing the challenges so that those who undertake it can be aware of the task ahead and the possible pitfalls. While Table 1 identifies success factors and challenges separately, in practice they should be seen as intertwined. For example, the risky nature of community engagement (mentioned under challenges) is addressed when we suggest starting small, working in partnership and seeking advice. Start small and safe with something well known and familiar to you, rather than being too ambitious. Derive the community engagement from your own studies and existing work as is the case with the USA AGSSS project and UK HEP example or tie with things that colleagues have done before. The studies reviewed in the paper, particularly the New Zealand case, show that the length or extent of community engagement does not have to be huge in order to make a difference to student learning.

The main message of this paper is that community engagements should strive to be win–win–win (community–faculty–student). However, the realities do not always match this ideal and sometimes there are significant time lags before positives appear. Benefits to students (such as challenging preconceived notions and developing skills) are often fairly immediate, but benefits to the community can be diffuse or delayed. We believe, however, that those considering embarking upon community engagement should not be discouraged—the literature reviewed earlier and our own case studies show largely positive experiences.

We argue, therefore, that the long-run benefits of community engagement, if carefully designed, can and should outweigh the associated costs. You, as geography practitioners from across the globe, are therefore strongly encouraged first to share your own experiences of community engagement, and second to consider how positive lessons learned in other contexts might be applied to enhance your own community engagement activities.

And finally, in making this call for engagement, dissemination and publication, we are mindful that the discussion and case studies presented in this paper (although illustrating different national and local circumstances) are drawn essentially from what might loosely be called Anglo-American countries. Our hope would be that our paper will serve not only to raise further the profile of community engagement amongst geographers in this group of countries but also to encourage geographers from other parts of the world to develop and share their practice too.

Acknowledgements

The authors would like to thank Aya Oda and Joann C. Vender for their input into this project, including the construction of a comprehensive bibliography of works on community engagement. The authors also wish to acknowledge the other members of the INLT geography workshop in Brisbane, July 2006, who gave constructive feedback during the drafting and redrafting of this manuscript, both at the workshop and online.

Notes

[1] We suggest that many of the ideas discussed in this paper could also be applied to geography learning, teaching and research at the secondary school or graduate/postgraduate levels.

[2] The term 'faculty' is used throughout this paper to refer to the academic staff or teachers employed within a university or other higher education institution.

[3] Not all geographers consider work-based learning or work placements a form of community engagement. See Dorsey (2001) for a discussion on this. If properly designed, workplace learning can be engaging, but work must be selective and learning objectives clearly outlined.

References

Astin, A. W., Vogelgsang, L. J., Ikeda, E. K. & Yee, J. A. (2000) *How Service Learning Affects Students* (Los Angeles: UCLA Higher Education Research Institute). Available at: http://www.gseis.ucla.edu/heri/service_learning.html (accessed November 2006).

Ballinger, R. C. & Lalwani, C. S. (2000) The role of internships in marine policy and Integrated Coastal Management higher education, *Ocean & Coastal Management*, 43(4–5), pp. 409–426.

Billig, S. H. & Waterman, A. S. (Eds) (2003) *Studying Service-learning: Innovations in Education Research Methodology* (Mahwah, NJ: Lawrence Erlbaum).

Buckingham-Hatfield, S. (1995) Student–community partnerships: advocating community enterprise projects in geography, *Journal of Geography in Higher Education*, 19(2), pp. 143–150.

Cantor, N. & Lavine, S. (2006) Taking public scholarship seriously, *Chronicle of Higher Education*, 52(40), p. B20.

Chalkley, B. (2000) *Improving Students' Skills through Work-based Learning* (Cheltenham: Geography Discipline Network).

Chalkley, B. & Harwood, J. (1998) *Transferable Skills and Work-based Learning in Geography* (Cheltenham: Geography Discipline Network).

Cohen, J. (2002) Public scholarship: serving to learn, in: M. E. Kenney, L. E. K. Simon, K. Kiley-Brabeck & R. M. Lerner (Eds) *Learning to Serve: Promoting Civil Society through Service Learning*, pp. 239–256 (Boston, MA: Kluwer).

Colby, A., Ehrlich, T., Beaumont, E. & Stephens, J. (2003) *Educating Citizens: Preparing America's Undergraduates for Lives of Moral and Civic Responsibility* (San Francisco: Jossey-Bass).

Connor, H. (2005) *Work-based Learning: A Consultation* (London: Council for Industry and Higher Education).

Dorsey, B. (2001) Linking theories of service learning and undergraduate geography education, *Journal of Geography*, 100(3), pp. 124–132.

Eflin, J. & Sheaffer, A. L. (2006) Service learning in watershed based initiatives: keys to education for sustainability in geography?, *Journal of Geography*, 105, pp. 33–44.

Foster, L., Jones, K. & Mock, D. (1979) Internships in the applied geography curriculum, *Journal of Geography in Higher Education*, 3(2), pp. 8–14.

Kenzer, M. S. (Ed.) (1989) *Applied Geography: Issues, Questions and Concerns* (Dordrecht: Kluwer).

Kolb, D. A. (1984) *Experiential Learning* (Englewood Cliffs, NJ: Prentice Hall).

Krumme, G. (2006) Service learning and other volunteer work related to economic and business geography. Available at: http://faculty.washington.edu/~krumme/207/service_learning.html.

Mohan, J. (1995) Thinking local: service-learning, education for citizenship and geography, *Journal of Geography in Higher Education*, 19(2), pp. 129–142.

Oberhauser, A. (2002) Examining gender and community through critical pedagogy, *Journal of Geography in Higher Education*, 26(1), pp. 19–31.

Pain, R. (2003) Social geography: on action-oriented research, *Progress in Human Geography*, 27(5), pp. 649–657.

Panelli, R. & Welch, R. (2005) Why community? Reading difference and singularity with community, *Environment and Planning A*, 37(9), pp. 1589–1611.

Shepherd, I. D. H. (1995) Small is beautiful: a 'short and thin' model for work experience, *Journal of Geography in Higher Education*, 19(2), pp. 182–188.

Smith, M. K. (2001) Community, in: *The Encyclopedia of Informal Education*. Available at: http://www.infed.org/community/community.htm

Spronken-Smith, R., Bullard, J., Ray, W., Roberts, C. & Keiffer, A. (2008) Where might sand dunes be on Mars? Engaging students through inquiry-based learning in geography, *Journal of Geography in Higher Education*, 32(1), pp. 71–86.

Waddington, S. (2001) Working with the community: improving the learning experience for large classes, *Journal of Geography in Higher Education*, 25(1), pp. 67–82.

Yarwood, R. (2005a) Geography, citizenship and volunteering: some uses of the higher education Active Community Fund in geography, *Journal of Geography in Higher Education*, 29(3), pp. 355–368.

Variations in International Understandings of Employability for Geography

PAUL ROONEY*, PAULINE KNEALE**, BARBARA GAMBINI[†],
ARTIMUS KEIFFER[‡], BARBARA VANDRASEK[§] & SHARON GEDYE[^]
*Faculty of Science and Social Science, Liverpool Hope University, UK, **Higher Education Academy Subject Centre for Geography, Earth and Environmental Sciences, University of Plymouth, UK, [†]PhD, Università degli Studi di Urbino, Italy, [‡]Department of Geography, Wittenberg University, Ohio, USA, [§]Department of Geography, University of Minnesota, USA, [^]GEES Subject Centre, University of Plymouth, UK

ABSTRACT *This research started from the premise that (a) employability is an internationally accepted concept with a confusion of interpretations and definitions; and (b) that an insight into the variation in understanding of employability and teaching employability would benefit geography curriculum development. Consequently, the views of the co-authors from Italy, the United Kingdom, United States, Chile, Estonia, Greece and Spain were sought to develop an international understanding of employability and its position in the geography higher education curriculum. Discussion shows that the definitions and implications are varied. There is common agreement that geography graduates are very employable, and that their degree work enhances their employability attributes. The extent to which employability can be enhanced within the curriculum is discussed.*

Introduction

While it may not be at the forefront of most academic geographers' minds, the majority of students in undergraduate and postgraduate classes do not continue to a professional career in geography. For the majority of geography students their degree is one step on the route from primary school to employment. It is therefore important to explore the ways in which employability is addressed within geography curricula internationally.

In this paper we present the views of a range of contributors from different national contexts in order to understand what is meant by 'employability.' These perspectives, together with those from the literature on employment, key skills and the curriculum for geography, are synthesized to summarize the views of geographers from different national contexts responding to employability and lifelong learning initiatives. The aim is curriculum development to help graduates fulfil their career goals.

Defining Employability

There is not a generally agreed definition of employability. In the UK, where discussion of the concept is current (Little, 2003), the definition used by the Enhancing Student Employability Co-ordination Team (ESECT, 2004) is:

> ... a set of achievements—skills, understandings and personal attributes—that make graduates more likely to gain employment and be successful in their chosen occupations, which benefits themselves, the workforce, the community and the economy.

This definition reflects the perspective that higher education (HE) is meant to serve the interests of *both* the graduate and the larger society. This view is not distinctive for public higher education, or to the UK. The notion that higher education receives public support because it produces a public good is pervasive across the globe.

In the Australian 'Employability Skills for the Future' study (DEST, 2002) the definition of employability used was:

> ... skills required not only to gain employment, but also to progress within an enterprise so as to achieve one's potential and contribute successfully to [the] enterprise strategic directions.

Curtis & McKenzie (2001) report that Australian universities tease out this concept to highlight the generic employability skills of graduates in terms of 'graduate qualities'. For example, a graduate of the University of South Australia:

- operates effectively with and upon a body of knowledge of sufficient depth to begin professional practice;
- is prepared for lifelong learning in pursuit of personal development and excellence in professional practice;
- is an effective problem solver, capable of applying logical, critical and creative thinking to a range of problems;
- can work both autonomously and collaboratively as a professional;
- is committed to ethical action and social responsibility as a professional and citizen;
- communicates effectively in professional practice and as a member of the community;
- demonstrates international perspectives as a professional and as a citizen.

Again, the link is strongly made to the community and society.

In Canada the definition used by the Conference Board of Canada (2005) is:

> Employability Skills 2000 + are the critical skills you need in the workplace—whether you are self-employed or working for others. Employability Skills 2000

+ include communication, problem solving, positive attitudes and behaviours, adaptability, working with others, and science, technology and mathematics skills.

In Europe the Bologna Declaration (1999, p. 3) places considerable emphasis on employability:

> Adoption of a system of easily readable and comparable degrees, also through the implementation of the Diploma Supplement, in order to promote European citizens' employability and the international competitiveness of the European higher education system.

The Bologna Declaration effectively contains an acknowledgement that signatory countries will work to reform their HE systems so that there is convergence at the European level, and that graduate qualifications and understandings of employability are shared:

> The Declaration reflects a search for a common European answer to common European problems. The process originates from the recognition that in spite of their valuable differences, European higher education systems are facing common internal and external challenges related to the growth and diversification of higher education, the employability of graduates, the shortage of skills in key areas, the expansion of private and transnational education, etc. The Declaration recognizes the value of coordinated reforms, compatible systems and common action. (Confederation of EU Rectors, 2001)

Geography as a discipline prides itself on being aware of, and concerned with, 'real' world issues (Chalkley, 1995). Most geographers are aware of the needs and demands of society. They are taught to look at issues from many perspectives, to be aware that the world is changing rapidly, and that in many cases there are no 'right' answers to environmental and societal issues. Neoliberalism asserts the importance of the stock of human capital as essential for economic growth (Lees, 2002). Geographers are particularly well qualified to respond creatively to the changing needs and demands of society and to operate in local, regional, national and international arenas.

Evaluating the extent to which the discipline has been successful in responding to the needs and demands of society in a rapidly changing world, especially in producing successful geographers who are employable and employed, presents a major research challenge. Geography graduates enter a job market that is changing rapidly in an increasingly uncertain world (Jenkins & Healey, 1995). They are employed in a variety of positions, in a wide range of careers (Kneale, 2002), but few positions carry the title 'geographer' (Frazier, 1994). There is an increased demand for practitioners to be able to solve environmental and spatial problems, but these problems are not the sole preserve of geographers, and the problems do not comfortably reside within traditional disciplinary boundaries (Kneale & Chalkley, 2001).

Identifying a geographer can be difficult for an employer. For example, with the widening availability and applications of desktop GIS, it has become increasingly difficult to distinguish between those who possess the geographer's unique world-view, and others who have mastered a particular IT skill set. The computer-science-trained GIS expert will not necessarily have the depth of understanding that will allow him/her to assess a problem knowledgeably, critique proposed solutions and arrive at the best plan of action. An employer understandably has trouble appreciating the difference, and the advantages of seeking the enhanced applied understandings that a geographer can bring to bear.

In exploring the concept of employability as it relates to geography, we aim to identify some international constructs that influence the discipline. These are valuable in their own right and of interest to graduates seeking employment internationally. In some national settings in particular, there is pressure to conform to social and economic agendas determined by the state, and these might already be directing the nature and quality of geography in higher education. One challenge for geography is to instil in students the value of the geographers' analytical and synthesizing approach to problems in the discipline and in 'real world' settings, and to show how these are relevant to many aspects of employment. We must encourage undergraduates to understand that the approaches taken in geographical research are also those used by practitioners effectively doing research as part of their jobs with voluntary and charity bodies, local government, national government, large and small companies and organizations. The skills of geographical researchers are also valuable for the self-employed, and these are lifelong learning skills as well.

International Views on the Concept of 'Employability'

Higher education in many parts of the world prioritizes career preparation for students. There is interest in the relationship between higher education and employment (Little, 2003). This is particularly the case in North America and Australasia (Jenkins & Healey, 1995) where some institutions have developed close links between the geography curriculum and industry. Each contributor was tasked to explore the understanding of employability in his/her HE context and the relationship with geography. Each perspective is unique and reported separately.[1]

An Italian view:

> The word employability does not have any equivalent either in Italian or in Spanish. In fact, the English term is sometimes used in Italy. Universities in Italy only occasionally address the issue of student employability, and this appears to be poorly suited to the new economic trends. While the national job market is becoming more and more flexible regarding dismissal, in fact, it seems to be keeping too much of its old rigidity in the recruitment system. In the case of geography, specific difficulties add up to the general shortcomings of the academic system, so that gaining disciplinary visibility and an adequate status are still the priority among Italian geographers, before they can systematically tackle the issue of employability.

A perspective from Chile:

> Employability is not an intuitively comprehensible term, although in Chile the need to enhance students' career perspectives is felt more and more. Accreditation has been the answer so far. In Latin America, the priority seems to be enhancing the students' initial competitiveness rather than maintaining an occupation, finding a new one if required, advancing in one's career or being satisfied with one's job. Given the characteristics of

the Chilean job market, enhancing professional flexibility and an ability to move easily within the job market should possibly be the priority.

A Spanish view:

In Spain, employability is a topic that worries a wide percentage of the academic community, but not everyone, and this is especially true among those who for many years have taught students to seek any service-sector job they can find, completely unaware of how to prepare students for these positions. These professors don't want to consider that the university is like a school of business, or to teach geography as a profession. Nevertheless, from the mid-nineties Spanish universities began to graduate students in geography who wanted to be employed as geographers. At the same time many faculty members retired and were replaced by younger people. The new graduates and the recently arrived lecturers have become allied with the professors who had predicted the growing importance of applied geography. The fruit of this alliance has been a series of collaborations that have improved the perspectives of all, such as the creation of the Colegio Profesional of geographers, the incorporation of technical geographers into public administration (at national, autonomous and local levels), the association of many geographers with other regional planning professionals, the multiplication of subjects, courses, Masters and seminars with a professional orientation, and so on. In spite of everything, university departments of geography, in general, make only a few efforts to increase the employability of their students. The inertia is still too great.

A view from Estonia:

Employability of geography graduates in Estonia has been rather good (Roosaare & Liiber, 2004). Of course, several peculiarities may be pointed out (e.g. a small country, liberal and transitional economy, one dominant university), but some three interrelated characteristics may have more importance: (1) The prestige of the subject (the university's curriculum and the profession studied) is a decisive factor in Estonian employability, since it determines the general abilities of students (communication and leadership capabilities, among other general skills). The fact that one has studied at the Institute of Geography is much more important than the discipline studied, while in HE the primary mode is self-learning, not teaching. (2) The integrity of teaching in geography, taking a very broad, systemic and spatial approach to the world, generates graduates who are, in many workplaces, more successful than 'specialized' graduates from other faculties. The breadth of the subject, with the IT and practical analytical skills, means that a human geographer knows ecology and GIS, for example. Geography is a good background subject for many jobs. Every concrete job needs its own specialization and the proficiency that comes with experience. (3) The long-held Estonian tradition is that students should already have professional contacts with their future (first) employer during the final stage of their study. Typically students work part time, doing projects and gathering materials for BSc or MSc projects. This process is a real help in focusing students on the demands and practicalities of the workplace and they consequently adapt quickly to 'real life'.

A perspective from Greece:

> Enhancing employment for geography graduates is a process that is more complicated and delicate than most academic geographers in Greece consider or would like it to be. In general, the process is characterized by three stages: the formulation of the curriculum represents the beginning of the process, which develops a set of achievements (skills) that in turn leads to employment. In this process, however, the most important and determining factors are not the stages themselves, but the transitional mechanisms, filters or constraints that lead into them. First are institutional pressures, which are generated by external curriculum boundary conditions (i.e. accreditation, national standards or specific school requirements) and necessitate the teaching of certain courses and the omission of others. Second, professional attitudes and conceptions of academic geographers result in providing geography students with 'real geography' courses and thus limiting their 'enhancement' prospects. Finally, market forces are generated by the demands of the market players who do not care who solves their problems, or how, as long as they solve them. In sum, enhancing employment for geography graduates requires that we understand, analyse and find in this rapidly changing employment world the optimum outcome for the three stages, by resolving the constraints imposed by the transitional mechanisms through these stages.

A view from the UK:

> Geography academics in the UK express the full gamut of opinions on the employability agenda from keen enthusiasm to 'it is not the business of the university to get students a job'. There are some programmes with career- and employability-focused modules (Leeds and Plymouth for example); and the majority of departments have opportunities for work placements or dissertation research undertaken in workplace settings, and a history of bringing non-academic 'experts' into the classroom. Applied geography topics help to keep a focus on the real world. Sandwich courses (Coventry University) and some Masters courses (MSc Environmental Technology, University of Tartu,) are focused on providing well-trained graduates to specific job sectors. On balance the employability agenda does appear to be seen as the province primarily of campus careers officers. But in practice one or two champions per department updating and implementing the skills and employability competence agendas and benchmarks can make a difference to students. However, national university league tables that highlight student employability, personal development planning and the Bologna Declaration are changing the broad picture. An online review of eight University Learning and Teaching strategies showed that all mentioned employability, enhancing opportunities and developing student skills. Each used either the ESECT or the Bologna Declaration nomenclature, indicating a top down awareness of, and commitment to, employability issues.

Each respondent has made different points, focusing in his/her own way on the issues of his/her own choosing. The UK and Estonian contributors concentrate more on curriculum and delivery approaches that help a student develop workplace experience, while clearly in Italy other issues take precedence over the employability agenda. These are, of course, the views of individuals and need to be treated conservatively.

Despite the variations, the authors agree that the concept of employability is useful and deserves continuing efforts to articulate a shared understanding of the term across international boundaries. Our discussions showed different countries and institutions to be at very different stages of delivery. Local cultural and social contexts are important. For one author, being made aware of the Australian approach to HE employees and students working for the benefit of their local community was revelatory and sparked ideas for innovation.

It is agreed that employability is a sophisticated and integrated concept that may be incorporated effectively into the geography curriculum for the benefit of geography students. As we develop curricular and other innovations to enhance employability, they will need to be adapted for particular settings.

Employability Issues, Agendas and Approaches

The next section arises from our discussions on the issues, agendas and approaches to employability. At one level, simply sharing approaches was very valuable. The whole showed that there are many gaps and opportunities for further development. We describe some of them here as a basis for starting a discussion and sharing ideas about how to enhance employability for our students, but we recognize that this is only a start at scoping the topic and that a more detailed analysis is warranted.

Responsibility for Developing Employability

It can be argued that HE should focus on intellectual development alone, and that employers should take the responsibility for imbuing the skills and traits that they want after they hire people. In some institutions we see a compromise position with the geography departments embedding writing, presentation and critical thinking skills into their curricula but looking to the institution to contribute more general preparation for students in all disciplines (for example self-assessment, interest inventories, job-portfolio preparation, placement briefings, personal development planning, skills workshops and so on). There is a tension between leaving these activities for self-motivated students to pursue in their own time, and recognizing the value of such activities, and making time and space within the curriculum such that all students have equality of access.

Further, we have to ask whether academic geographers are the correct group to lead employability-related teaching. Enhancing students' employability skills requires academics to have an understanding of professional life outside academe (Chalkley, 1995). However, the traditional route into academic geography does not typically include periods of employment outside academe. We argue that most academics acquire highly developed business skills through their research and wider university roles. They approach organizations for funding, network widely at professional academic meetings, and present the outcomes of their research as posters, in oral presentations, in discussions and in report and paper formats. Researchers think outside the box, take initiatives, develop ideas, manage their own time and learning, keep up to date and regularly acquire new skills. They are resourceful and proactive. These are the characteristics of employable people. While a relatively small proportion of academic geographers (in the UK and the US, at least) have strong links with business and industry, and consultancy activities that can be used as exemplars with students, we would argue that academic geographers have highly developed personal skills and attributes that characterize employability. Making this explicit to students can be very helpful in promoting the discipline.

Recognizing and Building on Current Strengths

An employability audit (Hughes, 2004) allows a department to identify current practices and gaps in provision. One critical and easily adopted strategy involves putting in place opportunities for students to reflect on the skills acquired from each module, project and assignment that can be drawn on later in CVs, interviews and applications for employment. Similarly, an audit of opportunities offered on campus that can be developed and integrated into the geography curriculum provides a good starting point.

Promoting Vocational and Placement Opportunities

Work-based learning is one of the major ways of producing and achieving the experience required for graduates to succeed in the job market. Although this concept may seem easy enough to understand, it implies a lot more than just work. Familiarizing students with both the discipline and the career opportunities available takes more work on the part of the *department* than on the part of the student. We describe here four initiatives that will attract students to a programme and allow them some flexibility regarding its outcome. These include internships, connections with alumni, maintaining a database of available jobs, and institutional and departmental outreach.

Internships come in many forms, such as placements, sandwich years, work shadowing and temporary project officer posts. Whether paid or unpaid, in the field or in the office, hands-on or observational, the exposure to a 'real' job is perhaps the best way to educate students through personal experience. Matching a particular student with the right experience is vital. Programmes should be monitored, and students should have frequent interactions with their job and university mentors. Ideally, students will leave an internship programme ready to write reflectively about the practical, workplace applications of their experience. Students should have input in tailoring internships to serve their career aspirations. Just as students are allowed to choose and petition for specific classes, their input in designing an internship is crucial. This fosters a sense of pride, willingness and encouragement to develop a programme that is of interest to them, selecting modules and classes to prepare themselves for their placement. For example, a student going into urban planning may be required to take a GIS class, whereas a student working on an ecological reserve may need preparation in soils, laboratory sciences, tourism or wilderness management. Although the discipline crosses many boundaries, it is important that there is enough flexibility in the curriculum to accommodate the necessary core classes to support a student on placement. It is arguable that a student intending to go into an applied field should undertake an internship or placement, and that a project from the placement might be of more value and replace a thesis-writing class.

Connections with alumni are important in establishing linkages within the discipline and external professions, as well as fostering a sense of accomplishment for the student. Alumni can spark enthusiasm in others to pursue a particular career path, and their enthusiasm for life after geography can help retention rates. Recent alumni are a great source of information about what employers really want.

An up-to-date *job database*, for employment purposes, *and list of alumni career destinations* is helpful for students as they approach graduation. It also is a good tool for reaching out to students who are on the cusp of deciding on a particular major, or on a thesis or dissertation topic.

Institutional and departmental outreach is also critical. While geography departments are familiar with the needs of their students for work-based learning, research placements, internships, projects and dissertations, they may not have the resources to pursue connections with large corporations or foundations on behalf of their students. Institutions can take a large role in arranging such positions for students. Career counsellors, placement and alumni officers can accomplish this daunting task much more easily. Where student placements are successful, the link can become an annual opportunity. Businesses appreciate connections with the departments and institutions that provide them with good employees. It is a reciprocal relationship that enhances employability for students and benefits all, but both the student and the employer need to see the HE partner as a visible and supportive element in what is a three-way relationship.

Highlighting Careers, Skills and Employability to School Pupils, Students, Graduates and Employers

A review of geography department websites shows variety in the approach to careers information. Many but by no means all sites have this link, essentially illustrating the relevance of geography to potential students. Some sites list the careers that geographers may enter (see for example University of Colorado at Denver; University of Minnesota, Duluth; Association of American Geographers; Ritsumeikan University Japan; University of Cape Town, South Africa); others articulate the skills associated with geography degrees (for example University of Newcastle, UK; University of North Carolina, USA; Flinders University, Australia; University of Queensland, Australia; University of Canterbury, New Zealand).

Developing embedded modules that address workplace issues (e.g. Hawksworth & Kneale, 2001) can raise awareness effectively. Collaboration with careers specialists, bringing human resources and graduate recruitment specialists from business and industry into the HE classroom, and using alumni to describe their experiences, broadens and grounds student understanding. Student assignments to research the changing workplace, economic influences on employment patterns, retail or charity sector marketing approaches, the development of start-ups and entrepreneurship are just a few examples that link employability themes to the geography curriculum. Grounding their research in real companies encourages students to explore organizational ethos and culture and, in passing, the graduate recruitment websites and opportunities for placements and internships.

Employability for Those with Employment Experience

Mature students, late starters and students studying part time while at work all bring a challenging diversity to the classroom. These students have experience in employment and established employability skills. Recognizing skills and attributes already developed is important and such students can be valuable advocates of work-related skills and can place research activities in a workplace context. It is important to distinguish between experiences in graduate-level and professional employment and stopgap college-support jobs. The MSc by Learning Contract programme at the School of Earth Sciences and Geography, Kingston University, UK takes this concept further by allowing mature and experienced professionals to tailor their own learning. The challenge is to provide appropriate support to students with diverse life and career goals and aspirations.

First-generation Students

UK data suggest that first-generation students are less likely to graduate to professional-status jobs, a situation influenced in part by a lack of family role models (Blasko *et al.*, 2002). Such students have a particular need for support in identifying and competing for graduate-level employment. Whether this is the case internationally is not clear.

Reporting Graduate Employability

We feel that is important to distinguish between employment rates (getting any job after graduation), graduate employment rates (the success of graduates in finding work at graduate level), and an emerging concept of employability, meaning the preparation and readiness for employment as a geographer, with the ability to adjust and adapt to changing conditions in the job market, and continuously to improve one's knowledge and professional situation (lifelong learners).

Geographers are typically inquisitive about the world, travelling and trying alternative employment opportunities before settling on a particular career path. Domestic circumstances, geographic mobility and the conditions of the national and regional economy influence employment opportunities, and may limit choices for first and future jobs. As our Estonian colleague has noted, employability is also a function of the prestige of the HE institution attended. In the UK, 'first destination' and questionnaire survey statistics are used to analyse employment and career patterns of geography graduates (Clark *et al.*, 1990; Gedye *et al.*, 2004). Such an approach is limited to snapshots of employment, usually six months after graduation. It does not reveal longer-term achievements. What data there are on employability in each national context were agreed to be partial and unreliable.

Developing an Internationally Consistent Language for Employability Skills

Curtis & McKenzie (2001, p.vii) highlight the nomenclature confusion around definitions of employability, as do others: "The lack of common understanding is reflected in the language being used in different circles and forums. Adjectives such as core; key; generic and essential are variously used to preface nouns such as skills; competencies; capabilities; and attributes. It is not clear whether these different terms reflect slight variants of the basic concepts ... or whether they signal genuinely new developments. In either case the lack of shared understanding makes it difficult to build the broad coalition of governments, employers and educators needed to drive substantial reform."

There is a significant difference between the skills agenda identified by employers as being essential for the graduate workplace, and the skills required by graduates to sustain their employment. Within the UK geography curriculum the focus to date has been on the former rather than the latter (Chalkley & Harwood, 1998; Gravestock & Healey, 2000; Lees, 2002; Kneale, 2003; Yorke, 2004). Addressing sustainable lifelong learning skills potentially adds a challenging new element to the agenda, which may face inertia and institutional resistance.

We found that, internationally, terms are not used in a consistent way (Little, 2003). Our discussions suggest that sharing a common understanding of the concepts would be helpful.

We argue that geography aims to equip its graduates with geographic understandings, skill sets and the professional acumen needed to either create or move into new professional situations. An objective of an employability agenda would be to ensure that all geography students can articulate and exemplify this in CVs and interviews—in essence, that they are comfortable with the language of employability. An accurate measure of the 'enhancement' that this would offer our students would need to draw on the satisfaction and perceived success of both graduates and their employers.

The Way Forward

Asking a diverse group of faculty to discuss and comment on employability in a range of countries inevitably leads to some idiosyncratic outcomes and includes personal views. The net result was more agreement than less, agreement that there is diversity, many unknowns and more anecdote than hard data. The profile of employability and its promotion to students internationally is very variable.

However, we agree that improving understanding of and embedding employability skills in HE qualifications, through curriculum innovation and in partnership with employers, is potentially very powerful. In theory a well-designed programme should attract more students initially and send them on to the workplace as better equipped employees. An employer benefits from new graduates who are ready to make an impact and who understand the workplace. This may be an ideal but we agree that we are nowhere near this position.

> The education system (should) ... be more responsive to the needs of employment and...ensure that the way subjects are taught at every level reflects the needs of students in their subsequent careers rather than the preferences of their teachers. (Jenkins & Pepper, 1988, p.67)

Embedding employability within the curriculum raises the potential issue of short-term, political agendas having an influence on the curriculum. Often this is seen as undesirable, as it may interfere with the independence of the academic institution (Johnston, 1997). However, geography graduates will work within their own societal and political employment contexts—the situation in Estonia, Chile and Italy is very different. But shielding students from knowledge of external influences and forces does not help to prepare them for the workplace. We argue here that it is appropriate for graduates to be equipped to make their way in the job market, serve their employers' goals as well as their own, and continually improve and advance as professionals working to solve the problems of society.

Geography at the higher education level can change and expand its role to understand the workplace, the employer and student employability better (Frazier, 1994). For geography there is no *single* way forward; we must imagine every possible useful innovation, whether in curricula or elsewhere, and cooperate across national contexts to position geography to continue its important work, both in the intellectual realm and in its application on the ground.

We *can* prepare students to operate comfortably in the zone of tension between, on the one hand, a completely instrumental approach to professional life and, on the other, a broader view that asserts the possibility of being a thoughtful, ethical, critical and highly skilled professional with much to offer to the job, the world and oneself. We need neither put our heads in the sand regarding the recent shifts in our world, nor give up on ideals of integrity and breadth of understanding.

Note

[1] The multinational contributions are from Barbara Gambini, Italy (co-author); Professor Osvaldo Muñiz, Universidad de La Serena, Chile; Dr D. José Somoza Medina, Universidad de León, Spain; Associate Professor Jüri Roosaare, University of Tartu, Institute of Geography, Estonia; Professor Konstantinos Koutsopoulos, National Technical University of Athens; Professor Pauline Kneale, University of Leeds (co-author).

References

Blasko, Z., Brennan, J. & Shah, T. (2002) *Access to What: Analysis of Factors Determining Graduate Employability* (Bristol: Higher Education Funding Council for England). Available at: http://www.hefce.ac.uk/pubs/rdreports/2002/rd14_02/ (accessed September 2005).

Bologna Declaration (1999) *Bologna Declaration on the European Space for Higher Education*. Joint declaration of the European Ministers of Education convened in Bologna on 19 June 1999. Available at: http://www.bologna-berlin2003.de/pdf/bologna_declaration.pdf (accessed September 2005).

Chalkley, B. (1995) Geography staff placements: nice work?, *Journal of Geography in Higher Education*, 19(2), pp. 234–239.

Chalkley, B. & Harwood, J. (1998) *Transferable Skills and Work based Learning in Geography* (Cheltenham: Geography Discipline Network, Cheltenham and Gloucester College of Higher Education). Available at: http://www.glos.ac.uk/gdn (accessed September 2005).

Clark, D., Healey, M. & Kennedy, R. (1990) Careers for geographers: the employment experiences of Coventry Polytechnic sandwich degree students, *Journal of Geography in Higher Education* 14(2), pp. 137–149.

Confederation of EU Rectors (2001) The Bologna Declaration on the European space for higher education: an explanation. Available at: http://www.crue.org/eurec/bolognaexplanation.htm (accessed September 2005).

Conference Board of Canada (2005) Employability Skills 2000+. Available at: http://www.conferenceboard.ca/education/learning-tools/employability-skills.htm (accessed September 2005).

Curtis, D. & McKenzie, P. (2001) Employability Skills for Australian Industry: Literature Review and Framework Development. Available at: http://www.dest.gov.au/archive/ty/publications/employability_skills/literature_research.pdf (accessed September 2005).

Department of Education Science and Training & Australian National Training Authority (2002) Employability Skills for the Future. Available at: http://www.dest.gov.au/archive/ty/publications/employability_skills/ (accessed September 2005).

ESECT (2004) (Enhancing Student Employability Co-ordination Team), Learning and Employability Guides. Recent and ongoing project covering generic employability within HE. (Available at: http://www.heacademy.ac.uk/employability (accessed September 2005).

Frazier, J. W. (1994) Geography in the workplace: a personal assessment with a look to the future, *Journal of Geography* 93(1), pp. 29–35.

Gedye, S., Fender, E. & Chalkley, B. (2004) Students' undergraduate expectations and post-graduation experiences of the value of the degree, *Journal of Geography in Higher Education*, 28(3), pp. 381–396.

Gravestock, P. & Healey, M. (Eds) (2000) *Key Skills in Geography in Higher Education: A Series of Eight Guides* (Cheltenham: Geography Discipline Network, Cheltenham and Gloucester College of Higher Education). Available at: http://www.glos.ac.uk/gdn (accessed September 2005).

Hawksworth, S. & Kneale, P. E. (2001) Geographers and the workplace: an embedded module, *Planet*, Special Issue 1, pp. 17–18, Available at: http://www.gees.ac.uk/planet/index.htm#PSE1 (accessed September 2005).

Hughes, I. (2004) The Employability Audit, Available at: http://www.bioscience.heacademy.ac.uk/issues/employability/resources.htm (accessed September 2005).

Jenkins, A. & Healey, M. (1995) Linking the geography curriculum to the worlds of industry, commerce and public authorities, *Journal of Geography in Higher Education*, 19(2), pp. 177–181.

Jenkins, A. & Pepper, D. (1988) Enhancing students' employability and self-expression: how to teach oral and group work skills in geography, *Journal of Geography in Higher Education*, 12(1), pp. 67–83.

Johnston, R. J. (1997) 'Graduateness' and a core curriculum for geographers, *Journal of Geography in Higher Education* 21(2), pp. 245–259.

Kneale, P. E. (2002) Careers for geography graduates, *Journal of Geography in Higher Education* 26(3), pp. 405–412.

Kneale, P. E. (2003) Context 2003—Enterprising Intrapreneurship Case Studies. Available at: http://www.geog.leeds.ac.uk/courses/other/casestudies/ (accessed September 2005).

Kneale, P. E. & Chalkley, B. C. (2001) Why careers in the curriculum?, *Planet*, Special Issue 1, p.3. Available at: http://www.gees.ac.uk/planet/index.htm#PSE1 (accessed September 2005).

Lees, D. (2002) Employability Literature Review. Available at: http://www.heacademy.ac.uk/resources.asp?process=full_record&section=generic&id=190 (accessed September 2005).

Little, B. (2003) *International Perspectives on Employability* (York: Enhancing Student Employability Co-ordination Team and the Learning and Teaching Support Network Generic Centre). Available at: http://www.heacademy.ac.uk/resources.asp?process=full_record&section=generic&id=230 (accessed September 2005).

Roosaare, J. & Liiber, U. (2004) e-Learning and Europeanisation as promoters of changes in geographical education, in: Estonian Geographical Society (Ed.), 9, pp. 211–223 (Tallinn: Estonian Academy Publishers).

Yorke, M. (2004) *Employability in Higher Education: What it is—What it is not*, Learning and employing Series, No. 1 (York: Enhancing Student Employability Coordination Team (ESECT) and the Learning and Teaching Support Network Generic Centre). Available at: http://www.heacademy.ac.uk/resources.asp?process=full_record&section=generic&id=336 (accessed September 2005).

Internationalizing Professional Development in Geography through Distance Education

MICHAEL SOLEM*, LEX CHALMERS**, DAVID DIBIASE[†], KARL DONERT[‡] & SUSAN HARDWICK[§]

*Asssociation of American Geographers, USA, **Department of Geography, Tourism and Environmental Planning, Waikato University, New Zealand, [†]Department of Geography, Pennsylvania State University, USA, [‡]Education Deanery, Liverpool Hope University, UK, [§]Department of Geography, University of Oregon, USA

ABSTRACT *This paper assesses the value and relevance of geography education in the realm of professional development. It explores the potential of distance education to support lifelong learners through courses or modules that operate across international boundaries and incorporate materials from local and global contexts. The authors argue that Internet-enabled distance education offers the potential to extend access to many prospective students who are unlikely or unable to participate in full-time residential courses, and that distance education can facilitate international collaboration among educators and educational institutions. A case is made for an internationalized programme of study for continuing adult education, as opposed to the primary, secondary and higher education sectors that are the focus of most existing geographical education programmes. Next, the authors document the ways in which recent commitments to internationalizing teaching and learning in geography have brought us to the point where professional development of lifelong learners is demonstrable, particularly in the fields of geographic information technologies and teacher professional development. They outline some of the main challenges that must be addressed if the potential of distance education as an enabling tool for professional development in geography is to be fulfilled: specifically, collaborative development and delivery of curricula and the articulation of quality assurance standards and certification agreements among participating institutions.*

Thinking Beyond Existing Primary, Secondary and Higher Education Models of Geography Education

Most of the literature on geographical education focuses on students and teachers in primary, secondary and higher education sectors. We focus instead on the needs of adults who seek further education but whose commitments to families, employers and communities prevent them from participating in full-time, residential programmes of study. We address this clientele for two reasons: first, demographic trends in most developed countries (OECD, 1998), combined with changes in the relationship between employers and employees (Robson, 2001), emphasize the importance of lifelong learning. Second, workforce development experts estimate that "one-third of all [US] jobs are in flux each year, meaning that they have recently been created or soon will be eliminated from the economy" (Kohl, 2000, p. 13). The generation of workers now reaching retirement age entered the workforce with the reasonable expectation that their entire careers might be devoted to a single employer but a more realistic expectation for graduates entering the workforce today is a succession of careers with different employers. Education is no longer just a prelude to a career; for many professionals it now spans a lifetime.

The question as to how higher education institutions can better prepare the next generation of professionals is already prompting change in higher education. Outside the academy, the value of a graduate degree has come under scrutiny in recent years, with questions raised about the abilities of new graduates to apply their knowledge and skills to serve a broad range of societal needs in many professions (Nyquist & Woodford, 2004). For example, a report by the Renewable Natural Resources Foundation in the United States warns of imminent retirements of large numbers of senior grade personnel in federal agencies and private research firms, and the current lack of orientation in graduate schools to preparing and encouraging graduates to consider careers in these sectors (Colker & Day, 2003). Indeed, a survey initiated by the Pew Charitable Trusts found a majority of American students in arts and sciences doctoral programs to be dissatisfied with their professional training and unprepared for their careers (Golde & Dore, 2001). The same survey revealed that many students enter programmes without a clear understanding of the nature of graduate education and what they can do to enhance their own abilities and prospects for success in their programmes and future careers. In response to these concerns, some institutions have introduced 'professional Master's' programmes in the sciences that integrate management training and internships with scientific education (Tobias *et al.*, 1995).

In Europe, an attempt to address the divide between the needs of society and what higher education provides is being addressed by the Tuning initiative. Tuning implies the development of points of reference, convergence and common understanding between institutions for curriculum design and evaluation (Tuning Project, 2002). The reference points have been developed for generic and subject-specific competences at Bachelor (first level) and Master's (second cycle) graduates in some subjects, with the aim of connecting what employers need with what graduates say they get and academics think they provide. This thus provides a vehicle to support the higher education reform being undertaken as part of the Bologna Process (DfES, 2005). European geography departments are undertaking a pilot study concerning these competences through the HERODOT Thematic Network (Donert, 2003).

In this article we also suggest that the emphasis on lifelong education should be explored first closest to home. So, despite international concerns about the future of traditional educational institutions (Gallagher, 2000), there is evidence that education can be provided across borders (Cunningham *et al.*, 2000) by 'capable' technology (IBM, 2004). Much of this evidence comes from work being done in the discipline of geography.

Building on Success

Geographers have already laid the foundation for success in internationalized education for adult professionals, particularly in the areas of GIS education and teacher professional development. They have created excellent 'proof-of-concepts' that explore the internationalization of courses and programmes through projects including the NCGIA Core Curricula, the Virtual Geography Department and the UniGIS Consortium (Kemp et al., 1998). More recently, as part of their 'Digital Libraries in the Classroom' initiative, the US National Science Foundation (NSF) and the European Joint Information System Committee (JISC) jointly funded a research and development project that combines the efforts of geographers, education specialists and computer scientists at the University of California at Santa Barbara, Pennsylvania State, Southampton and Leeds Universities. The aim is to develop and deploy reusable digital learning objects for geographic education through the Alexandria Digital Library (http://www.dialogplus.org). Among the various definitions of 'learning object' (e.g. IEEE Learning Technology Standards Committee, 2001; Wiley, 2002), the most practicable is L'Allier's (1997): "the smallest independent structural experience that contains an objective, a learning activity and an assessment".

To illustrate some of the potential of internationalized distance education for lifelong learning in geography, we continue by examining two successful areas of cross-border professional development: GIS and teacher professional development.

GIS Education and Training

As noted above, some of the greatest activity in geography has been in developing online courses and programmes in geographic information systems (GIS). However, even relatively high investment in online courses like UNIGIS is no guarantee in providing products that really meet the needs of students (Buckley & Donert, 2004).

The need for formal quality assurance mechanisms is particularly great in the realm of GIS education. In their popular college text *Geographic Information Systems and Science*, Longley et al. (2000) sketch both optimistic and pessimistic scenarios about the future of GIS. Their optimistic scenario envisions pervasive location-enabled technologies. "Within the next five years", they predict, "geographic information and maps will be everywhere" (Longley et al., 2000, p. 446). Their pessimistic scenario involves an identity crisis that threatens the potential of geographic information science to improve the quality of life. "As GIS technology becomes increasingly fragmented and embedded into specialist areas", they fear, "there is a danger that some may lose sight of core GIS values" (Longley et al., 2000, p. 445). Even as ESRI, the pre-eminent software vendor and host of the world's largest annual gathering of GIS professionals, promotes GIS as 'the language of geography', academic geographers are ambivalent about the discipline's identification with the technology. Currently, geography retains a central role in GIS higher education. We argue that the sustainability of this role is by no means assured, but that it will be strengthened to the extent that geography educators are able to (a) adapt our offerings to the needs of lifelong learners, many of whom need to study away from campus; (b) minimize curricular redundancies and stimulate collaboration and internationalization by sharing students within a marketplace of distance education providers; and (c) embrace accountability through voluntary participation in peer review and accreditation.

To advance their careers, professionals need credentials as well as the educational achievement that credentials denote. Colleges and universities are entrusted by society to confer educational credentials. More than 4000 higher education institutions are accredited in the US. However, none of the hundreds of GIS certification and degree programmes in the US have submitted to any formal, voluntary quality assurance mechanism such as those embodied in organizations like the Accreditation Board for Engineering and Technology. As the GIS profession matures and society's reliance on geographic information technologies increases, GIS education will be expected to be more accountable. Mindful of the fact that accreditation is essentially a peer review process, analogous to the quality assurance mechanism long institutionalized in academic publishing, DiBiase (2003) proposes that the GIS education community implement accreditation as a form of peer-reviewed publication. If GIS educators in geography departments do not accept responsibility to develop and participate in accreditation initiatives, it seems possible that authority for GIS education may migrate to accredited engineering programmes. The resulting marginalization of geography and kindred faculty could exacerbate the 'erosion of core GIS values' that so worries Longley and his colleagues.

Professional Development and Geography Teachers

Healey (2003, p.1) makes the point that while professional development of teachers of geography in primary and secondary schools was a "major achievement in geography education of the twentieth century, promoting the professional development of faculty teaching geography in higher education is one of the major challenges that faces us". We concede this point, but suggest several factors make the promotion of internationalized, online professional development options for school teachers also a worthy target for collaboration. Despite curriculum and language variation, we argue that an internationalized programme for teacher professional development would attract universal interest. The demographics, working lives and widespread distribution of geography teachers make online professional development particularly attractive.

For the past several years, geography faculties active in the Association of American Geographers' *Committee on College Geography*, in partnership with officers of the National Council for Geographic Education, have been engaged in an ongoing discussion about how best to develop, assess and disseminate a collaborative online degree programme in geography education. Building on a foundation of online degrees already in place at other institutions as early as the mid-1990s, and online geography courses offered at institutions such as the University of Colorado, Pennsylvania State University, the University of Oregon and Texas State University, this initiative provides a model programme designed to meet the needs of the adult learners discussed in this paper. Preliminary plans for launching this international degree program centre on offering graduate-level courses for teachers at three or more institutions that, in tandem, would meet the requirements of a rigorous, standards-driven and inclusive Master's degree.

A similar programme is being developed by the Institute of Education in London and the University of Waikato in New Zealand. The Institute of Education in London has a long history of providing learning experiences in geographical education for teachers located throughout the former British Commonwealth and beyond, and the progressive move to email- and Internet-based servicing of these adult learners has been a feature of developments since 2000. The Institute's collaborative work with the University of Waikato began in the late 1990s when an emphasis on the importance of including some reflexive work in theory relevant to the teaching and learning of geography was established. In part, this emphasis was adopted to address a growing divide (Goudie, 1993): the gap between new cultural geographies and skills and competences of a teacher body trained in methodologies of the 1970s and 1980s. In short, a professional development need that could be addressed by cooperative, cross-border provision of an online resource was identified. The early steps in establishing a module based on awareness of different 'perspectives' in geography is described in Chalmers *et al.* (2002). Bell & Gilbert's (1996) framework that emphasizes social and political dimensions of professional development was a key focus in the initiative.

Perhaps more important than the content was the constructivist model of teaching and learning that has been adopted at the University of Waikato. Based on more than a decade of teaching online courses in distance education mode, using a variant of the WebCT tutorial system known as ClassForum, the Waikato professional development option advocated a strong 'communities of practice' (Schlager & Fusco, 2003) approach to professional development. The principles used to articulate this approach to online distance education for professional development are described in Keown & Chalmers (2004). Early experiences with learners from a variety of cultural backgrounds have shown that some of the benefits of teaching and learning across (cultural) borders can be realized. Maori, Pakeha (New Zealanders of European Heritage) and Pacific Island teachers have all completed the module successfully.

Within Europe there are new opportunities available that target international audiences. The Erasmus Mundus programme is a cooperation and mobility programme that addresses the growing educational markets of Latin America, Africa and Southeast Asia with the provision of relevant, high-quality products with a European seal of approval. Erasmus Mundus is intended to strengthen European cooperation and international links in higher education by supporting high-quality European Master's courses. It will enable students and visiting scholars from around the world to engage in postgraduate study at European universities, as well as encouraging the outgoing mobility of European students and scholars towards countries in Asia, Africa and Latin America.

Internationalizing e-Learning for Professional Development

International partnerships leading to the sharing of Internet-based courses between institutions involved in teaching and learning is a positive development, yet there are some significant issues related to the design and quality assurance of such online provision. In this section of the paper we discuss three major challenges that we believe set the conditions for the success of internationalized professional development programmes in geography. The first challenge concerns international collaboration and the development and implementation of professional development programmes through distance learning. A second challenge is that of finding technical and practical solutions for sharing courses and students internationally. Third, we consider the challenge of programme accreditation, quality assurance and certification. Drawing on prior work and relevant theories in distance education and professional development, we offer some practical guidance to faculty, departments and institutions as they explore the prospects of internationalizing an online curriculum for professionals and lifelong learners.

Collaborative Development and Delivery of Internationalized Curricula

In recent years geographers have pursued a variety of strategies to design courses through international collaborations. Hurley *et al.* (1999) developed a course in which teams of students from the University of California, Santa Barbara and Westminster College, Utah collaboratively analysed problems of human-induced environmental change. Similarly, Reed & Mitchell (2001) and Warf *et al.* (1999) collaboratively developed and taught courses that linked students in the US and Europe. In each case, the authors reported the need to prepare students with the skills necessary to learn in online environments, an intercultural challenge that is especially daunting where the curriculum is specifically intended for an international audience.

This is an important issue because researchers are finding that students tend to learn geography differently from country to country. Healey *et al.* (2005) examined the learning styles of geography students in 12 different universities (three each in Australia, New Zealand, the United Kingdom and the United States). Students were asked in a survey to describe how they preferred to learn geography, with the results categorized using Kolb's (1984) learning style dimensions: *converger* (those who like to learn using abstract concepts and active experimentation, including labwork and fieldwork), *diverger* (those who like to learn using reflective observation and concrete experience, including writing journals and brainstorming), *accommodator* (those who like to learn using concrete experience and active experimentation, including simulations and case studies), and *assimilator* (those who like to learn using abstract concepts and reflective observation, usually by taking notes and listening in lectures). The study found that students in beginning geography courses are predominantly assimilators (46% of the sample). The next most common identified learning styles, in order, were convergers (24%), divergers (17%) and accommodators (14%).

Healey *et al.* (2005) also found significant variations in learning styles among students in the sampled universities, a phenomenon the authors attribute to international differences in faculty pedagogy training, course content and academic culture. Though these differences are likely to complicate internationalization, Foote's (1999) analysis of recent online curriculum projects in geography provides some clues as to how institutions can facilitate collaborative curriculum development. Based on his review, Foote recommends a number of strategies for collaboratively planning and designing international courses: spreading the work of preparing materials among many departments and instructors; providing faculty with training to learn effective practices for using instructional technology; offering compensation and rewards to faculty through existing academic mechanisms; and making use of existing funding models for developing international courses and programmes that meet shared educational goals. Even more complex is the intercultural aspects, where students from different backgrounds collaborate online within communities of learning, as these multi-dimensional aspects of engagement and participation are not well understood.

Efforts to internationalize geography education have also been assisted by the involvement of professional organizations and networks. In 2003, the Association of American Geographers launched an Online Center for Global Geography Education (http://www.aag.org/Education/center/) to provide college and university instructors with materials to engage students worldwide in collaborative projects that address contemporary global issues, while simultaneously teaching geographical skills and perspectives that have broad relevance for citizenship in a highly interdependent world (Solem et al., 2003). The Center's instructional modules are appropriate for introductory and advanced undergraduate courses in geography. Each module is a self-contained, Internet-supported collaborative learning environment featuring data-rich, highly interactive activities. Each module includes an instructor's guide to help professors plan an international teaching collaboration. All of the materials were collaboratively developed and tested by academic staff working in a broad range of higher education contexts and international settings (Klein, 2005); we believe their strategies are also applicable to the development of internationalized courses and degree programmes for adult professionals (Table 1).

A related challenge is the need to train course instructors as international collaborators. According to a survey examining patterns of international collaboration in post-secondary American geography, three out of every four professors have no previous experience with an international collaboration focused on teaching, course or curriculum development (Solem & Ray, 2005). These individuals cited a lack of professional incentives, training and departmental support as reasons for avoiding international collaboration. Unless these concerns are addressed constructively by those in leadership positions, the prospects of advancing an internationalized e-learning programme for professionals will be limited by the energies of an enthusiastic minority.

In Europe, funded Thematic Networks were intended to lead to the creation of an environment conducive to a more effective European cooperation and educational innovation by promoting discussions on improving teaching methods and developing Europe-wide joint projects (Almeira-Texeira, 1997). Since 2003, the HERODOT network (http://www.herodot.net) has grouped more than 100 European higher education geography departments in such debate, from which a number of collaborative international curriculum development proposals have been made. The establishment of a distinctive European curriculum dimension is acknowledged by the European Commission as a high priority, as education becomes increasing global (European Commission, 1993). However, recognition understanding and dealing with international issues as part of joint courses such as cultural differences and second/third language usage and related mutual understanding has yet to be addressed (van der Vaart et al., 2005).

Sharing Courses and Sharing Students

The direct benefits of learning new skills and the international credentialing associated with this training have meant that very sustainable programmes have been offered by both private providers and traditional institutions. We suggest that the use of new e-learning platforms could also be applied in more discursive, learner-centred programmes that address core issues of professional development in disciplines (Bell & Gilbert, 1996). The oldest of the major Internet tutorial systems claims initial authorship in the 1980s but the major platforms have been developed in the last five years. Landon (2002) points out that the institutional choice regarding the systems used for online teaching and learning is dependent on needs and budget, and his review identifies four of the major players: Blackboard, TopClass, Webcrossing and WebCT. These e-learning platforms create virtual environments that allow engagement with the more abstract (thinking) and less technical (skills) components of the geography curriculum. They develop communities of practice where a group of people share knowledge, learn together and create common

Table 1. Strategies for managing the development and delivery of internationalized curricula

Issues related to internationalization	Development and delivery strategies
Supporting collaborative learning activities among geographically distributed groups of instructors and students	• Develop instructional materials based on social constructivism • Adapt and develop collaborative technology (e.g. virtual classrooms, discussion boards) and digital media (Web pages, electronic mail) to facilitate asynchronous and synchronous communication
Complementing international differences in curricular content, scheduling, language, culture, learning style, teaching practices and philosophies of geography	• Collaboratively write lessons and activities with faculty members from multiple nations • Enable faculty to search for appropriate collaborators on the basis of course subject, lesson topic, type of activity, language, instructor location, desired dates of collaboration, student audience/division level, etc. • Diversify the length, complexity and pedagogy of lessons and activities • Produce materials in multiple languages
Emphasizing global perspectives in instruction	• Draw on international collaborative research findings for lesson content • Subject modules to international peer review • Design lessons that allow students to collaborate with peers in different world regions
Increasing participation from developing regions	• Make concerted efforts to include institutions from underrepresented regions
Facilitating international teaching collaborations	• Coordinate materials development and dissemination through disciplinary organizations • Provide faculty incentives and rewards (e.g. publish faculty projects, honouring exemplary collaborations with teaching awards)
Address uneven technical skills and access to technology	• Offer local, national and international training workshops held at professional conferences • Make training materials available via distance learning and digital media • Create low-technology and mobile-technology options whenever possible
Determining how international collaborative learning can enhance student achievement and faculty teaching	• Conduct systematic research on the process and outcomes of online international collaborative learning and teaching
Promoting broad adoption of and providing long-term access to high-quality international learning materials	• Adapt materials and strategies from earlier disciplinary projects to enhance the development of innovative materials • Use existing models and relationships with geography departments and organizations to disseminate materials nationally and internationally

practices. The challenge for online course developers is probably how to use these technologies in a creative, meaningful and effective way that will actually enable learning for some who might otherwise be excluded and really enhance the learning experience for many.

In the next decade, the institutions that thrive most in international partnerships serving lifelong learners may be those that develop online distance learning offerings that enable adult students to study at convenient times and places. These are likely to build partnerships with kindred distance-learning providers to share students and minimize redundancies in shared curricula. If university geography departments accept the responsibility to provide the kind of flexible, responsive educational offerings that adult professionals need, questions remain about how they do this while maintaining all the existing offerings that serve traditional resident students. Part of the solution may be to share students as well as curricula. Credit transfer systems like those being implemented in university exchange programmes and course agreements through international collaborative projects will be essential if this is to be achieved.

The impetus to share curricular materials runs counter to the practice of higher education institutions that provide similar courses in multiple locations to serve students who study in residence. Residency is defensible in the context of traditional undergraduates, for whom the resident experience is a valuable opportunity for personal development. But residency is often impractical for adult professionals. In principle, online distance education eliminates some of the barriers to higher education, such as inconvenient locations and schedule conflicts. Certainly, the required computing technologies, dependable Internet connections and access to specialized software pose barriers for some students, particularly in developing nations, and capacity building in these areas must be a key component of a truly internationalized system but enabling longstanding international academic collaboration will be critical if the global opportunities afforded by technology are not to be wasted.

In principle, while e-learning can help lifelong learners to access educational opportunities not otherwise available locally, it also enables them to engage the services of multiple institutions regardless of the institutions' physical location. In this way, distance education offers the possibility of sharing professional development options among partner institutions, each of which offers its own unique, and ideally complementary, learning opportunities. Common elements can sit comfortably alongside course components that emphasize local specificity and expertise.

Adult learners ought to be able to earn degrees and certificates by successfully completing curricula that they design in consultation with qualified advisers, within a marketplace of distance learning providers that is coordinated by one or more educational brokerages such as the Worldwide Universities Network (http://www.wun.ac.uk). Technological advances currently in development will make it easier to for institutions to share students in this way. One such technology is Shibboleth, an Internet2 middleware product that supports inter-institutional sharing of Web resources subject to access controls (http://shibboleth.internet2.edu). Shibboleth and related solutions promise to enable students to navigate among institutional course management systems without having to re-authenticate every time they cross virtual institutional boundaries. Boundary-bridging technologies like Shibboleth challenge education providers to develop meaningful articulation agreements that will reduce redundant content production and encourage collaborative inter-institutional and international curriculum design and development. The prospect of truly adaptive curricula that can accommodate students' unique goals, interests, prior knowledge and experience ought to justify the effort and expense required to negotiate the necessary inter-institutional agreements and to create the technological infrastructure needed to mediate those agreements in a way that is transparent to students and educators. We believe that such goals are obtainable well within a decade.

Accreditation, Quality Assurance and Certification

Accreditation is a system or process for providing a certain standard of quality and a tool for improvement used by educational institutions. This is normally undertaken through a system that examines the content, procedures and processes involved. Institutions of higher education and the courses they offer can thus be evaluated against established standards (Institute for Higher Education Policy, 2000), normally through a peer-review process including external scrutiny (CHEA, 2002). Accreditation is thus a system that provides an indication of the value of the courses in which students enrol. Ultimately it is also a benchmark against which employers recognize qualifications, skills and competences.

Higher education needs to have quality evaluation as well as formal periodic accreditation of new programmes. The question of accreditation is relatively new or is poorly developed in many countries. In the US, UK and many countries of the British Commonwealth the power to award degrees is normally vested in the higher education body of the national state. At present, most courses are designed, delivered and validated by that institution. Some university degree courses are moving towards a system of basing their courses on subject benchmark statements, which provide a means for the academic community as a whole to describe the nature and characteristics of the programmes in their specific subject. These benchmarks also represent general expectations regarding the standards for the award of qualifications at any given level and articulate the attributes and capabilities that those possessing such qualifications should be able to demonstrate. In the UK the benchmarking statement for geography has been drawn up by a group of invited subject specialists representing the broad spectrum of the subject area (QAA, 2000).

Academic qualifications need to have legal value if they are to be valued in the different countries. Quality assurance and certification mechanisms are normally the responsibility of the institution conferring credit for virtual courses and these processes are normally governed by state and national regulations. In the case of cross-border learning arrangements, both the sending and receiving countries need to share responsibility for these issues.

Dixon & Tammaro (2003) discuss issues raised by collaboration between European universities in the joint delivery of Master's courses. They comment that though international collaboration is often high on many university agendas at the most senior level, this often remains an intention only, and does not necessarily translate easily into truly collaborative ventures. Similar experiences are reported in Australia (Gallagher, 2000). The drawing up of legal contracts is likely to be difficult but necessary, and cultural adaptability, determination and the high motivation of professionals in geography education will be required.

With regard to quality assurance and certification, we suggest a multi-national agency is needed to establish an agreed set of rules that will operate at the national (and perhaps sub-national) level for disciplines interested in professional development for lifelong learners.

While the quality assurance and certification systems of universities are focused on accountability, in an international context what is needed is comparability standards for professional qualifications that do not create a jungle of degrees, standards and criteria (Haug & Tauch, 2001). In Europe, quality standards in higher education are being recommended by the establishment of a European Network for Quality Assurance in Higher Education (ENQA, 2004). Much of the former British Commonwealth uses the wide-ranging NARIC system. NARIC is the national agency under contract to the Department for Education and Skills (DfES). The agency is a source of information and advice on the comparability of international qualifications from over 180 countries worldwide. It also provides information on education systems and qualifications to higher education institutions, professional bodies and commercial organizations.

Opsomer & Van den Branden (2003) considered the collaborative efforts of traditional universities in a networked environment with the aim of exchanging and sharing learning materials, courses, packages and even full programmes in a virtual context. They investigated the possibilities and obstacles that would accompany the creation of a collaborative European Virtual University by considering technical or organizational issues including interoperability, language, accreditation, IPR and copyright and policy issues, such as marketing, ethical questions and quality assurance. They comment that quality assurance is of paramount importance in a collaborative model but that it differs from the quality assurance in a single university. They suggest that institutions which share and jointly develop online learning materials have to respect joint quality standards that will fundamentally affect their way of working. They comment that national or local quality control systems are unlikely to be sufficient in an academic environment. Establishing international courses requires that quality assurance and certification in e-learning consider the e-learner first but also that they explicitly address the institutional, national and international perspectives on teaching and learning. This implies the establishment of an interactive, online system with trained tutors that will facilitate cross-cultural dialogue and intercultural understanding.

Other issues of concern with e-learning in higher education relate to whether employers and professional credentialing authorities will value the skills, wider professional development and qualifications provided through cross-border online courses. There will be questions about how transferable credits are from cross-border online courses to domestic institutions and workplaces. We also anticipate that institutions will require these course providers to demonstrate evidence of a rigorous and worthwhile educational experience.

In Europe, the e-learning action plan (European Commission, 2000) establishes a series of targets associated with access, equipment, connectivity, support services and educational resources with the aim of integrating new learning methods and professional development based on information and communication technologies; this process has involved consultation with employer groups and professional credentialing authorities. The EU has set targets for member states with a higher education focus on virtual campuses to ensure that the quality and efficiency of learning processes and activities are maximized (European Commission, 2002). So, the issues of e-learning in higher education provide the need for national and wider-scale policy (ESRC, 2002). These issues are being debated as part of the Bologna Process, which requires the international transparency of higher educational systems and degrees, easily readable and comparable degrees, the establishment of a system of credits and European cooperation in quality assurance. This has been a top-down approach to major reform but it has attempted to involve higher education institutions, departments, academics, subject and even student associations (ESIB, 2005) as well as the policy-makers and politicians. We are, however, still some distance from creating accepted international standards.

Conclusion

Geographers are poised to lead higher education into an innovative era of internationalization by tapping the potential of distance-learning technologies to deliver high-quality professional education to an international market. They have the expertise, experience and constituency that prefigure a successful enterprise, yet as this paper, it is hoped, demonstrates there are any number of issues that could easily derail the process. As efforts to internationalize professional development move forward, we urge consideration of issues of fairness, equity and opportunity. Programme developers must attend to the diverse needs of the international community and strive to maximize the benefits of intercultural interaction. Care must be taken to avoid erecting barriers— whether cultural, technical or financial—that would limit participation to the privileged few. By attending to the lessons learned from the past, geographers ought to be able to introduce models of internationalization that account for international differences in academic culture and the expectations and professional needs of students while simultaneously integrating the perspectives and talents of faculty around the world. Internationalization will not have a broad impact on geography education unless students, faculty, departments and institutions understand its value for teaching, learning and professional development. Achieving this vision will require leadership and a tremendous amount of coordination on the part of academics, institutions and professionals. If done right, the outcome will be a professional workforce with the knowledge, skills and mindset for lifelong learning in a modern economy and globalized society.

Acknowledgements

The authors wish to thank Mick Healey, Steve Gaskin and others involved with organizing the International Network for Learning and Teaching Geography in Higher Education (INLT) Post-IGC Workshop in Glasgow, Scotland. They also acknowledge the anonymous referees who provided helpful suggestions for improving an earlier draft of this paper.

References

Almeira-Texeira, M. A. (1997) Thematic Network Projects: first years results, in: *Proceedings of the 1st European Thematic Network Forum*, 15–16 October 1997 in Dublin, pp. 10–30 (Barcelona: European Universities Continuing Education Network).

Bell, B. & Gilbert, J. (1996) *Teacher Development: A Model from Science Education* (London: Falmer Press).

Buckley, C. & Donert, K. (2004) Evaluating e-learning courses for continuing professional development using the Conversational Model: a review of UNIGIS, *European Journal of Open and Distance Learning* (online). Available at: http://www.eurodl.org/materials/contrib/2004/Buckley_Donert.html (accessed September 2005).

Chalmers, L., Keown, P. & Kent, A. (2002) Exploring different 'perspectives' in secondary geography: professional development options, *International Research in Geographical and Environmental Education*, 11(4), pp. 313–324.

CHEA (2002) Accreditation and Assuring Quality in Distance Learning, CHEA Monograph Series, Number 1 (Washington, DC: Council for Higher Education Accreditation). Available at: http://www.chea.org/Research/Accred-Distance-5-9-02.pdf?pubID=246 (accessed September 2005).

Colker, R. & Day, R. (2003) (Eds) Educational institution responsibilities and new skill sets, in Federal Natural Resources Agencies Confront an Aging Workforce and Challenges to Their Future Roles, *Renewable Resources Journal*, 21(4), Winter 2003–2004.

Cunningham, S., Ryan, Y., Stedman, L., Tapsall, S., Bagdon, K., Flew, P. & Coaldrake, P. (2000) *The Business of Borderless Education* (Canberra: DETYA). Available at: http://www.dest.gov.au/archive/highered/eippubs/eip00_3/bbe.pdf (accessed September 2005).

DfES (2005) Bologna Secretariat Website, Department for Education and Skills. Available at: http://www.dfes.gov.uk/bologna/ (accessed September 2005).

DiBiase, D. (2005) On accreditation and the peer review of geographic information science education, *Journal of the Urban and Regional Information Systems Association*, 15(1), pp. 7–14. Available at: http://www.urisa.org/Journal/Vol15No1/Dibiase.pdf (accessed September 2005).

Dixon, P. & Tammaro, A. M. (2003) Strengths and issues in implementing a collaborative inter-university course: the international master's in information studies by distance, *Education for Information*, 21(2–3), pp. 85–96.

Donert, K. (2003) HERODOT: European networking in geographical education, in A. Kent & A. Powell (Eds) *Geography and Citizenship Education: Research Perspectives*, pp. 129–136 (London: Institute of Education).

ENQA (2004) European Network for Quality Assurance in Higher Education. Available at: http://www.enqa.net/ (accessed September 2005).

ESIB (2005) An Introduction to Bologna, The National Union of Students in Europe. Available at: http://www.esib.org/BPC/intro/introbologna.html (accessed September 2005).

ESRC (2002) Working Towards E-Quality in Networked E-Learning in Higher Education: A Manifesto Statement for Debate. ESRC Research Seminar. Available at: http://csalt.lancs.ac.uk/esrc/manifesto.htm (accessed September 2005).

European Commission (1993) *White Paper on Growth, Competitiveness and Employment: The Challenges and Ways Forward into the 21st Century* (Brussels: Commission of the European Communities).

European Commission (2000) *e-Learning: Designing Tomorrow's Education* (Brussels: European Commission). Available at: http://europa.eu.int/eur-lex/en/com/cnc/2001/com2001_0172en01.pdf (accessed September 2005).

European Commission (2002) eEurope 2005: an information society for all. Available at: http://europa.eu.int/information_society/eeurope/2002/news_library/documents/eeurope2005/eeurope2005_en.pdf (accessed September 2005).

Foote, K. (1999) Building disciplinary collaborations on the World Wide Web: strategies and barriers, *Journal of Geography*, 98(3), pp. 108–117.

Gallagher, M. (2000) Corporate Universities, Higher Education and the Future: Emerging Policy Issues. Available at: http://www.dest.gov.au/archive/highered/otherpub/corp_uni.htm (accessed September 2005).

Golde, C. M. & Dore, T. M. (2001) *At Cross Purposes: What the Experiences of Doctoral Students reveal about Doctoral Education* (Philadelphia: Pew Charitable Trusts). Available at: http://www.phd-survey.org (accessed September 2005).

Goudie, A. (1993) Guest editorial: schools and universities—the great divide, *Geography*, 78(4), pp. 338–339.

Haug, G. & Tauch, C. (2001) Trends in learning structures in Higher Education (II). Follow-up report to the Bologna Declaration. Paper prepared for the Salamanca and Prague Conferences of March/May 2001.

Healey, M. (2003) Promoting lifelong professional development in geography education: international perspectives on developing the scholarship of teaching in higher education in the twenty-first century, *Professional Geographer*, 55(1), pp. 1–17.

Healey, M., Kneale, P. & Bradbeer, J. with other members of the INLT Learning Styles and Concepts Group (2005) Learning styles among geography undergraduates: an international comparison, *Area*, 37(1), pp. 30–42.

Hurley, J. M., Proctor, J. D. & Ford, R. E. (1999) Collaborative inquiry at a distance: using the Internet in geography education, *Journal of Geography*, 98(3), pp. 128–140.

IBM (2004) In the Future: Learning will Reshape our World at Work, at Home and at School. Available at: http://www.sric-bi.com/LoD/meetings/2004-12-06/IBMpaper.pdf (accessed September 2005).

IEEE Learning Technology Standards Committee (LTSC) (2001) Draft Standard for Learning Object Metadata Version 6.1 (New York: Institute of Electrical and Electronics Engineers). Available at: http://ltsc.ieee.org/wg12/files/LOM_1484_12_1_v1_Final_Draft.pdf (accessed September 2005).

Institute for Higher Education Policy (2000) *Quality on the Line: Benchmarks for Success in Internet-based Distance Education* (Washington, DC: National Education Association).

Kemp, K. K., Reeve, D. E. & Heywood, D. I. (1998) Report of the International Workshop on Interoperability for GIScience Education. Available at: http://www.ncgia.ucsb.edu/ige98/report/ige98.pdf (accessed September 2005).

Keown, P. & Chalmers, L. (2004) Continuing professional development of geography teachers, in: A. Kent, E. Rawling & A. Robinson (Eds) *Geographical Education: Expanding Horizons in a Shrinking World*, pp. 26–39 (Glasgow: Commission on Geographical Education).

Klein, P. (2005) Summative Evaluation: The Online Center for Global Geography Education. Available at: www.aag.org/education/center (accessed September 2005).

Kohl, K. J. (2000) The Post-baccalaureate learning imperative, in: K. J. Kohl & J. B. LaPidus (Eds) *Post-baccalaureate Futures: New Markets, Resources, Credentials*, pp (Phoenix, AZ: Oryx Press).

Kolb, D. A. (1984) *Experiential Learning* (Englewood Cliffs, NJ: Prentice-Hall).

L'Allier, James J. (1997) Frame of reference: NETg's map to the products, their structure and core beliefs. NetG. Available at: http://web.archive.org/web/20010712183454/www.netg.com/research/whitepapers/frameref.asp (accessed September 2005).

Landon, B. (2002) Hardware and Software used in Online Education. Available at: http://edutools.info/landonline/ (accessed September 2005).

Longley, P. A., Goodchild, M. F., Maguire, D. J. & Rhind, D. W. (2000) *Geographic Information Systems and Science* (Chichester: Wiley).

National Recognition Information Centre (2004) *UK NARIC* (London: Department for Education and Skills). Available at: http://www.naric.org.uk/ (accessed September 2004).

Nyquist, J. & Woodford, B. (2004) Re-envisioning the PhD: A challenge for the twenty-first century, in: D. Wulff & A. Austin (Eds) *Paths to the Professoriate: Strategies for Enriching the Preparation of Future Faculty*, pp. (San Francisco: Jossey-Bass).

OECD (Organization for Economic Co-operation and Development) (1998) *Staying Ahead: In-service Training and Professional Development* (Luxembourg: OECD).

Opsomer, A. & Van den Branden, J. (2003) Quality in a collaborative European Virtual University (cEVU), EuroPACE. Available at: http://www.cevu.org/Infos/Eden/cEVU%20workshop%20EDEN%20summary.pdf (accessed September 2005).

QAA (Quality Assurance Agency) (2000) *Benchmark Statement for Geography* (Gloucester: QAA). Available at: http://www2.glos.ac.uk/gdn/qaa/index.htm, accessed September 2004.

Reed, M. & Mitchell, B. (2001) Using information technologies for collaborative learning in geography: a case study from Canada, *Journal of Geography in Higher Education*, 25(3), pp. 321–339.

Robson, W. (2001) *Aging Populations and the Workforce: Challenge for Employers* (Washington, DC: British-North American Committee).

Schlager, M. & Fusco, J. (2003) Teacher professional development, technology and communities of practice: are we putting the cart before the horse?, *The Information Society*, 19, pp. 203–220.

Solem, M., Bell, S., Fournier, E., Gillespie, C., Lewitsky, M. & Lockton, H. (2003) Using the Internet to support international collaborations for global geography education, *Journal of Geography in Higher Education*, 27(3), pp. 239–254.

Solem, M. & Ray, W. (2005) AAG Report for the American Council on Education 'Where Faculty Live' project. Available at: http://www.aag.org/AAG_ACEfinalreport.pdf (accessed September 2005).

Tobias, S., Chibin, D. & Aylesworth, K. (1995) *Rethinking Science as a Career: Perceptions and Realities in the Physical Sciences* (Tucson, AZ: Research Corporation).

Tuning Project (2002) Tuning Educational Structures in Europe. Available at: http://www.relint.deusto.es/TuningProject/background.asp (accessed September 2005).

Van der Vaart, R., Beneker, T. & Paul, L. (2005) Getting geography students involved in European integration, in: K. Donert & P. Charnzynski (Eds) *Changing Horizons in Geography Education*, pp. 283–286 (Torun, Poland: HERODOT Network).

Warf, B., Vincent, P. & Purcell, D. (1999) International collaborative learning on the World Wide Web, *Journal of Geography*, 98(3), pp. 141–148.

Wiley, D. A. (2002) Connecting learning objects to instructional design theory: a definition, a metaphor, and a taxonomy, in: D. A. Wiley (Ed.) *The Instructional Use of Learning Objects*, pp. (Bloomington, IN: Agency for Instructional Technology).

Reflecting on Student Engagement

ERIC PAWSON, MICK HEALEY & MICHAEL SOLEM

The chapters in the four sections of this book have each focused on different aspects of active learning: re-imagining ourselves as learners; inquiry-based methods; new spaces of learning; and learning beyond the classroom. They are written from the premise that students who are encouraged to take responsibility for their own learning will be more readily engaged. This premise is in line with the first of the goals of the INLT, which is concerned with "critical reflection on learning and teaching of geography". In this concluding chapter we seek to reflect critically on the future of student engagement. We do this first by revisiting the concept as it has been understood in the past, and then discuss the results of national surveys of student engagement which give a picture of the extent of engaged behaviours amongst students today. We then consider the ways in which the changing dynamics of higher education might shape the future of active learning and engagement.

Revisiting student engagement

The idea of student engagement is not new, even if education continues to be widely practised as a process of transmission of knowledge, rather than as something that is actively transformative for individuals. As Mark Twain famously put it, "I have never let my schooling interfere with my education". This was a theme that concerned the great anarchist-geographer Peter Kropotkin when a post-imperial future for geography was being debated in the 1880s. He argued that the discipline was ideally placed to awaken the curiosity of the child in the world (Kropotkin, 1885). He called for greater self instruction and discovery-based learning, not only "as an instrument for the general development of the mind", but also to "teach us, from our earliest childhood, that we are all brethren, whatever our nationality" (Kropotkin, 1885, 941-2).

    The philosopher John Dewey had not dissimilar views. He portrayed geography, with history, in *Democracy and Education* (1916), as "the two great school resources for bringing about the enlargement of the significance of direct personal experience". "Geography is a topic that originally appeals to imagination .. the variety of peoples and environments .. furnishes infinite stimulation" (Dewey, 1985, 226). But like Kropotkin, he was critical of standard school practices that taught the subject as "isolated heaps" of information devoid of social meaning (Dewey, 1985, 218). In *How We Think*, published in 1933, he wrote that "[u]nderstanding, comprehension, means that various parts of the information acquired are grasped in relation to one another – a result that is attained only when acquisition is accompanied by constant reflection upon the meaning of what is studied" (Hickman and Alexander, 1998, 274).

As early as 1897, Dewey had begun to expound an approach favouring inquiry over passive education. He urged that the interests of the child, which he wrote "represent dawning capacities", be encouraged because to "repress interest is to substitute the adult for the child, and so to weaken intellectual curiosity and alertness, to suppress initiative, and to deaden interest" (Hickman and Alexander, 1998, 233). By contrast he saw successful methods of education as those which "give pupils something to do, not something to learn; and the doing is of such a nature as to demand thinking, or the intentional noting of connections; learning naturally results" (Fournier 2009, 88). Since then, many theorists have explored how the process of learning occurs. It is not hard to see echoes of Dewey in Piaget's influential work about the development of learning in children, or in the critical pedagogy of Friere and his condemnation of the role of the teacher as "filling up" rather than "drawing out" the student. Similarly, Kolb's theory of experiential learning and learning styles, outlined in our chapter 1 of this book, builds on Dewey's focus on the learner.

In 1975, Graham Little codified key aspects of the relationship between learning and student engagement in his book *Faces on the Campus*. He derived a typology that identified four types of learning environment based on two axes: one of levels of "challenge" and one of levels of "support" (Little, 1975). He argued that the "cultivating climate" is the most productive for student learning, because it is characterised by high academic standards, or levels of challenge, along with provision of support and recognition from faculty, in the form of encouraging features such as availability and feedback.

Patterns of student engagement

The extent to which students have access to, or take advantage of, such cultivating climates can be assessed from responses to campus surveys or those carried out at larger inter-institutional scales. The primary sources here are the NSSE (the National Survey of Student Engagement) initiated in 1999 amongst American students, and later in Canada, and the AUSSE (the Australasian Survey of Student Engagement), begun in 2007 (Coates, 2006; Kuh, 2009). In 2008, the NSSE was administered at more than 700 institutions in the United States, whilst 29 higher education institutions in Australia and New Zealand participated in the AUSSE, ie more than half the universities in the region. An intentional characteristic of such surveys is that they are not self-referential, i.e. they report the experiences of students, rather than faculty interpretations of those experiences. Their most important purpose is to provide high quality data that institutions can use to improve the undergraduate experience (Kuh, 2009).

The analysis of NSSE data reveals that colleges and universities that perform well in two areas, namely student engagement and graduation rates, have higher than predicted scores on five clusters of educational practice (Kuh *et al*, 2005). These five clusters reflect and also unpack the two dimensions of Little's model. The first is level of academic challenge, as indicated by the nature of intellectual and creative work and the value that the institution places on this. The second is active and collaborative learning, encouraging students to take responsibility for their own developing thinking, to reflect on it, and to do so in conjunction with others. The third is student interactions with faculty members, so that the latter are seen to act as role models, mentors and guides for effective learning. The fourth is enriching educational experiences, on campus, in the community and through internships and study abroad programmes, echoing the concern of Kropotkin more than a century ago that formal and informal curricula provide opportunities to work with others different to oneself. The fifth is a supportive campus environment that puts student experience at the centre of institutional strategy (Kuh *et al*, 2005).

If these are the practices that are exhibited by those schools that perform well in terms of student engagement, what are the overall patterns of experience as reported by students in the student engagement surveys? The 2008 AUSSE survey results map those from Australasia onto those from the United States. These reveal significant differences, which may reflect a number of factors, including real differences in practice. In terms of "challenge", for example, whilst a quarter of students in Australasia report that there is "very much" institutional emphasis given to "spending significant time on academic work", in the USA, the figure is more than 35 percent (ACER, 2009, 14). In respect of more concrete activities, reported for the current academic year, the same divergence shows up. Only five percent of American students above first year had not made a presentation in class, whereas in Australasia the figure was almost one fifth. About 43 percent of the first group compared to three quarters of the second group had not tutored other students during the year, even though teaching fellow students is an excellent way to learn (ACER, 2009, 19).

There are likely to be a range of explanations for such differences. Universities in Australia and New Zealand are almost without exception publicly funded and usually quite large. They have a number of strategic objectives of which generation of research outputs and of research income are seen as being of as great if not greater significance than undergraduate learning and teaching. Many of the institutions in the NSSE sample are smaller, often focused on teaching undergraduates and lacking a postgraduate element. Nonetheless there are also large, public research-oriented universities in the American sample. The picture of student engagement revealed by the surveys will therefore hide considerable within-sample variation. Similar differences would likely be revealed should such surveys be undertaken in other countries with quite different educational traditions, such as France, Germany and Britain.

Distinctions borne of culture and opportunity can make a dramatic difference to student experiences. Nearly two thirds of American later year students have participated in service learning, compared to only a quarter of Australasian students (ACER, 2009, 26). The vast majority of students in Australia and New Zealand have therefore not had the opportunity to expand their horizons through such work despite the frequent commitment of their universities to community engagement in high-level plans. Nor do the majority interact, or feel able to interact with faculty. Whereas half of American first year students and 59 percent of those in later years have discussed their grades or assignments with teaching staff, the equivalent figures for Australasia are 24 percent and 18 percent. Only 30 percent of first year Australasian students have "often" or "very often" sought advice from academic staff; the level for later year students is just over 40 percent (ACER, 2009, 22-3).

These figures suggest that even amongst American students, there are large numbers who are not actively engaged in the ways that Kuh *et al* (2005) assess as beneficial to learning. The next section of this concluding chapter looks at how the changing dynamics of higher education might either rectify or exacerbate this state of affairs.

The changing context of student engagement

The sort of strategies that have been discussed in this book to promote active learning are being implemented within systems of higher education that have been changing rapidly. The key shifts in many countries are towards massification and internationalisation (Teather 2004). This has been accompanied by what has been called "decentralized centralization", i.e. enhanced institutional autonomy alongside increasing accountability to both governments and educational consumers (Shin and Harman, 2009). Such accountability takes a range of forms. Quality audit processes are a tangible expression of it, but the more direct contribution to public discourse has been debate about the knowledge economy and the role of universities in research, innovation and commercialisation. Therein lies the potential conflict between the growing demands of teaching more students and the business of doing successful research.

Outside the United States, which has long had a large number of universities and colleges as well as high participation rates, massification – or rapid growth in size – has become an obvious characteristic of many systems of higher education. For example, in Britain in the early 1960s, only 6 percent of under 21 year olds went to university; by the early 2000s, when the system had diversified considerably, 43 percent of those aged 18 to 30 attended some form of tertiary level institution. As elsewhere, this expansion was accompanied by a sharp fall in funding levels per student during the 1990s, but with the expectation that participation rates would be raised still further, to around 50 percent of all 18 to 30 year olds (DES, 2003). In part the decline in unit funding has been countered, particularly in Canada, the United Kingdom, Australia and New Zealand, by internationalisation of the student body (Scott and Dixon, 2009). It is not unusual for between 15 and 30 percent the roll of universities in these countries to be from overseas.

The student body has therefore changed dramatically. So, John Tagg (2008) asks, why can't colleges? Earlier, in a well-known article co-authored with Robert Barr, he had announced a shift "taking hold in American higher education" from teaching to learning (Barr and Tagg, 1995, 13). The newer article was written in response to a concern that institutional change in this respect has been much slower than they had anticipated. In it he identifies a series of issues underlying what Inderbitzin and Stoors call "the conflict between transformative pedagogy and bureaucratic practice" (2008, 47). These include structural, informational, incentive and cultural barriers (see also Scott and Dixon, 2009). Not many institutions have set out, as has the University of Central Lancashire, for example, "to develop a culture in which excellence in developing learning is recognised and rewarded at individual and team levels". To do this, "[t]he University will, as a priority, raise the status, recognition and rewards for the learning and teaching role of staff to a level equivalent to that given to research" (DES, 2003, 51).

Tagg, however, argues that in most institutions, the investment in faculty training to encourage "a more learning-centered approach to teaching" has had limited success because "the incentives contradict the training". By this he means that the penalties for being research inactive are "public and visible", whereas those for not improving one's teaching are "private and invisible" (Tagg, 2008, 18-19). Not everyone would agree: for many poor teachers, the failure is immediate and recurrent; for good teachers, the approbation is ongoing. In many institutions and countries awards for teaching excellence have some profile (Higher Education Academy, 2006; Ako Aotearoa, 2008). In chapter 3 of this collection, Scheyvens *et al* seek to dispel what they call the "myth" of "significant institutional barriers to promoting active learning". One not insignificant reason for this is the evidence of a body of literature that demonstrates that there can be strong, if variable, links between teaching and research (Jenkins *et al*, 2002; Healey, 2005). These include the consequences to faculty in terms of student disengagement should they not be research active, or if they do not encourage their students to benefit from co-learning through research-based inquiry (Gardiner and D'Andrea, 1998, 1-2). Although students do identify negative effects where there is an over-emphasis on research, many see "the connection between teaching and research as positive, finding the proximity to research stimulating" (House of Commons, 2009, 76).

Student voice

If there is one feature that is often absent from "the majority of academic research, practice, and policy formulation" it is student voice (McMahon and Zyngier, 2009, 167). It seems an appropriate place to end a book that discusses and promotes active learning and student engagement with a renewed emphasis on student perspectives. No matter how much the context of higher education has changed in recent decades, from the point of view of the learner, it is individual experience that remains paramount, and it is the good and bad aspects of that experience that are remembered and learned from. Put in official language, this means that the higher education sector must simultaneously meet "the needs of the economy in terms of trained people, research, and technology transfer [as well as] enable all suitably qualified individuals to develop their potential both intellectually and personally" (DES, 2003, 21).

These two goals are not mutually exclusive, as the chapters in this book have demonstrated. Students learn most readily when they are enabled to work in a cultivating atmosphere, one that provides space for and listens to their voices. Echoing chapter 1 by Le Heron *et al* on co-learning, this means "[i]nstead of teachers teaching students, I want it to be people teaching people" (McMahon and Zygnier, 2009, 173). Another way of putting this is to long for "dialogue rather than monologue" (Perry 2009). This inevitably involves a degree of pedagogical reciprocity, where "a power-sharing teacher [is] authorised to make higher demands on the students because students have been authorised to make higher demands on the teacher" (Shor, 1996, 125). As one student put it, "the teachers I found were most positive had high expectations" (McMahon and Zygnier, 2009, 175), again echoing a key characteristic of Little's cultivating environment (cf. Friere 1972; Finkel, 2000).

High expectations however need to be matched by interest and support. "The lecturers .. provide good feedback and are genuinely interested in your progress. They stimulate [us] to find out more as well" (ACER, 2009, 13). Feedback is not evaluation: it is information and encouragement that helps someone to improve (Tagg, 2008). Hattie (2009) has identified the significance of feedback that, from students' point of view, is perhaps the most tangible expression of "genuine interest" in their progress. Knowing that such interest is there is much more likely to lead to self-learning: "[l]iving on campus is a good way to learn to motivate self learning and to have others around you who are doing the same helps" (ACER, 2009, 25). But not everyone will feel included without active forms of learning that facilitate student learning interactions. It is questionable for instance whether the internationalisation of higher education has helped students to discover that "we are", in Kropotkin's phrase, "all brethren" (1885, 942). As an engineering student put it, "[t]here should be more group projects and teachers should encourage local students to engage with students from different ethnic backgrounds while working on these projects. There is hardly any interaction between local and international students" (ACER, 2009, 25).

There are, however, a number of ways to engage with diversity, as the chapters in this book have shown: for example, problem-based learning, community engagement and service learning, international collaborative learning. Students may initially struggle with such approaches, but as Spronken-Smith *et al* observe, with facilitation this can be transformed into a "new awareness of learning". Such awareness comes with accepting responsibility, with a willingness to take a few risks, and with a growing capacity to reflect. As one student notes in chapter 3 by Scheyvens *et al*, reflecting on concepts highlighted in an e-portfolio improved understanding of them "and became far greater than ... if no reflection occurred". This consciously internalised a process of knowledge construction, "developing an understanding of how the concepts relate to me ... making my learning appear more valuable for the future".

Active, supportive, challenging and inclusive learning experiences therefore not only encourage engagement; they underwrite a process of life long learning. Such experiences and those who facilitate them may also be remembered for a lifetime.

References

ACER (2009) *Engaging Students for Success. Australasian Student Engagement Report*. Camberwell, Vic.: Australian Council for Educational Research.

Ako Aotearoa (2008) *Supporting Excellence in Tertiary Education, Tertiary Teaching Excellence Awards 2008*, Wellington: National Centre for Tertiary Teaching Excellence.

Barr, R. and Tagg, J. (1995) "From teaching to learning: a new paradigm for undergraduate education," *Change*, 27(6), pp. 12-25.

Coates, H. (2006) *Student Engagement in Campus-based and Online Education. University Connections*, Abingdon: Routledge.

DES (2003) *The Future of Higher Education*, London: Department for Education and Skills.

Dewey, J. (1985) *Democracy and Education 1916. The Middle Works of John Dewey 1899-1924 Volume 9*, Carbondale: Southern Illinois University Press.

Finkel, D. (2000), *Teaching with Your Mouth Shut*, Portsmouth, NH: Boynton/Cook.

Fournier, E. (2009) "Active learning," Solem, M., Foote, K. & Monk, J. (eds.), *Aspiring Academics. A Resource Book for Graduate Students and Early Career Faculty*, pp. 86-99, Upper Saddle River, NJ: Pearson Education.

Friere, P. (1972) *Pedagogy of the Oppressed*, Harmondsworth: Penguin.

Gardiner, V. & D'Andrea, V. (1998) *Teaching and Learning Issues and Managing Educational Change in Geography*, Cheltenham: Geography Discipline Network.

Hattie, J. (2009) *Visible Learning: A Synthesis of over 800 Meta-analyses Relating to Achievement*, London: Routledge.

Higher Education Academy (2006) *Celebrating Excellence. Six Years of the National Teaching Fellowship Scheme*, York: Higher Education Academy.

Healey, M. (2005) "Linking research and teaching to benefit student learning," *Journal of Geography in Higher Education*, 29(2), pp. 183-201.

Hickman, L. and Alexander, T. (eds.) (1998) *The Essential Dewey. Volume 1: Pragmatism, Education, Discovery*, Bloomington: Indiana University Press.

House of Commons (2009) *Students and Universities: Eleventh Report of Session 2008-09*, Volume 1, Innovation, Universities, Science and Skills Committee, London: The Stationery Office.

Inderbitzin, M. and Storrs, D. (2008), "Mediating the conflict between transformative pedagogy and bureaucratic practice," *College Teaching*, 56(1), pp. 47-52.

Jenkins, A., Breen, R., Lindsay, R. and Brew, A. (2002) *Re-shaping Teaching in Higher Education: A Guide to Linking Teaching with Research*, London: Routledge.

Kropotkin, P. (1885) "What geography ought to be," *The Nineteenth Century*, 18, pp. 940-56.

Kuh, G. (2009) "The National Survey of Student Engagement: conceptual and empirical foundations," *New Directions for Institutional Research*, 141, pp. 5-20.

Kuh, G., Kinzie, J., Schuh, J., Whitt, E. & Associates (2005) *Student Success in College. Creating Conditions that Matter*, San Francisco: Jossey-Bass.

Little, G. (1975) *Faces on the Campus. A Psycho-social Study*, Carlton, Vic: Melbourne University Press.

McMahon, B. & Zyngier, D. (2009) "Student engagement: contested concepts in two continents," *Research in Comparative and International Education,* 4(2), pp. 164-81.

Perry III, L. (2009). Personal communication, 15 September, University of Canterbury.

Scott, S. & Dixon, K. (2009) "Partners in a learning organization: a student-focused model of professional development," *The Educational Forum*, 73(3), pp. 240-55.

Shin, J. C. and Harman, G. (2009) "New challenges for higher education: global and Asia-Pacific perspectives," *Asia Pacific Education Review,* 10, pp. 1-13.

Shor, I. (1996) *When Students Have Power: Negotiating Authority in a Critical Pedagogy*, Chicago: University of Chicago Press.

Tagg, J. (2008) "Changing minds in higher education. Students change, so why can't colleges?" *Planning for Higher Education,* 37(1), pp. 15-22.

Teather, D. (2004) "The changing context of higher education: massification, globalisation and internationalisation," D. Teather (ed.) *Consortia. International Networking Alliances of Universities*, pp. 8-27, Carlton, Vic.: Melbourne University Press.

Index

Page numbers in *Italics* represent tables.
Page numbers in **Bold** represent figures.

Aboriginal communities 30
active learning 2, **75**; approaches 40-1; direct support 52; exercises 43; geography 4-6, 39-56; geography course strategies *42-3*; rationale and theory 3; strengths 40; student workload 51; variety of learning strategies 39
active learning implementation 41-8; case studies 43-8; e-portfolios 46-8; literature reports 41-3; online discussions 44-5; problem-based learning 44; reading journals 45-6
active learning myths 48-53; first time students 49; institutional constraints 51-2; just doing is active learning 48-9; knowledge transmission 52-3; lecturing 49-50; too much work 50
active learning successful integration 53-5; appropriate assessment activities 54; introduced from start of degree 53; student guidance 53-4; student reflection 55-6; written into course objectives 53
actor-network thinking 17
Adams, W.M.: and Stoddart, D.R. 89, 95
Advanced Geospatial Skills in Science and Social Science (AGSSS) 173-4
Alexander, B. 122
Alexandria Digital Library 196
Altbach, P.G. 105
alumni: connections with 188
alumni advice 144
American higher education 158-9; curricular innovations 159; multicultural initiatives 159

anti-terrorism bill: United Kingdom (UK) 27
applied geography 18, 172; growing importance 185
Association of American Geographers (AAG) 126; Centre for Global Geography 27, 77-8, 107, 199-200; Committee on College Geography 197; Enhancing Departments and Graduate Education (EDGE) 134; Sauer's presidential address (1956) 89
Australasian Survey of Student Engagement (AUSSE) 209, 210
Australia: Master's level education 132; overseas postgraduate students 133

Baldwin-Evans, K. 124
Barnett, R.: and Coata, K. 1
bebo.com 123
behaviour: perceived norms 111
Beringer, J. 65
Besio, K. 155
best practice initiatives 107-8
Bigelow, B.: *et al* 159-60
Biggs, J. 48
blended/distance/flexible learning 123-4
Bologna Declaration 183
Bologna Process 134, 195, 204
Bournemouth University 175
Boyd, B.: and Taffs, K. 30
Boyer Commission 81
Boyer, E. 15
Bradbeer, J. 64

California State University: World Regional Geography 44

campus-based students and distance learners 78
career planning 141
Carpenter, J.: and Kern, E. 91, 93
Carr, R.E. 120
Casey, M.B.: and Howson, P. 61
Castree, N. 13
Centre for Active Learning (CeAl) 2, 107; approach to active learning **3**; teaching for understanding 3
Centres for Excellence in Teaching and learning (CETLs) 107
Chalmers, L.: and Keown, P. 198
Cheltenham Climate Change Forum (2001) 19
Chickering, A.W.: and Gamson, Z.F. 2
Chile: employability 184-5
Chronicle of Higher Education 173
Ciardiello, A.V. 72-3
Clark, R.E. 117
co-learning 9, 11-20; beyond geography 14; definition 11-12; dimensions of 15; problem-solving activities 18
co-learning communities 20, 140-1
Coata, K.: and Barnett, R. 1
Cochrane, P. 122
Colegio Profesional of geographers 185
collaboration: developing and enhancing 112; many faces 103-5; positive sense 104; sinister meaning 104; transnational projects 104-5
collaborative learning 111; initiatives 105, 112, 113
communication skills: capitalizing on diversity 142-3; development 78, 172; professional posters 142; writing for different audiences 143
community engagement: benefits 177-8; challenges 179; community of interest 169; context 168; definition 169; dependent factors 171; geographic knowledge and skills 171; goals and learning outcomes **169**; learning and teaching tool 168-71; long-run benefits 179; moral and civic responsibility 172; physically proximate groups 170; project goals 171; range of geographical scales 170; rational and purposes 171-3; research 168; service requirements 173; strategies *178*; student learning in geography 167-79; temporal dimensions 170; three-stage process 169-70; transnational vision 168; United States of America (USA) 167-8; win-win-win 179

community engagement case studies 173-7; consultancy projects, Australia 176; indigenous values, New Zealand 174; research-based 174-5; service-based 173-4; supporting emergency planning 175-6; work-based 176-7
Conacannon, F.: *et al* 125
Conference Board of Canada 182-3
Connor, H. 172
Cribb, A.: and Gewirtz, S. 151
cross-disciplinary groups 20
Cuban, L.: and Tyack, D. 117
cultural geography 30
Curtis, D.: and McKenzie, P. 182, 190

deep learning and understanding 52
degree: life after 94
degree courses: outcome-based assessments 134; subject benchmark statements 203
Democracy and Education (Dewey) 208
Development and Inequality course: Massey University, New Zealand 45, 50
Dewey, J. 73
distance education 194-205
distance learners and campus-based students 78
distance/blended/flexible learning 123-4
diversity: defining 136; drawing strength from 139-40; and learning design 146; and learning environment 137-9; postgraduate education *138*; postgraduate learning environments *139*; student peers and staff 145
Dixon, P.: and Tammaro, A.M. 203

e-learning 77-8, 84, 101; accreditation 203; certification 203-5; collaborative

development 199-200; effective practice **124**; geography's teaching 116-27; initiatives 126; materials 107; open content initiatives 123; platforms 200; professional development 198-205; quality assurance 203-5; as research topic **118**; sharing courses and students 200-3; student and employer interest 125-6; types 116-17; ways to implement 124-6; websites *119*
e-portfolio 46-8; assessment 48; options 51; student home-page **47**; student remarks 47-8, 49, 50, 55
e-tools 118-21
Earth Surface Processes and Landforms: Loughborough University 76
education and technology 117
Eflin, J.: and Sheaffer, A.L. 172
Elliott, D. 52
employability: Chile 184-5; Estonia 185; for geography 181-91; Greece 186; international views 184-7; Italy 184; skills 191; Spain 185; United Kingdom (UK) 186
employability definitions 182-4
employability issues: agendas and approaches 187-91; current strengths 188; developing employability 187-8; employment experience 189-90; first-generation students 190; graduate employability reporting 190; institutional and department outreach 189; skills language 190-1; vocational and placement opportunities 188-9
employers: skills agenda 190
employment rates 190
enquiry: independence of 60
Environmental Hazards course: University of New South Wales 46, 54
environmental management 30
environmental and social indicators 46
Estonia: employability 185; Institute of Geography 185
ethical considerations 29
ethical dilemmas 143
ethical geographer 4; geography curricula 22-32

The Ethical Geographer, Oxford Brooks University 31-2; assessment 32; coursework ethics 31-2; ethical component 32
ethical issues: advanced professional context 143
ethical learning 9
ethical practice: literature 26; research 30
ethical skills 24
ethics: concepts and behaviours 25-7; disengaged graduate **24**; empowered graduate **25**; and ethical behaviour 30-1; and ethical considerations 24-5; institutional and personal components 26; refugee case study 27-8; research focus on 29; research methods course 29; teaching and learning 23; university geography education 22-32
ethics committees 27
European Network for Quality Assurance in Higher Education (ENQA) 204
European Union: SOCRATES Programme 107
European Virtual University 204
experiential learning 171

Faces on the Campus (Little) 209
feedback: online discussion 45
Fenwick, T.J. 59, 63
field data: collection 78
Field Research Studies: University of Otago, New Zealand 78
field school: ban 51
field study 5
fieldwork teaching: role of technology 90
Fink, L.D. 92
flexible/blended/distance learning 123-4
Flinders University, South Australia 176
Fluck, A.: and Robertson, M. 123
Foote, K. 199
Fournier, E.J.: and Wu, C.V. 61
Freire, P 155
French, D.: and Russell, C. 81
Fuller, I.C.: *et al* 91

Fusco, J.: and Schlager, M. 121
FutureLab 122

Gardiner, V.: and Unwin, D. 90
Geocast 123
geographers: careers list 189; and diversity 4; equity and social justice 150; humanities approach 145; interdisciplinary and multidisciplinary debates 144
geographic information system (GIS): certification and degree programmes 197; desktop applications 183; education accreditation 197; education and training 196-7; emergency response situation 175; prototype software 175
Geographic Information Systems and Science (Longley) 196
geographical language: international geography 18; river environments 18
geographies of children: University of Manchester 52
geography: active learning strategies 42-3; active learning and student engagement 4-6; case material 5; engaging with other disciplines 19-20; ethical teaching 29; faculty development 5; hands on subject 55; innovation in education practice 17; inquiry-based learning 72-84; international collaborative learning 113; learning processes 12; problem-based learning 58-69; professional career 181; professional development 194-205; promoting cultural empathy 154; re-linking research and teaching 11-20; relationship with government 153
geography curricula: employability 181; ethical geographer 22-32; ethics and ethical behaviour 30-1; problem-based learning 63-5
geography department websites 189
geography education 5; building on success 196-8; lifelong learners 194-5
Geography Faculty Development Alliance workshop 137

geography fieldwork: definitions and forms 88-9; high regard 89; history 89-90; overseas component 95; positive perceptions 92; research needed 96; residential overseas fieldtrip 95; teaching 91; types 89
geography fieldwork effectiveness: case studies 98-100; cohort identity and engagement 93-4; employability skills and lifelong learning 94; international case 92-3; international perspectives 88-100; Liverpool Hope University, United Kingdom (UK) 98-9; Massey University, New Zealand 99-100; National University of Singapore 99; recommendations 93; recruitment and image 95; research questions 93-5; surveys 92; University College Chester, United Kingdom (UK) 98; what works 90-2
geography graduates: job market 183
Geography and Related Disciplines: University of Gloucestershire 78-9
geography in schools 153
geography sub-disciplines 157
geography teachers 197
geography teaching 152; e-tools 118-21
geography textbooks 17
Gerber, R. 94
Gewirtz, S.: and Cribb, A. 151
Gibbs, G. 2, 41
Gold, J.R.: *et al* 89, 91
Greece: curriculum boundary conditions 186; employability 186
Gregory, D. 153
Gregson, N 19
gross domestic product (GDP) 151
group work 63

Haig, M. 31
Hamble Estuary Partnership (HEP) 174-5
Hanson, S.: and Moser, S. 39-40, 50
Hardwick, S.W. 28
Hay, I. 25, 29, 152
Healey, M. 15, 197
Healey, R.L. 28

Index

Hellstén, M.: and Ninnes, P. 104
higher education: collaborative arrangements 104; graduate and larger society 182; information and communication technology (ICT) 116; internationalization 109, 113; quality evaluation 203; and social transformation 154; teachers of geography 156-7
Higher Education Council for England (HEFCE) 14, 132
Higher Education Institutions (HEIs) 134
higher education systems: European convergence 183; South Africa 158
higher-level thinking skills 40, 47-8
Homeland Security restrictions 28
How We Think (Dewey) 209
Howson, P.: and Casey, M.B. 61
human geography 43; research and teaching 157
Human Subjects Protocol 28
Hurley, J.M.: *et al* 199

ice-breaker activities: student diversity 140-1
Inderbitzin, M.: and Stoors, D. 211
India: geographies of gender 154
Indian higher education: government policies 158; instigating change 158
Indiresan, J. 158
Informal Mobile Podcasting and Learning Adaptation (IMPALA) 123
information and communication technology (ICT) 116
innovative methodologies: designing 143-4
inquiry-based learning **75**; active learning 74; assignment as part of course 77; benefits and challenges students 79-80; benefits and challenges teaching staff 80-2; component of a field course 76-7; contemporary scope 75; contested landscapes 73-5; course 78; degree programmes 78-9; emotional turmoil 82; essential and optional attributes *73*; facilitated or scaffolded learning 74; geography 72-84; geography examples of 75-9; how to facilitate 83-4; inquiry process model **74**; modules of a course 77-8; problem-based learning and active learning **75**; question-driven 73; research oriented 73; short in-class activity 76; social transformation 156; student engagement 81; student or learner-centred 74; student learning outcomes 79; teaching implications 82-4; teaching staff practical suggestions 83; teaching team management 82-3; teaching-research links 80; umbrella term 79; which type to use 82
International Alliance of Research Universities (IARU) 109
international collaborative learning: cultural issues 113; developing and enhancing 103-13; educational benefit assumption 111; establishing collaboration 109-10; forms and context 105-9; geography 113; intercultural differences 110; joint degree programmes 108; joint module programmes 107; managing collaboration 110-12; module logistics 107; network of practitioners 106-7; partnership hierarchies 110; strategic alliances 108-9
International Network for Learning and Teaching Geography in Higher Education (INLT) 1; extensive literature 16; purposes 106; University of Strathclyde workshop 20
internationalized curricula: development and delivery *201*
Internet-based courses 198
internships 176, 188
Italy: employability 184

Jenkins, A. 60
Jocoy, C. 44
Johns, K. 69
joint degree 108; number of students 108
Journal of Geography in Higher Education 1
Justice, C.: *et al* 79

Kahn, P.: and O'Rourke, K. 75, 83
Keown, P.: and Chalmers, L. 198
Kern, E.: and Carpenter, J. 91, 93
key transferable skills 94
Kimmel, A.J. 25
King, S. 81
Knight, C.: *et al* 125
knowledge-production strategies 16
Kolb, D.A. 3, 4, 43
Kolb's learning styles 80, 199
Kozma, R.B. 117, 118
Kropotkin, P. 208
Kuh, G.D. 2

learner-centred programmes 200
learners: re-imagining ourselves as 4; virtual communities 101
learning: by doing 73; constructivist approaches 121; effects of activity 48; inquiry approach classification 75; new spaces 5; and previous experiences 41
learning communities: flexible to diversity 146; integrating alumni 144
learning design: and diversity 146
learning environment: co-learners community 20; and diversity 137-9
learning spaces 121-4; communities of learners 121-2; versatility and geography's **127**
Learning and Teaching Support Network 65
lectures 63; passive listening 40; theoretical knowledge 50
Lee, D.O. 157
lifelong learners: demographic trends 195; geography education 194-5; international partnerships 202
Liverpool Hope University 98-9
Loughborough University: Earth Surface Processes and Landforms 76; Social and Cultural Field Course 76-7

m-learning 120, 122
McKenzie, P.: and Curtis, D. 182, 190
Maori community 174
map-reading skills 44
Massey University, New Zealand 99-100; Development and Inequality course 45, 50
Master's level courses 131-47
Master's level education: Australia 132
Memorandum of Understanding 30
Merritt, C.D. 152
metaethics 25
mobile learning 122
mobile phone ownership: United Kingdom (UK) 125
mobile technology 122
Moser, S.: and Hanson, S. 39-40, 50
myspace.com 123

Nairn, K. 112
National Institute of Education, Singapore 44, 52
National Survey of Student Engagement (NSSE) 209, 210
National University of Singapore 99
neoliberalism 183
New Zealand: Performance Based Research Funding (PBRF) 12
Ninnes, P.: and Hellstén, M. 104

One Laptop for Every Child Project 118
online discussion: feedback 45
online environments 199
online technology: communication 112
O'Rourke, K.: and Kahn, P. 75, 83
Oxford Brooks University: The Ethical Geographer 31-2

Paloff, R.M.: and Pratt, K. 105
Peach, L. 26
Performance Based Research Funding (PBRF) 12
personal digital assistant (PDA) 122
Pew Charitable Trusts 195
physical geographers: inter-disciplinary discussion 19
physical geography 43, 64
plagiarism 51-2
podcasting 122-3; *A Very Spatial Podcast* (VSP) 123
postgraduate 'bar' and diversity 133
postgraduate education: changing

directions 131-3; diversity *138*; Dublin learning level *136*; environment diversity *139*; international models 132; learning descriptors *135*; skills 140-2
postgraduate study 140
postgraduate-workspace study 132
postgraduateness: defining 133-6
postgraduates: career planning 141-2; time management 142; value, skills and resources audit 141
Pratt, K.: and Paloff, R.M. 105
problem-based learning **75**; active learning and inquiry-based learning **75**; benefits and risks *62*; best practices *68*; case study **66**; definitions **60**; experiences 61-3; geography 58-69; geography curricula 63-5; geography use of 65-8; group dynamics 63; medicine and engineering 61; multi-dimensional scenario 64; nature and development 58-9; New Zealand-based study 64; potential disadvantages 80; published definitions 59; time commitments 61; web-based resources *67*; websites 65; what is 59-61; world regional geography course, Chile 65
public scholarship 156

Quality Assurance Agency (QAA) 88

Raju, S. 154
Ramasundaram, V. 120
Real, K.: and Rimal, R.N. 111
refugee research: dilemma 28; ethical view 27
research: ethical practice 30; social context 27
research assessment exercise 12
Research Methods in Geography: Flinders University, South Australia 176
research problems: innovative approaches 143
research and teaching: co-development 11; priorities 12
researcher: positionality 155
residency 202

Rimal, R.N.: and Real, K. 111
Robertson, M.: and Fluck, A. 123
Robinson, R. 154
Russell, C.: and French, D. 81

Sauer, C.O. 89
Savin-Baden, M. 59
Schlager, M.: and Fusco, J. 121
Serafin, E. 120
service learning 156; American students 210; United States of America (USA) 167-8
Sheaffer, A.L.: and Eflin, J. 172
skills agenda: employers 190
Smith, W. 17
social change agenda 150
Social and Cultural Field Course: Loughborough University 76-7
social and environmental indicators 46
social justice: and inclusivity 151; teaching 159-60
social network: websites 125
social skills: group-based exercises 94
social transformation 151-3; activism and academy relationship 152; higher education 154, 158-9; inquiry-based learning 156; teaching 153-4, 156-7
socialization strategies 16
South Africa: Black institutions 158; higher education system 158
South Australian Country Fire Service 176
Southeast Asia: observation-based fieldwork 90
Spain: employability 185
Spanish universities 185
Spronken-Smith, R. 64, 80
Stoddart, D.R.: and Adams, W.M. 89, 95
Stoors, D.: and Inderbitzin, M. 211
student engagement 84, 208-13; American students 210; campus surveys 209; changing context 211-12; definition 1; geography 4-6; patterns 209-10; rationale and theory 3; student perspectives 212
student exchanges 105
student learning: constructivist approach 41

student mobility 17
student placements 177
student voice 212-13
student-centred learning 84
student-led inquiry: effective practices 37
students: cultural differences 110; diversity 137, 157; employability 90; employability preparation 187; enhanced communication with 103; ethical capacity 28-30; feedback 212; knowledge base 76; migration 105; note-taking sharing 141; positionality 155; prescribing ethical practices 32; research skills 76; vocational experience 143

Taffs, K.: and Boyd, B. 30
Tammaro, A.M.: and Dixon, P. 203
teachers: above moral censure 23; content-oriented 81; geography in higher education 156-7; positionality 155; student-focused 81
teaching: social justice 159-60
teaching geography: for social transformation 150-60
teaching practice: versatility 124-6
teaching and research: co-development 11; priorities 12; separately judged 12
Teariki, C. 28
Techniques in Geography: National Institute of Education, Singapore 44, 52
technology and education 117
Texas A&M University 173
Texas State University: geographic information system (GIS) program 175-6
Thematic Networks 200
Thorne, P. 133
Thrupp, S.: and Tomlinson, S. 151
time log 142
time management: postgraduates 142
Tomlinson, S.: and Thrupp, S. 151
Toohey, S. 41, 49
travelling knowledge and experts 17-18
Tuning initiative 195

tutorial software 121
Twain, M. 208
Tyack, D.: and Cuban, L. 117

undergraduate and research postgraduate pathways 24
United Kingdom (UK): anti-terrorism bill 27; career and employment focused modules 186; employability 186; geography departments 153; Learning and Teaching Support Network 65; national university league tables 186; research assessment exercise 12; teaching and research 12; university participation 211
United Nations Decade of Education for Sustainable Development 32, 152
United States of America (USA): community engagement 167-8; service learning 167-8
University Centre for Excellence in Teaching award 79
university exchange programmes 202
University of Gloucestershire: Geography and Related Disciplines 78-9
University of Leicester: e-learning website 119
University of Manchester: geographies of children 52
University of New South Wales: Environmental Hazards course 46, 54
University of Otago, New Zealand: Field Research Studies 78
University of South Australia: graduate qualities 182

Valentine, G. 152
A Very Spatial Podcast (VSP): podcasting 123
virtual field course 120
virtual field trips 120
Vygotsky, L.S. 41

web-based modules 107
Wenger, E. 155-6
wider learning community 144
Wilson Gilmore, R. 153

women geographers: concerns 136; survive and thrive 136
work-based learning 176; assessment 177; real benefits 177
work-type environments 146
working: interdisciplinary context 143-4
workplace: integrating students 146
workplace skills 143-4, 172
World Regional Geography: California State University 44, 49
Worldwide Universities Network 202
Wu, C.V.: and Fournier, E.J. 61

Yan, L. 44